RETIREMENT SECURITY

RETIREMENT SECURITY

Understanding and Planning Your Financial Future

David M. Walker
Partner, Arthur Andersen LLP

JOHN WILEY & SONS, INC.
New York • Chichester • Brisbane • Toronto • Singapore • Weinheim

Library of Congress Cataloging-in-Publication Data:
Walker, David M. (David Michael), 1951–
    Retirement security : understanding and planning your financial
future / David M. Walker.
        p.   cm.
    Includes index.
    ISBN 0-471-15207-2 (cloth : alk. paper)
    1. Retirement income—United States—Planning.   2. Old age
pensions—United States.   3. Social security—United States.
4. Individual retirement accounts—United States.   5. Medicare.
6. Insurance, Health—United States.   7. Saving and investment-
-United States.   8. Income tax—United States.   9. Finance.
Personal—United States.   I. Title.
HD7125.W35   1996
332.024'01—dc20   96-24022

Printed in the United States of America

10 9 8 7 6 5 4 3 2 1

Acknowledgments

There are many people who have helped to make this book a reality. First and foremost, I want to thank my wife, Mary, for sacrificing many nights and weekends during the past year while I was writing and rewriting this book. She was supportive of my efforts from the first day that I thought about writing this book. Second, I would like to thank our children Carol and Andy for doing well in college, thereby enabling me to concentrate on my career, in general, and this book, in particular. Third, I would like to thank my partners at Arthur Andersen for their support of this book project and my related efforts.

Creating a book of the size and scope of this one is a major undertaking. As such, it can't be done well without the help of others. There are many who gave of their time, treasure (information), and talent to support me in this effort. While many could be acknowledged, I'd like to thank a few here. Barbara Buchholz and Meg Crane for their concerted editing efforts designed to assure that this book is interesting, informative, and readable. They clearly made a number of significant improvements to my original work. Frank Butitta for coordinating the editing efforts with Barbara and Meg. Philly Jones and Lisa Mahaffey for their extensive research assistance. Len Podolin, Stan Ross, Mike Andrew, Judy Hunt, Richard Hinz, Dick Helfand, Jim Sullivan, Jon Cook, Gregg Buckalew, Frank Butitta, Bruce Meyer, and my wife Mary for reading a draft of the book and providing their valuable comments and insights. Marla Bobowick of John Wiley & Sons for her interest in and enthusiasm for the book. Barrett Avigdor for her legal assistance in connection with the book contract. And, finally, my assistant, Arleen Ricotta, who provided valuable administrative assistance and "hung in there" through the stress and strains of my attempts to perform my many ongoing roles during the day while writing this book on evenings and weekends.

All of these individuals made real and meaningful contributions in their own way. For that, I am truly thankful.

About the Author

David M. Walker is a Partner and Global Managing Director of the Human Capital Services Practice of Arthur Andersen LLP and a member of the Board of Arthur Andersen Financial Advisors, a registered investment advisor. Mr. Walker is a CPA and consultant with over 13 years of retirement policy and planning experience in both the government and the private sector. His government positions include serving as one of two Public Trustees of the Social Security and Medicare Trust Funds, as Assistant Secretary of Labor for Pension and Welfare Benefit Programs, and as Acting Executive Director of the Pension Benefit Guaranty Corporation. Mr. Walker has also held a number of leadership positions in the retirement policy community and his profession. For example, he is a member of the Board of the Association of Private Pension and Welfare Plans and a former Chairman of the American Institute of Certified Public Accountants' Employee Benefit Plans Committee. Mr. Walker's public and private sector experience make him uniquely qualified to address the important issue of retirement security for the twenty-first century. As a result, his views on this and other issues have been sought out by a various congressional committees, government task forces, and a variety of media and publications such as ABC, CNBC, CNN, *Fortune* magazine, *The Wall Street Journal, The Washington Post, The New York Times,* and *Pensions and Investments Age.*

Mr. Walker is married to the former Mary Etheredge of Jacksonville, Florida. They have two children, Carol Marie and James Andrew. Mr. Walker has a B.S. degree in Accounting from Jacksonville University and an S.M.G. certificate from the John F. Kennedy School of Government at Harvard University.

Preface

When many people think about retirement, they envision a condominium in a warm climate, relaxed days spent driving golf balls, quiet cruises with cocktail in hand, big monthly dividend and interest checks to support their new life of leisure, and money and property left over to leave to their children and grandchildren. Most also imagine receiving some monthly Social Security and pension checks and Medicare to help pay hospital and doctor bills if they get sick.

But a bleaker picture is likely to emerge for many Americans in the twenty-first century. Try this scenario: a part-time job, the same home because they can't afford to move to a condo in a warmer climate, and a stack of bills that eat up the next few months of Social Security and dividend checks. Not so enticing, is it?

It's time for a reality check. Retirement security is neither a right nor an entitlement. It is a goal that requires informed planning and disciplined action. Chances are that if you don't take the necessary steps, you may be forced to reduce your retirement standard of living or work longer than you'd like. This reality check includes facing up to the impending changes in government entitlement programs like Social Security and Medicare and figuring out ways to make the most of your earnings and investments both now and later.

There is a "looming retirement crisis" in this country, a phrase that I coined in connection with my work as an adviser to the Committee for Economic Development (CED), a committee of CEOs of major American-based enterprises that produced a report in 1995 entitled "The Looming Crisis—Who Will Pay for Your Retirement?"

Numerous factors endanger our retirement security and are helping to create an increasing generational conflict over who should pay for what. These factors also foment the current rancorous debate between political parties and individual members of Congress in connection with attempts to reform Social Security, Medicare, and other entitlement programs.

There are a number of main triggers igniting this concern: life expectancies that stretch longer than previously estimated, declining pension coverage and contribution rates, losses in some pension funds, retiree health-care cutbacks, expensive new medical treatments, diminished Social Security benefits, and a Medicare system that will go bust unless fundamentally restructured.

Need more bad news? How about a stagnant economy, mercurial stock and bond markets, fluctuating interest rates, and our own improvidence? Most Americans are lousy savers.

While my primary objective in writing this book is to help individuals in their retirement education and planning efforts, I will also present a clear and concise history of the various programs affecting your retirement security such as Social Security, Medicare, and employer-sponsored pension and retiree health plans. I'll also take a candid, nonpartisan look at these programs in the context of the current economic, political, and social climate, and discuss likely reforms.

The book contains straightforward advice to help you separate retirement security fact from fiction and show you how to develop your own retirement security plan. This two-pronged approach, available under one cover, is something other retirement books have failed to take. It is presented in a highly readable and understandable format so that you won't give up and put it back on the shelf.

I have used the pronouns he or his in most cases, though the information certainly applies equally to women. I have also tried to address several scenarios, including divorcees, widows and widowers, and single people. No longer can planning for the future be aimed only at the "perfect" 1950s family.

Specifically, this book will give you information to enable you to make intelligent and informed decisions regarding what the federal government's social insurance programs currently provide, how they may be changed, what the ramifications of these and other changes will be for your retirement security, what you can expect from your employer, and what you need to do both now and in the future (see Time Clock/Line at the end of this chapter, Exhibit P-1). This book will also help you know where to turn for related information on your retirement benefits, savings, and investments at or before the times you need them.

Some of the information in these pages is based on my own family's legacy, beginning with how my parents and grandparents saved scrupulously, and moving on to my efforts to protect the financial future of my immediate family, which includes my wife and two children. My family's experience has mirrored changes in our society in many ways.

I came from a typical nuclear family where my mother did not work outside the home. Lord knows she had her hands full raising three boys. My father worked for one company throughout his adult life. He was covered under a relatively generous and well-funded defined-benefit pension plan as well as a company-paid retiree health program. My parents planned for retirement and counted on Social Security and Medicare benefits as an integral part of their retirement package.

In contrast to my parents, my wife and I work at full-time jobs. I have worked for five organizations, including the U.S. government since my graduation from college in 1973. All of my employers have relied primarily on defined-contribution plans as their primary retirement vehicle (see Chapter Four). Only the government offered some employer-subsidized retiree health care (see Chapter Eight). Unlike many other baby boomers (those born between 1946 and 1964), my wife and I are discounting, but not eliminating, the value of Social Security and Medicare benefits in our own retirement planning (see Chapters Two and Three).

Our son is in college and our daughter just graduated. As Generation Xers (those born between 1965 and 1980), both are concerned about the future of government-sponsored programs and the related tax burdens they may be asked to bear. Already they are aware of their need to assume responsibility for their retirement security early in their working careers. Our 19-year-old son, Andy, has already started to save. He saves and invests at least 50 percent of the annual amount that Mary, my wife, and I award him for winning an NROTC scholarship at Villanova University. His savings are invested primarily in stock and balanced (stock and fixed-income) mutual funds. Our daughter Carol also has recognized the need to incorporate a savings and investment strategy into her financial planning now that she has entered the full-time workforce. She plans to contribute regularly to the 401(k) plan sponsored by her employer, once she becomes eligible.

While I draw on some family experiences, most of the information contained in this book is based on my close-up view of working on retirement security and planning issues in both the public and private sectors over the last 13 years. My credentials include serving as one of two public trustees of the Social Security and Medicare programs from 1990 to 1995, as U.S. Assistant Secretary of Labor for pension and welfare benefits from 1987 to 1989 and as head of the U.S. Pension Benefit Guaranty Corporation from late 1984 to mid 1985. I am now a partner and global managing director of the Human Capital Services Practice of the international accounting and consulting firm of Arthur Andersen LLP, based in the Atlanta, Georgia, office.

Arthur Andersen's motto is "Think straight and talk straight," a credo that I have attempted to follow throughout my adult life. It's one that I also adhere to in this book because it is both valid and vital in planning for your financial future.

The moral of this book is simple and succinct: If we don't individually plan now for retirement, we will all pay a heavy price in the future. We all want to be financially secure when we retire, but most of us don't understand what it takes. Many of us fail to heed the ominous signs. A vast majority of Americans plan for their retirement too late, save too little, and don't invest wisely what they do save. Studies show that most people don't start thinking about retirement until age 50.

Many people put it off, saying they're too busy building their careers and families during their 20s and 30s. They also believe other savings needs have to be addressed in their 40s to buy cars, make home improvements, and afford children's education. Most don't realize the importance of another type of early saving—not to spend for a particular purchase, but to set aside for retirement planning. This should be done as soon as people take their first job after completing their education.

Many don't think about retirement until they get that first jolt—their invitation to join the American Association of Retired Persons (AARP), which automatically comes in the mail shortly before their 50th birthday. Interestingly, the first baby boomers reached 50 this year.

Despite past actions, we must face the facts today. Unless we step up our savings pace, most retirees will not glide gently into their golden years. Rather, they may face a bumpy ride and possible crash-landing.

This book is divided into two parts. Part One provides valuable information and insights into a number of important retirement issues and trends relating to Social Security, Medicare, employer-sponsored pension and retiree health programs, and other personal savings arrangements. This segment is designed to provide you with a foundation of knowledge from which to make intelligent and informed retirement planning decisions.

Part Two shows how to design and implement a personal retirement security plan based on the knowledge that you gain from Part One and using a seven-step method, which I have adopted for my own family. Part Two also includes valuable information on a range of retirement savings and investment principles and strategies. Much of the information in Part Two is presented through a hypothetical couple, James and Carol, who represent a typical hardworking forty-something family with one stepchild, two children, and several aging parents.

Some people may be tempted to go directly to Part Two of this book to get started with their own retirement plan. While the design of the book makes this possible, I don't recommend it. Part One contains important information that you need to engage in informed long-range planning.

I believe this book can make a real and lasting difference in your efforts to gain economic security and peace of mind before you retire. The risk of not following the advice is that you may find yourself in the untenable position of being too old to work and too poor to retire. The time to address your retirement security planning is now. The clock is ticking.

RETIREMENT PLANNING TIMELINE

<u>Typical Age</u>   <u>Suggested Actions</u>

Early - Mid 20s
- Get into the habit of preparing and following an annual budget which includes a savings component.
- Be sure to take advantage of employer sponsored savings vehicles, especially Section 401(k) arrangements with employer matching contributions.
- Take advantage of IRA's as a supplemental savings vehicle, if possible.
- Invest for the long-term and do not withdraw your retirement savings.

30
- Prepare your first retirement security plan, if you have not already.
- Review your spending, savings and investment patterns and adjust accordingly.
- Maintain a long-term investment strategy and do not withdraw your retirement savings.

40
- Review and update your plan, at least annually.
- Increase savings as disposable earnings increase.
- Maximize employer sponsored savings opportunities.
- Consider supplemental savings arrangements (e.g., insurance products).
- Update your retirement plan annually from here until retirement and beyond, as applicable.
- Maintain a long-range investment policy.
- Prepare a will if you have not already.

50
- Join AARP.
- Get serious about your retirement planning, savings and investments, if you have not already.
- Review and update your plan at least semi-annually.
- Maximize employer and supplemental savings arrangements.
- Maintain a longer-range investment strategy.
- Prepare an estate plan if you have not already.

60
- Review and update your plan quarterly.
- Reassess your estimated retirement date.
- Begin to consider Social Security retirement strategy.
- Maximize employer and supplemental savings arrangements.
- Consider a mid-range investment strategy.
- Begin distribution planning process.

63
- Re-run your plan to see if you can afford to retire.
- Adjust your objectives or actions (e.g.; spending, savings, investment patterns), as appropriate.
- Review and update distribution planning.

65 or at Retirement
- See if you can afford to retire.
- Franchise and implement your social security benefit strategy supplement.
- Implement your distribution plan.
- Modify your investment strategy, as appropriate, based on your estimated investment horizon.
- Adjust your spending patterns.

Note: If you want to retire before age 65, you'll need to accelerate your timeline accordingly.

Exhibit P-1   Things people should do at various ages

Contents

PART ONE

The Elements of Retirement Security—A Retirement Education Primer

SETTING THE STAGE FOR CHANGE: THE NEED TO PLAN

Failure to plan for retirement is a little like ignoring chest pains when your family has a history of heart trouble. The problem isn't going to go away and will only get worse the longer you wait. The fact that many of us ignore the need to plan for retirement is somewhat surprising given two recent press reports:

- A recent national survey noted that 85 percent of Americans believe they will have to assume more responsibility for their retirement security in the twenty-first century, just four years away.
- Washington and the press keep hammering home the challenges that future retirees will face given the projected financial imbalances in the Social Security and Medicare trust funds, yet these messages fail to spur widespread action.

The need for change in our retirement system is now. As insidious as the future looks to the current crop of retirees, who could well be the last group to enjoy traditional retirement benefits, it gets more precarious for the generations coming up behind them.

1

Regardless of the findings in the Committee for Economic Development's 1995 report on the "looming retirement crisis," politicians and private-sector experts disagree about the nature and extent of a crisis in the United States and in other industrialized nations. They also disagree about who's responsible. At the same time, an overwhelming majority, will acknowledge, at least privately, that we face a retirement crisis based on our current path.

The U.S. government bears much of the blame for many of the uncertainties due to long-standing policies or lack thereof. Among the many telling indicators in recent years, and the most publicized, is that the country's Social Security and Medicare programs are not financed adequately to meet the future needs of the swelling baby boom generation.

More specifically, the factors that may derail your retirement security include the following:

Demographic trends. The seniors population, those age 65 and over, is growing like Topsy, and these people are living longer. In 1995, one in eight Americans was over 65 years, and the percentage will climb to one in five within a decade according to the U.S. Census Bureau (Exhibit I-1). Part of the reason is that the baby boom generation that will turn 65 beginning in 2011 is larger than any in previous history. The baby boom generation is followed by the baby bust or Generation X, who under current government policies will be asked to pay a significant part of the check for the boomers' retirement. Worse than sheer

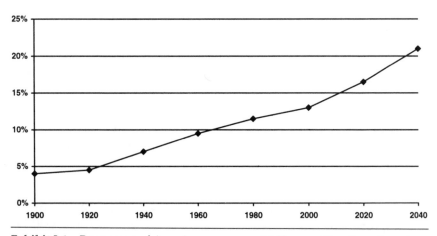

Exhibit I-1   Percentage of Americans over age 65 (*Source: Bipartisan Commission on Entitlement and Tax Reform, Final Report to the President,* January 1995.)

numbers is the fact that old age is not always a guarantee of good health—or good times. Medical costs pose a staggering threat as we live longer. There were 260,000 bypass operations in 1993 versus 12,000 in 1976, according to the National Center for Health Statistics. The least expensive such operation now costs over $6,000 for the procedure alone when performed in a major teaching hospital. More than one in two Americans over the age of 85 is said to face the possibility of Alzheimer's, a debilitating and costly disease that has gained more visibility through former president Reagan's bout with it. Six percent of all Americans aged to 74 are afflicted with Alzheimer's. Cancer strikes one of every two men and one of every three women in America and also wreaks havoc with personal finances. Eighty percent of all cancer cases involve individuals over 50, and virtually all Alzheimer's cases involve this age group. In addition, annual medication costs alone for certain cancer patients can top $30,000.

The projected financial imbalance in the Social Security and Medicare programs. A likelihood exists that the two chief sources of retirement funds for many—Social Security and Medicare—will not provide the same level of benefits they do today. Between 1965 and 1995, spending on Social Security and Medicare for the elderly has risen from 14 to 34 percent of the annual federal budget, and is projected to hit 39 percent by 2005. Most people recognize that we can't sustain this type growth and something must be done to curb it.

Changes in employer-provided pension and retiree health plans. Increased domestic and global competitive pressures on private-sector companies are compelling more businesses to look for techniques to cut costs and increase their bottom lines. One sure-fire way, which shows no signs of abating, has been to reduce expenditures for pension and health plan funding. This affects current employees and retirees, both of whom will have to spend more of their money to pay for such benefits or assume additional financial and health risk if they reduce or drop their health insurance coverage.

Instead of traditional retirement plans such as defined-benefit pension plans, which asked nothing of employees yet guaranteed them a fixed income upon retirement, more employers are turning to defined-contribution plans (such as 401(k) plans for for-profit entities or 403(b) arrangements for nonprofit organizations). These plans typically require workers to kick in some of their own funds. Many also may allow individuals to choose how their retirement savings money are invested. Still, only approximately one-third of individuals who are eligible to participate in voluntary defined contribution plans chose not to.

Anemic personal savings. Many people fail to save. Some don't put away sufficient funds due to ignorance. Others just don't have much discretionary income left to save at least early in their working careers, especially if they have children. Still others are neglectful, enjoying an overly lavish lifestyle and piling on personal debt during their working years. Too many Americans are concerned with keeping up with the Joneses and living for today.

According to a 1994 report by Merrill Lynch entitled "The Merrill Lynch Baby Boom Retirement Index," the average baby boomer needs to triple his or her retirement savings rate in order to maintain their standard of living in retirement. While this report did not consider home equity, which may be converted for retirement income purposes, the message is clear—boomers and others need to save more for retirement.

Moreover, a wave of inflation, for which the seeds were planted in the late 1960s after President Lyndon B. Johnson failed to raise taxes to pay for his "guns and butter" spending policies, continued until the early 1980s. While current inflation rates are low compared to the 1970s and early 1980s, higher inflation could reappear and erode the value of individuals' savings, especially if government doesn't get control of the longer-term fiscal budget deficits—beyond the call for a seven-year balanced budget.

As Congress debates the federal deficit, Americans are becoming increasingly confused and worried about what they can expect to receive from the Social Security and Medicare programs. Don't rely on what most politicians tell you, however. Many slant the message or don't tell you the whole story to serve their own political purposes.

The reality is that whether you are in your 20s and embarking on a career or in your later 50s and edging closer to retirement, you need to take charge of your retirement planning today. While it's never too early or too late to begin, if you wait too long, you may have to downsize your expectations or re-enter the work force after you retire.

To begin focusing on your retirement planning, ask yourself the following questions, which this book will help you answer:

- What is the likely future of the Social Security and Medicare programs, and how will the changes affect me?
- What type of pension and savings plan(s) does my employer offer?
- What will these plans provide, and are they likely to change?
- What type of retiree health-care access or financing does my employer provide? Is it likely to change?

- How much will I need when I want to retire, and what will I need if I'm forced to retire early?
- How much in savings and investments do I have today? Am I investing my savings wisely?
- What is the likely future trend in home prices, and what does this mean to me?
- Can I count on receiving an inheritance?
- When do I need to begin?

Let's get down to the real nitty-gritty and focus on the specific elements you need to address.

CHAPTER ONE

The Elements of Retirement Security and Selected Retirement Security Models

RETIREMENT MYTHS

Many pride themselves on how much they think they know about retirement. Yet myths abound because the perception of what constitutes retirement security today can be as murky as old sherry. Test yourself on this myth and the others that follow in subsequent chapters.

Baby boomers won't receive Social Security benefits.

MYTH 1 False. While a recent *USA TODAY* article noted that more baby boomers believe in UFOs than the likelihood that they will receive Social Security benefits, they are in the wrong orbit. Clearly, the Social Security retirement system faces financial challenges, which must be addressed. Program changes are inevitable, but the system can, should and will be saved from extinction. In my view, the system will likely eventually switch from today's total defined-benefit approach to a two-tiered one. Under the new approach, individuals would receive a reduced defined-benefit pension and a portion of Social Security (OASI) payroll taxes will go into an individual account in the worker's name. Workers will have control over how their individual account funds are invested. The individual will then convert their account balance to an annuity at retirement.

For nearly 60 years, the retirement security model in the United States has been based on a "three-legged stool" metaphor, which stresses that a person's retirement should be funded by his or her Social Security, employer-sponsored pension and savings programs and personal savings. This idea was an outgrowth of the establishment of the Social Security retirement system and the increase in employer-sponsored pension and savings arrangements after World War II. According to this theory, the amount to be funded and the condition of each leg differed, based on a person's age, work history, and economic status.

Now the traditional "stool" paradigm has been thrown out of kilter. Some of the givens can no longer be counted on. The financial condition of the Social Security system has worsened since the major reforms were enacted in 1983, and it is expected to continue to deteriorate. The increase in the number of divorces and single parent households has resulted in many of these individuals finding themselves in retirement hell, especially if they're not protected by a qualified domestic relations order (QDRO). (More on this in Chapter Four.) Furthermore, the three-legged stool concept has failed to address a crucial and increasingly troublesome need of individuals in their retirement years: access to affordable health care, especially catastrophic care.

NEW RETIREMENT SECURITY MODEL FOR THE TWENTY-FIRST CENTURY

The three-legged stool obviously needs rebuilding. I have developed a new model that recognizes the primary needs of all Americans during retirement: an adequate stream of income and access to affordable health care. My model takes into account the availability of the traditional as well as new public and private sector program elements, all of which provide the necessary retirement security. Here they are, arranged by type and source:

Program Element	Primary Control Agent	Income	Health
Social Security	Govt.	X	
Medicare	Govt.		X
Employer pension/savings programs	Employers	X	
Employer retiree health programs	Employers		X
Personal savings and inheritance	Individuals	X	
Earnings from continued employment	Individuals	X	
Health Care from continued employment	Individuals		X

Before I discuss each element, it's important to stress that the largest single impact on all public or private programs in the next century and on everybody's retirement security will be the change in the demographic makeup of the U.S. population. This is true for several reasons.

First, the population of seniors, those 65 years and over, has exploded since 1935 and is expected to continue to increase in both numbers and average life expectancies. In 1935, there were 7.8 million Americans 65 and over and 2.4 million Americans age 75 years and over. In 1995, there were 33.6 million Americans 65 years and over and 14.8 million Americans 75 years and over. These numbers are projected to escalate to a total of 69.8 million Americans 65 years old and 32 million Americans 75 and over by the year 2030 (Exhibit 1-1).

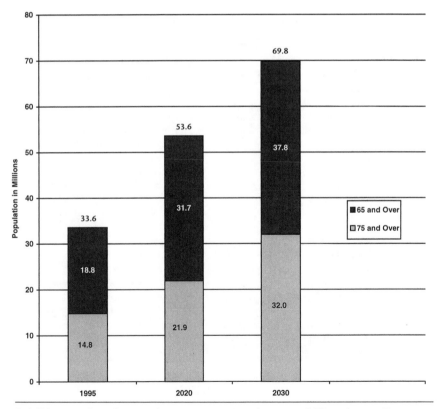

Exhibit 1-1 Population of Americans 65 and over and 75 and over (*Source:* Employee Benefit Research Institute, *Issue Brief,* August 1993.)

Second, Americans are living longer. The average current life expectancy for an individual (men and women) born in 1995 is 75.8 years. This is up from 61.4 years in 1935, when the Social Security program was enacted into law, and from 70.3 years in 1965, when the Medicare program began (Exhibit 1-2). When you eliminate mortality statistics prior to age 65, the average person born in 1935, 1965, and 1995 who makes it to age 65 will live 12.6, 14.6, and 17.5 years longer, respectively (Exhibit 1-3).

Conversely, concurrent with longer life expectancies, the average retirement age for Americans has declined significantly in recent years, in part due to early retirements as a result of businesses downsizing. In 1965 about 57 percent of the population 55 and over was in the workforce.

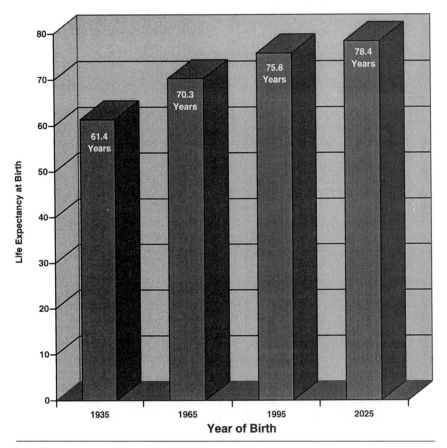

Exhibit 1-2   Life expectancy (1995) (*Source: Bipartisan Commission on Entitlement and Tax Reform, Final Report to the President*, January 1995.)

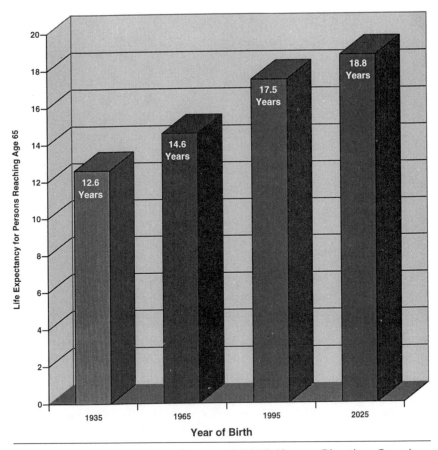

Exhibit 1-3   Life expectancy after age 65 (1995) (*Source: Bipartisan Commission on Entitlement and Tax Reform, Final Report to the President*, January 1995.)

By 1995, this percentage had dropped to about 38 and was still declining. Longer life spans and earlier retirement ages mean that an increasing number of Americans plan to spend more years retired than they do at work, another reason early and proper planning is crucial.

Third, the average number of workers available to support Americans over age 65 has declined significantly, and this trend will continue into the twenty-first century. In 1950, there were approximately 16 Americans between the ages of 20 and 64 for every American age 65 and over. Today that ratio is approximately 4.7:1, and by the year 2020, it will decline to about 2.7:1 (Exhibit 1-4). The related decline in the so-called seniors support ratio will have profound impacts on Social Security,

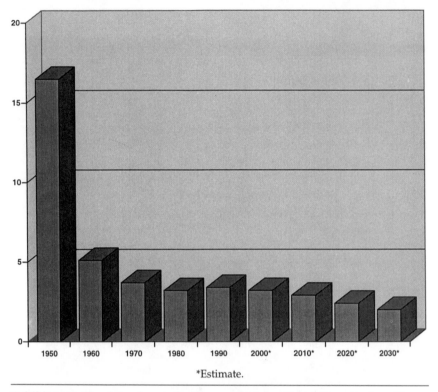

*Estimate.

Exhibit 1-4   Number of contributing workers per Social Security beneficiary (1995) (*Source: 1995 Annual Report of the Board of Trustees of the Federal
Old-Age and Survivors Insurance and Disability Insurance Trust Funds.*)

Medicare, and employer-sponsored pension and health programs and,
in turn, on your retirement security.

Fourth, the challenges relating to the baby boom generation are
monumental. Currently, there are over 77 million baby boomers in the
United States, and this group represents approximately 30 percent of
the country's current population. The number of baby boomers affects our nation's major retirement systems (Social Security,
Medicare, employer pension, and retiree health arrangements) and
the boomers' own retirement security because many of these programs aren't financed adequately to pay promised benefits. In addition, taxes alone won't make up the difference in the social security
and medicare program imbalances.

Though the challenge to baby boomers is considerable, it is modest
compared to that facing the baby bust generation (those born between

1965 and 1980), who will receive a double hit. By their retirement, projected deficits will be greater and there will be proportionately fewer workers. Furthermore, their tax rates will be increased during their lifetime to provide for the baby boomers.

Have I grabbed your attention yet? The point is, regardless of which group you fall into, the increasing population and the U.S. government's declining ability to provide funds will cause all Americans to assume a greater share of responsibility for their retirement security than their parents and grandparents did to maintain a reasonable lifestyle in their retirement years.

The question looms: What are you doing to assure you and your family's retirement security? Let's address the major sources of retirement security in the twenty-first century, beginning with Social Security.

CHAPTER TWO

Social Security

**MYTH
2**

Current retirees paid for their Social Security (OASOI) benefits. False again. Most of today's retirees believe they have completely paid for their Social Security retirement and disability benefits through the payroll taxes that were taken out of their paychecks, and their employer's contributions, during their working lifetime. Sorry. This is not the case. A married man who retires at 65 in 1996 is expected to live for another 13.7 years. Assuming that he earned the average wage each year throughout his working lifetime (for example, approximately $23,750 in 1994, $12,513 in 1980 and $6,186 in 1970), the total lifetime payroll taxes (employee and employer) paid on his behalf would represent only 56 percent of his expected Social Security retirement benefit (100/356 per × 2 Exhibit 2-9). Current and past retirees have paid even less of the cost. The upshot: early Social Security beneficiaries got a great deal but the deal gets worse for each year's retirees, especially since these figures do not consider interest on Social Security contributions.

Few people buy a pricey item like a car based solely on an advertisement. Obviously the advertiser is not objective, and if the car conks out after a few thousand miles, you're the one left holding the keys. As a result, most car buyers do their homework in advance. They may read *Consumer Reports* to check prices and reliability; they may ask others who have similar models for a critique; they go to several dealerships and examine a few cars to see if they look well made. Finally, they take a test drive to see how the cars sound and feel.

People need to do the same when planning for retirement. They need to do their homework to make sure that their assumptions are valid and their plans realistic. Yet most of us still save too little and rely too much on government-sponsored programs such as Social Security, even when these systems appear to be headed south.

Social Security is arguably the country's most successful public sector program. It has raised many elderly from poverty and the Social

Security Administration has won a number of awards for its efficiency and effectiveness. But Social Security is at risk. Don't grab the valium yet, however. Some needed reforms can be undertaken before the bottom falls out.

BACKGROUND/HISTORY

Despite the Social Security program's relative success, the program has been maligned and misunderstood in light of its original role and whom it was intended to help. Some think of Social Security as an umbrella of all government programs fashioned to assist seniors—those over age 65—including the Social Security retirement program and Medicare. Others consider it the retirement and disability programs that the Social Security Administration oversees.

In this book Social Security refers to the retirement income program tailored for seniors and enacted into law in 1935 during President Franklin D. Roosevelt's administration. It is sometimes referred to as the Old Age Survivors Insurance (OASI) program. (The name was selected before the days of political correctness, when people aged 65 were considered old.)

Roosevelt's social insurance program wasn't the first federal retirement program. In the 1860s, President Abraham Lincoln promised postwar pensions to Civil War (Union) soldiers to increase the number of recruits. Several decades later, that program became the first federal income security program, helping the elderly in the late 1890s.

While the U.S. Social Security program is well known, the United States was not at the forefront in providing social insurance for the elderly. The first government-sponsored retirement program was started in Germany by Otto von Bismarck in the 1870s. Bismarck, a shrewd politician, wanted to take a step toward providing economic security for Germany's elderly without breaking the bank. His solution was a program of income support for Germans 65 years and over, even though the average life expectancy in Germany at that time was 55 years. As a result, the program wasn't expected to cost much.

Some would consider Bismarck's creation a masterstroke of political genius because it combined a liberal approach to making government promises with a conservative stance toward fiscal responsibility. Others would view Bismarck's action as an example of a politician's empty promises.

In this country, our version of Bismarck's program, Social Security, was crafted with the assistance of Robert J. Myers and others in 1935, as a by-product of the Great Depression. Social Security was intended to serve as a foundation of financial security that seniors could count on in their retirement years, though not as their sole source of retirement income. It was meant to supplement, not supplant, employer-sponsored pension plans and personal savings arrangements. Stated differently, Social Security's foundation, like a house, had to be built on—or added to—to make a livable and lasting dwelling.

The initial age of eligibility for the Social Security retirement program was set at 65, in part because that was the average life expectancy when it was enacted. In addition, the average remaining life expectancy of a person who was 65 in 1935 was 3.3 years or 68.3 years. While our Social Security system was not as empty a promise as Bismarck's, it was not expected to pay benefits to most individuals for extended periods of time.

The initial average annual benefit level was quite modest—just $58. The initial payroll tax rate and wage base cap were also nominal (2 percent and $3,000, respectively, for employers and employees). Neither the taxable wage base nor the benefit levels were automatically indexed to inflation as they are today.

Since its enactment 61 years ago, the OASI program has undergone many incarnations in tax rates, taxable wage bases and benefit structure. Despite the fact that early Social Security beneficiaries paid little or nothing for their benefits, the program sustained itself largely as a result of a growing population and high support ratios—the number of workers per beneficiary.

While some alterations in program benefits and the financing structure took place from 1935 until 1965, they were not dramatic in real terms. Major changes began to occur in the late 1960s and early 1970s. As a result a variety of factors, including the indexing of the OASI benefit in 1972 and a decline in the support ratio that began after World War II and accelerated since in the mid-1960s, the Social Security system began to stagger.

The stress on the system escalated to the point that the OASI Trust Fund, used to finance the retirement income portion of Social Security, was threatened with insolvency in the early 1980s. This impending insolvency led to the creation of a bipartisan Commission on Social Security Reform, headed by Alan Greenspan, currently Chairman of the Federal Reserve System.

The Greenspan Commission recommended a number of benefit and tax changes designed to ensure the OASI program's solvency for more than 75 years, or until 2062. These recommendations resulted in legislative changes designed to bolster the overall financial integrity of the OASI program through a combination of staged payroll tax increases and benefit changes. Arguably the biggest change resulted in a

Annual Operating Balance of the Social Security Cash Benefit Trust Funds

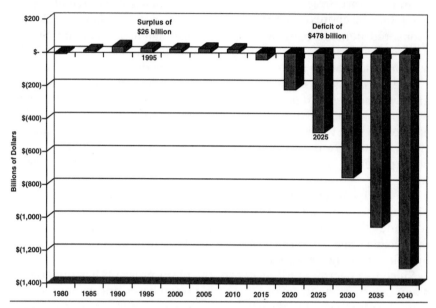

Exhibit 2-1   Financial position of Social Security (1995) (*Source: Bipartisan Commission on Entitlement and Tax Reform, Final Report to the President,* January 1995.)

staged increase in the normal retirement age under the OASI program from age 65 to 67. However, the early retirement eligibility age for OASI of 62 was not modified.

While the changes that were enacted into law as a result of the Greenspan Commission recommendations made sufficient changes to temporarily revive the long-term financial condition of Social Security, the program now faces midrange financial challenges and a deteriorating financial condition, which must be addressed (Exhibit 2-1).

ELIGIBILITY, LEVEL OF BENEFITS, AND TAXES

General

The OASI program of Social Security pays retirement benefits to eligible beneficiaries, all of whom have worked and paid taxes into Social Security to receive benefits upon retirement. More than 95 percent of all American workers are covered by the OASI program. The major exceptions are federal government workers hired before 1984, railroad workers, and about 20 percent of state and local government workers whose employers have not elected coverage under this program. At the end of 1995, approximately 140 million workers were covered by the OASI program and 39 million individuals were receiving OASI benefits.

If you work and pay OASI taxes, you earn Social Security credits. As of 1996, you earn one credit for each $640 in earnings. This amount increases yearly. You can earn a maximum of four credits per year, and it takes 40 credits to quality for Social Security retirement benefits. It generally takes 10 years of work to qualify for any OASI benefits. But it's like a cliff. You either get the 10 years or you don't.

Most people earn many more credits than they need to qualify for full Social Security retirement benefits. The extra credits don't increase your benefits. Individuals who don't earn the necessary 40 credits may be eligible for Supplemental Security Income (SSI) benefits, which provides income for the poor. Some people with fewer than 40 credits may qualify for disability payments if they meet the physical or mental disability standards under the federal Disability Insurance (DI) program. The DI program is also administered by the Social Security Administration. The amount of OASI benefits that you receive also varies according to your date of birth, retirement date, and average lifetime earnings.

The Social Security retirement program is progressive, designed to provide higher relative benefits levels for people with lower incomes. Social Security now replaces 58 percent of lower-paid workers' wages, about 43 percent of the average pay workers, but only 24 percent of higher-paid workers salaries (Exhibits 2-2 and Appendix A). It also contains an annual normal retirement benefit cap of about $1,300 per month in 1996.

The Basic Benefit Formulas

The most important factor in determining your Social Security retirement benefit is the amount of earnings in your working lifetime and your average annual earnings, subject to the overall wage base cap ($62,700 in 1996). OASI benefits are based on the following formulas:

1. Your total number of years of earnings is used as a base. For most individuals, the maximum number of years for this base is 35. The base number of years is lower for individuals born in 1928 or earlier. Irrespective of an individual's birth year, the highest years of relative earnings are counted.

2. Your earnings during these years are adjusted for inflation to make the numbers comparable.

3. Your average adjusted earnings are determined by dividing the number arrived at in step 2 by the number of years figured in step 1.

4. Your average earnings are multiplied by a percentage specified by law. This percentage is about 42 for individuals who had earnings equal to the national average each year during their working years ($23,750 in 1994).

Most OASI benefits are determined in accordance with the preceding formula. There are, however, minimum and maximum benefit formulas. These benefit limits are adjusted annually, based on changes in the overall inflation rate.

The Social Security Administration uses two special formulas to calculate the benefits of certain lower-income workers who were covered under the OASI for 10 to 30 years. These individuals receive the higher of the two formulas. In a vast majority of cases, the benefit determined under the preceding formula is higher.

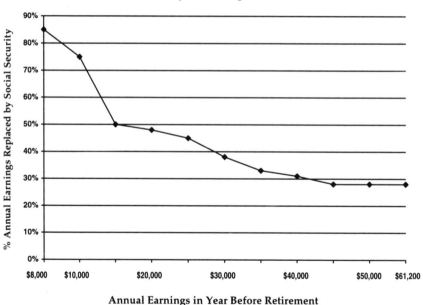

(For Retirement at Normal Retirement age—65 Until 2003, Then Gradually Increasing to 67 After 2026)

Annual Earnings in Year Before Retirement

Exhibit 2-2   Social Security replacement ratios (*Source: Guide to Social Security and Medicare*, 1995.)

Effect of Different Retirement Ages

Today, as a result of changes recommended by the Greenspan Commission, the retirement age under the OASI program is starting to inch up. Your normal retirement age (the age at which your earned benefits will not be increased due to delayed retirement or decreased due to early retirement) under Social Security will vary depending on when you were born. Those born before 1938 are eligible for full Social Security retirement benefits at age 65. Individuals born after that year are eligible for full retirement benefits at later ages. Specifically, beginning in the year 2000, the year of eligibility for full Social Security retirement benefits will gradually increase from 65 to 67 (Exhibit 2-3).

For example: If you were born in 1940, your age for full retirement eligibility is 65 and six months. If you were born in 1950, full retirement eligibility age is 66. Anyone born in 1960 or later will not be eligible for full retirement benefits until age 67.

Regardless of your age for normal retirement eligibility, you currently can receive benefits as early as age 62. However, the benefits will be reduced by a small percentage for each month before your normal retirement eligibility age (Exhibit 2-4). For example, if you turned 62 in 1995 and decided to begin receiving benefits, you would receive 80

Birth Year	Full Retirement Age
1937 and before	65
1938	65 and 2 months
1939	65 and 4 months
1940	65 and 6 months
1941	65 and 8 months
1942	65 and 10 months
1943-1954	66
1955	66 and 2 months
1956	66 and 4 months
1957	66 and 6 months
1958	66 and 8 months
1959	66 and 10 months
1960 and after	67

Exhibit 2-3   Eligibility for full Social Security retirement benefits (*Source: Research Institute of America Client Guide: What You Should Know about Your Social Security*, 1995.)

percent of your normal benefit (Exhibit 2-4). The benefit reduction percentage will increase in future years as the full retirement eligibility age increases (Exhibit 2-4). These monthly benefit reductions due to early retirement are permanent.

You may also prefer to work past the age of full benefit eligibility and not apply for Social Security benefits. This will increase your retirement benefit in two ways. First, your extra income may increase your average earnings, which is used to calculate your benefit. Second, if you delay your retirement, your OASI benefits are automatically increased by a stated percentage per year (Exhibit 2-4). For people turning 65 in 1995, the increase is 5.5 percent a year. This rate gradually increases as the retirement age for full eligibility increases until it hits a peak of 8 percent in the year 2008 or later. (However, as noted later, if you start receiving Social Security benefits and keep working, your benefits may be reduced.)

Appendix A summarizes projected Social Security benefits based on different retirement dates and alternative average wage assumptions. This will help you understand the ramifications of opting for early or later retirement on your Social Security benefit levels.

Retirement Age	Born		
	1937 and Before	1943-1954	1960 and After
62	.800	.733	.667
63	.867	.800	.733
64	.933	.867	.800
65	1.0	.933	.867
66	N/A	1.0	.933
67	N/A	N/A	1.0

Note: If you were born between the years 1938 and 1942 or between the years 1955 and 1959, then determine your early retirement factor as follows:
1. Determine your desired early retirement age.
2. Using Exhibit 2-3, determine your age of eligibility for full Social Security benefits.
3. Determine the difference, in months, between the results of steps 1 & 2, for example, if you were born in 1940, then your full retirement age (from Exhibit 2-3) is 65 & 6 months. However, if you desired early retirement age is 63, then there is a 30 month difference between the results of steps 1 & 2.
4. Divide the result of step 3 by 180 (30 ÷ 180 = .167).
5. Finally, subtract from 1.00 the result of step 4 in order to determine your early retirement factor. (1 − .167 = .833) For the example, the early retirement factor is .833.

Exhibit 2-4 Social Security early retirement factors (*Source: Social Security Explained,* 1995; *Research Institute of America Client Guide: What You Should Know about Your Social Security,* 1995.)

Retirement Age	1916 and Before	1917-1924	1925-1926	1927-1928
65	1.0	1.0	1.0	1.0
66	1.01	1.03	1.035	1.04
67	1.02	1.06	1.07	1.08
68	1.03	1.09	1.105	1.12
69	1.04	1.12	1.14	1.16
70	1.05	1.15	1.185	1.20

Retirement Age	1929-1930	1931-1932	1933-1934	1935-1936	1937
65	1.0	1.0	1.0	1.0	1.0
66	1.045	1.05	1.055	1.06	1.065
67	1.09	1.10	1.11	1.12	1.13
68	1.135	1.15	1.165	1.18	1.195
69	1.18	1.20	1.22	1.24	1.26
70	1.225	1.25	1.275	1.20	1.325

Note: If you were born after 1937, then determine your delayed retirement factor as follows:
1. Using Exhibit 2-3, determine your age of eligibility for full Social Security benefits.
2. Using the following table, begin with a factor of 1.0 and add the correct annual percentage for each year you delay your retirement up to age 70.

Born	Annual Percentage
1938	6.65%
1939-1940	7.0%
1941-1942	7.5%
1943 or later	8.0%

Example: If you were born in 1941, then based on Exhibit 2-3, your age of eligibility for full social security benefits would be 65 years and 8 months. However, if you delay your retirement until 67 and 8 months then your delayed retirement factor is 1.15 (1.0 + .075 + .075).

Exhibit 2-4   *(Continued)* Social Security delayed retirement factors (*Source: Social Security Explained,* 1995.)

Benefit Limits and Minimums

There are some overall limits on the amount of retirement benefits that an individual and family can receive. The individual annual benefit limit in 1996 is $12,500. The overall family limit is 150 to 188 percent of the higher earner's benefit rate. If the family's combined total benefits exceed the family limit set by the government, the benefits paid to other family members—a spouse or dependent children—are reduced.

The overall family limit is more applicable to situations where more than two family members are receiving OASI or DI benefits. Typically, where a child may be receiving DI benefits. In addition, there are certain minimum OASI benefits applicable to married couples. Specifically, the lower earning spouse will receive a benefit equal to the greater of what they earn or 50 percent of the higher earning spouse's benefit. For example: John is entitled to a monthly Social Security benefit of $1,200 per month at his normal retirement age (65). Jackie, who was in and out of the workforce raising a family, is entitled to $500 per month in benefits at age 65. However, as a couple Jackie would receive an additional $100 per month ($1200 ÷ 2 − $500) if she and John retire at age 65, due to Social Security's minimum benefit formula.

If both you and your spouse work, you may be eligible for higher benefits. If the two of you earned the maximum OASI benefit, you would both receive your respective benefits.

Effect of Divorce

If you are divorced, your ex-spouse may be eligible for retirement benefits based on your OASI record. This occurs even if you remarry. In some situations, your current or former spouse may be able to receive benefits even if you don't. If your ex-spouse receives benefits based on your account, it will not affect the benefits paid to you or to other family members.

Effect of Death

Once you start collecting OASI benefits, your beneficiaries may be eligible for payments upon your death. A surviving spouse who is 62 or older is entitled to certain benefits unless the spouse collects a higher OASI benefit based on the spouse's own earnings record. Usually your surviving spouse and possibly other family members such as dependent children will be eligible for a benefit of up to 50 percent of your full retirement benefit.

If you die before receiving any of your Social Security retirement benefits, certain family members may be eligible for some of your OASI benefits if you earned enough credits. The amount payable usually ranges from 75 to 100 percent of your personal benefit with an overall family cap of 150 to 180 percent of your benefit.

The Retirement Income Test

Individuals who begin receiving OASI benefits and continue to work may have their benefits reduced. In a unusual show of bipartisanship, in April 1996, President Clinton signed a Republican-backed bill to more than double the earnings limit on Social Security benefits. Under the new law, the 1996 annual outside earnings limit was raised from $11,520 to $12,500 for beneficiaries age 65–69. This limit will increase to $30,000 by the year 2000. For beneficiaries under age 65 the 1996 limit is $8,280, up from $8,160 in 1995. Generally, individuals between 65 and 69 lose $1 in Social Security benefits for every $3 earned over this limit. People who are age 70 and above are not currently subject to any benefit reductions based on outside earnings.

These limits are related only to earnings from employment and self-employment such as salaries and consulting payments. They do not include other types of income such as pensions, annuities, investment income like interest and dividends (including municipal bond interest), Social Security and Medicare benefits, veterans and other government benefits, severance payments made on account of retirement, sick pay received after retirement, expense reimbursements, and contest or lotto winnings.

These earnings limits will have an impact on how much you may wish to earn after applying for Social Security benefits and what form your earnings take. They may also affect when you choose to apply for benefits to maximize your overall benefits. If you decide to work part-time, it may make sense to delay applying for OASI benefits. Delaying benefits will avoid any related benefit reductions due to earnings and may increase the amount of benefits that you receive when you start receiving

For Beneficiaries Who *Have Not* Reached Normal Retirement Age 65		
Annual Earnings	Monthly Wages	Reduction in Monthly Benefits
$8,280	$690	$1 for each $2 of earnings above $8,280
For Beneficiaries Who *Have* Reached Normal Retirement Age 65		
Annual Earnings	Monthly Wages	Reduction in Monthly Benefits
$12,500	$960	$1 for each $3 of earnings above $12,500

Exhibit 2-5   Retirement benefits reduction due to too much earnings
(*Source: Annual Statistical Supplement to the Social Security Bulletin, 1995.*)

Social Security (Exhibit 2-5). However, you may need to draw on your savings or other investments to maintain your desired standard of living.

OASI FUNDING AND PROJECTED IMBALANCES

The financing of the OASI program is controversial and not well understood. The three primary Social Security financing questions that most people have are:

- How is the Social Security retirement program financed?
- How well is the Social Security retirement program financed?
- What is likely to be done to address the long-range financial integrity of the Social Security retirement program?

The OASI program is currently financed by three primary sources of revenue. The first is payroll taxes imposed on individuals and employers, up to stated annual limits. Individuals with self-employment

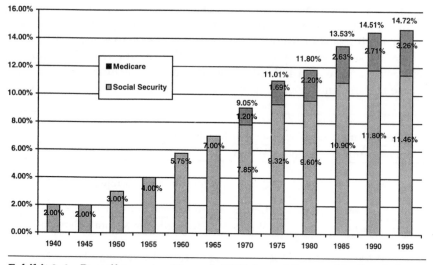

Combined Employer and Employee Total

Exhibit 2-6 Payroll tax rates (*Sources: 1995 Annual Report of the Board of Trustees of the Federal Old-Age and Survivors Insurance and Disability Insurance Trust Funds; 1995 Annual Report of the Board of Trustees of the Federal Hospital Insurance Trust Fund.*)

earnings, including me since I am a partner in Arthur Andersen, pay both the individual and employer portion of these payroll taxes. The 1996 payroll tax for Social Security retirement benefits is 5.26 percent of taxable wages or earnings, up to a cap of $62,700. As a result, the maximum tax that an individual would pay in 1996 is $3,887.40 and the maximum tax for self-employed individual is $7,774.80. The tax is not generally imposed on passive income like interest, dividends, rents, and capital gains. The annual tax rates and limits have increased substantially through the years from the initial level of 2 percent on the first $3,000 in wages or $60 (Exhibits 2-6 and 2-7).

The second source of revenue is income taxes received from the taxation of certain Social Security retirement benefits. Here, individuals who earn over $34,000 per year and families that earn over $44,000 per year have 85 percent of their Social Security benefits subject to income tax. Of this 85 percent, the tax on the first 50 percent goes to the OASI Trust Fund and the tax on the remaining 35 percent goes to the Hospital Insurance Trust Fund (HI), or Medicare Part A.

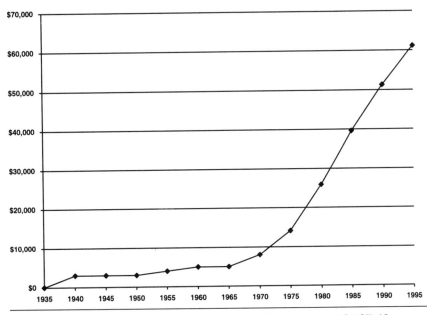

Exhibit 2-7 Maximum taxable earnings for Social Security (OASI) (*Source: Bipartisan Commission on Entitlement and Tax Reform, Final Report to the President,* January 1996; *1995 Annual Report of the Board of Trustees of the Federal Old-Age and Survivors Insurance and Disability Insurance Trust Funds.*)

The third source is interest on the U.S. government securities such as Treasury Securities with maturities from one to 15 years held in the OASI Trust Fund. OASI program funding works much like a money market account since interest is earned on the accumulated balance and the government writes checks on the OASI Trust Fund.

All of the tax revenues—payroll and income taxes—relating to the Social Security retirement program are transmitted to the OASI Trust Fund. All Social Security retirement benefit payments and administration expenses are paid out of the OASI Trust Fund. Under current law, OASI benefits and administrative expenses can be paid only out of OASI Trust Fund assets. Unless something changes, when the OASI Trust Fund is exhausted, the Social Security retirement benefits spigot will be shut off.

Finally, by federal law, any annual excess of OASI receipts over disbursements must be invested in U.S. government securities such as U.S. Treasury and selected agency securities. Conversely, any annual deficit would result in the liquidation of any government securities in the OASI Trust Fund until such securities are exhausted, at which time Social Security retirement benefits could no longer be paid on a timely basis.

To maintain its credibility and integrity, the OASI Trust Fund is overseen by a board of trustees, comprised of six individuals, who are appointed by the president of the U.S. and confirmed by the U.S. Senate. Four of the trustees have executive-level positions in the current administration—the secretary of the treasury, the secretary of health and human services, the secretary of labor and the commissioner of the Social Security Administration. The executive branch trustees wear more than one hat. They hold cabinet-level positions in the administration and also serve as trustees on a part-time basis. This can lead to conflicting interests between their respective responsibilities as members of the current administration with specific full-time responsibilities and their part-time responsibilities as trustees of the Social Security Trust Fund.

For example, the secretary of the treasury is both the chairman of the board of trustees and the nation's chief fiscal officer. As chairman of the board of trustees, his primary concerns include assuring the financial integrity of the program and the trust fund assets while maximizing the interest paid on trust fund assets such as the government securities held by the trust fund. As the nation's chief fiscal officer, he is concerned with minimizing the interest paid on the federal debt and avoiding default on the federal government's obligations.

These conflicting interests have been manifested on at least two occasions when the secretary of the treasury effectively borrowed from the Social Security and Medicare Trust Funds (HI and SMI) by temporarily suspending interest payments on the government bonds held in trust to avoid violating the federal debt limits. The most recent examples of this were in late 1995 and early 1996, when Treasury Secretary Robert Rubin employed various techniques to avoid violating the debt ceiling limit due to the Clinton Administration's budget stalemate with Congress. A similar situation occurred when James Baker was Secretary of the Treasury during the Reagan Administration. In both cases, the suspended interest payments were made after the fiscal crisis passed.

While such historical actions were criticized by certain members of Congress and the press, no definitive action was taken. Interestingly, similar actions by a trustee of a private sector pension plan would result in an enforcement action by the Department of Labor because it would represent a violation of the fiduciary responsibility provisions of the Employee Retirement Income Security Act (ERISA). While there are some obvious differences between this government social insurance program and employer sponsored pension and savings plans, many people believe that these actions represent just another example of the government's double standard: do as I say rather than as I do.

In addition to the four administration representatives, two trustees serve as representatives of the public, one from each major political party. These two public trustee positions were also a result of the Greenspan Commission's recommendations. While they represent part-time positions, the public trustees spend significantly more time dealing with Social Security and Medicare Trust Fund matters than the administration trustees. The same six trustees also serve as trustees of the Disability Insurance (DI) Trust Fund, Hospital Insurance (HI), and Supplemental Medical Insurance (SMI) Trust Funds.

One big dispute surrounding the financing of the OASI program concerns the legal requirement that any annual Social Security or Medicare surpluses must be invested in U.S. government securities. Some believe this means there are no assets in the trust fund, only IOUs. Others think it represents a scheme to allow Congress to use OASI Trust Fund surpluses to finance the annual federal fiscal budget deficits. Still others contend that the government is raiding the trust fund.

The primary reason that the trust fund assets were invested in government securities related to shorter-term benefit security issues. Namely, most legislators wanted to protect the principal balance in the trust fund. They were concerned with the potential implications of swings in the value of trust fund assets due to changes in market conditions. Others were concerned with the possibility that the Social Security and Medicare Trust Funds might be used as a means for the government to pick winners and losers and inappropriately influence private enterprises through trust fund investments in stocks and corporate bonds. Most recognized the financial soundness of government securities because they are backed by the full faith and credit of the U.S. government.

Investing OASI surpluses in U.S. government securities clearly helps hold down interest rates on government securities by creating a standing demand for these securities in years when OASI tax revenues exceed program benefits and expenses. The OASI Trust Fund also serves as a ready source to finance a portion of continuing government fiscal budget deficits. At the same time, the U.S. government securities held by the trust fund are backed by the full faith and credit of the federal government.

Based on the 1996 Annual Trustees' Reports, approximately $639 billion in government securities were held in the Social Security (i.e., OASI and DI) and Medicare (i.e., HI and SMI) Trust Funds at the end of 1995, of which $458 billion was attributable to the OASI Trust Fund and $143 billion was attributable to Medicare. The balance was attributable to the Disability Insurance (DI) Trust Fund.

While $639 billion in government securities were held in the Social Security and Medicare Trust Funds at the end of 1996, more than $4 trillion in such securities were held by others such as pension plans, individuals, mutual funds, and foreign governments. Many of these parties consider such U.S. government securities to be among the safest investments in the world.

Some individual's attempts to assert that the trust funds have no assets is wrong and somewhat analogous to a scare tactic. At the same time, we need to address the important fiscal challenges posed by the current federal budget treatment of the Social Security trust funds. We also need to reexamine the effect of investing all trust fund assets in lower-risk and lower-yielding investments such as U.S. government securities. For example, a 1995 study published by the Brookings Institute in Washington, D.C., asserted that a significant portion of the existing OASI Trust Fund imbalance could be eliminated through more aggressive investment of trust fund assets.

The second major program debate deals with how well the OASI program is financed. There is considerable misinformation being transmitted in this regard. The OASI program is the most soundly financed of the four Social Security and Medicare Trust Funds. The OASI Trust Fund has never had more money in it and these amounts are growing daily. Yet this statement poses a paradox. While the OASI program is the best financed of the four Social Security and Medicare programs, it faces financial challenges in the future because of the demographic shifts previously discussed.

Based on the 1996 Social Security and Medicare Trustees Annual Report, the OASI Trust Fund had $458.5 billion in assets—U.S.

government securities as of December 31, 1995. Furthermore, according to the 1996 Annual Report the OASI Trust Fund was estimated to have adequate assets to pay benefits until the year 2031 (the same as the 1995 Annual Trustees' Report). This represents a significant improvement from the precipice of insolvency the program faced in 1983.

But these facts tell only part of the story. After enactment of the 1983 Social Security Amendments, the OASI Trust Fund was projected to have adequate assets to pay benefits until 2060. However, actual experience has resulted in a quicker insolvency date than projected in 1983 (Exhibit 2-8). In addition, each of the five annual reports from 1991 to 1995 with which I was associated included a reduction in the estimated years until the fund would become insolvent. In addition, the 1996 Annual Report, which was released over two months late, noted that the OASI trust fund is now projected to become insolvent in 2031. The same as the Trustees' 1995 estimate.

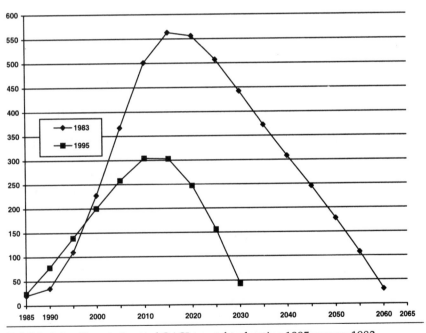

Exhibit 2-8 Comparison of OASI trust fund ratios 1995 versus 1983 trustees' report (*Sources: 1983 and 1995 Annual Reports of the Board of Trustees of the Federal Old-Age and Survivors Insurance and Disability Insurance Trust Funds.*)

Some of the deterioration in trust fund solvency since 1983 is due to variances from the economic and demographic assumptions that Congress used in 1983. Some of the assumptions were overly optimistic, hardly surprising given the fact that projecting key economic and demographic factors over a 75-year-period reflects more of an art than a science. The 1983 projection assumptions were also part of a political process and were made during the later stages of a recession.

The current assumptions are more realistic than the ones used in 1983, yet they are not beyond question. After all, the trustees are still required to select key demographic assumptions such as birth rates, mortality rates, immigration rates, and key economic assumptions such as gross domestic product (GDP) growth, inflation, interest rates, real wage growth, and productivity growth over the next 75 years. To put this in perspective, imagine yourself being asked in 1921 to predict these assumptions for the period 1922 until 1996.

The more realistic OASI projections are due in part to the creation of two public trustee positions in 1984. As noted earlier, these trustees serve as the public's watchdog for the preparation of the Social Security and Medicare annual reports, and part of their job, stated bluntly, is to be sure the books aren't cooked.

Some variances from the 1983 projections are due to Congressional actions. In 1993, Congress increased the (maximum) percentage of Social Security benefits that were subject to federal income taxation from 50 percent (based on a 50/50 split of employer and employee contributions) to 85 percent (predicated on the assumption that the current average retiree paid for 15 percent of his benefits based on his contributions, excluding employer contributions and interest).

However, these additional tax revenues did not go to OASI but into the HI Trust Fund, which pays hospital benefits and was considered to be in worse financial condition at the time. HI's financial condition has worsened since that time. The redirection of the additional income tax revenues from the OASI to HI Trust Funds was a prime example of politicians shifting funds, essentially robbing Peter to pay Paul.

Another more recent example of Congress reallocating funds to the detriment of the OASI program occurred in 1994. According to the Trustees Report that year, because the Disability Insurance (DI) Trust Fund, which provides income benefits to the disabled, was projected to become insolvent in 1995, Congress passed a law to reallocate the existing payroll tax attributable to the combined Social Security retirement and disability programs (respectively OASI and DI).

This was a short-term reallocation of the payroll tax to shore up the financial condition of the DI program at the expense of OASI, a move that was supported by the board of trustees, although reluctantly by the public trustees, including myself, who generally oppose such reallocations as a matter of principle. Specifically, Congress maintained the overall 6.2 percent combined payroll tax attributable to the combined OASI DI program but changed the relative allocations of the tax by reducing the amount payable to the OASI Trust Fund and increasing the amount payable to the DI Trust Fund. DI's projected date of insolvency was moved from 1995 to 2015, while the date of insolvency for the OASI program dropped from 2036 to 2031. The public trustees were not only philosophically opposed to reallocations, they were also concerned with certain recent trends in DI program costs. For example, one of the many DI program red flags has been a significant escalation of disability claims by younger individuals and claims for nonphysical impairments such as mental disorders. As a condition for their support for the reallocation, the public trustees insisted the board make it clear that any short-term reallocation should be temporary and accompanied by a review of the DI program toward enactment of needed program reforms.

Possible Future OASI Reform Options

Although the OASI program is the best financed of the four Social Security and Medicare programs, it is not awash in money. While based on the 1996 Annual OASI Report, the OASI trust fund is projected to have enough assets to pay benefits until 2031, it will start to run a negative cash flow, excluding interest on government securities in the trust fund, in 2014, just three years after the first baby boomers hit 65.

To address this shortfall, the federal government will have to take action: raise the OASI payroll tax, cut OASI benefits, refinance some Social Security government obligations by selling them to others for cash, or take a combination of these actions. In addition, refinancing these obligations only serves to delay the inevitable fiscal challenge. Unfortunately, the negative cash flow will grow progressively worse each year after 2014 (Exhibit 2-1).

Can this program (OASI) be saved? What effect will it have on your retirement? I believe it can and must be saved, though today's programs won't resemble tomorrow's benefits. Changes must be made. The longer politicians wait to enact needed reforms, the tougher it will be to do so and the more dramatic the reforms will have to be because of the burgeoning seniors population. Some reforms must and will be made. I don't believe the politicians can, will, or should let the Social Security program go bust.

Reforms that I consider more likely include:

- Gradually raising the early retirement age from 62 to between 65 and 67 similar to what Congress did in 1984 when it raised the normal retirement age from 65 to 67.
- Eliminating any early retirement subsidy under OASI.
- Increasing the normal retirement age from 67 to 70 on a gradual basis.
- Making the OASI benefit formula more regressive (providing even greater relative benefit weighting to lower wage earners) by creating an additional bend point—individuals with higher lifetime earnings histories would receive lower percentages of their average preretirement wages than under the present Social Security system.
- Modifying the Social Security cost-of-living adjustment formula to more accurately reflect actual inflation. (The government is reviewing the appropriateness of the current method of calculating the inflation rate since a number of economists believe that it overstates the actual inflation rate, especially for seniors.)
- Lowering the overall income replacement rates for a majority of all Social Security recipients.
- Revising the current spousal benefit structure and possibly increasing such benefits in some cases.
- Broadening the OASI payroll tax base by including the dollar value of certain employer-provided fringe benefits such as health care and disability insurance.
- Increasing but not eliminating the OASI wage base cap ($62,700 in 1996). This amount is indexed annually.
- Increasing the payroll tax rate from the current combined OASI/DI combined rate of 6.2 percent.
- Revising the investment restrictions applicable to the OASI Trust Fund to allow a portion of assets to be invested in higher-yielding but passive investment vehicles such as stock index funds.

These steps are plausible and, if combined, could assure the financial condition of a reformed OASI program for the next 75 years and beyond. These actions represent a combination of revenue enhancements—political jargon for tax increases—and benefit restructuring—typically referred to as benefit cuts. While I've listed the reforms which I consider to be more likely, their listing herein does not mean that I personally would support all of these potential changes.

People are lining up and taking sides concerning OASI. Some call for drastic changes—outright termination or benefit enhancements. Others call for full means testing of the program (tying entitlements directly to a recipient's income/assets) and fully privatizing it. In my view, such ideas are overly dramatic and inappropriate.

Any attempt to terminate the Social Security program outright would be the equivalent of political suicide. While many politicians may not be held in high public esteem, they aren't stupid, either. Termination of the Social Security program is a non-starter. Likewise, significant enhancements to existing OASI benefit levels are inappropriate given the projected financial condition of the program and continued pressure to reduce and eliminate the country's budget deficits.

Full means testing of Social Security benefits could mean that some who pay OASI taxes their entire lives would not receive any Social Security retirement benefits. (According to one related legislative proposal, singles who make above $75,000 and couples who earn in excess of $150,000 would lose some or all of their OASI benefits.) I believe that taking such a step would be unnecessary, inequitable, and counterproductive. While some noted billionaires suggest this step, they do not represent mainstream America. After all, while they may not need Social Security benefits, these benefits comprised approximately 50 percent of the average retirement income of retirees in 1992. While this is down from approximately 62 percent of average retiree income in 1970, it still represents a significant percentage. In addition, full means testing of OASI benefits would likely cause a significant reduction in public support for the program.

Privatization in the context of Social Security reform is another hot issue being bandied about and pumps a breath of fresh air into the debate versus more traditional approaches such as raising taxes and the retirement age(s). To do this would require dramatic changes. It would mean moving away from the existing government-run defined benefit system to a more flexible one including mandatory personal savings arrangements, which would rely more on private and semi-private sector investment vehicles. The CATO Institute, a conservative think tank based in Washington, D.C., has been a proponent of privatizing Social Security for some time, based in part on the Chilean experiment.

In the 1980s, Chile reformed its national social security retirement system from a program like OASI to a mandatory defined-contribution savings approach. Under the Chilean system, both employees and employers are required to contribute a stated percentage of their salary into an individual retirement account. The worker can then invest the retirement savings in one or more private investment vehicles. People must take their benefits in the form of an annuity (periodic payments rather than a lump sum) when they retire. To take a U.S. related example, if an individual turns 65 in 1996 and has a 401(k) plan or IRA account balance of $100,000, based on current individual annuity rates he or she could receive a monthly payment of approximately $925 per month for life in lieu of a lump sum based on a 6.8 percent annuity rate. That individual could receive even more if he or she is eligible for group annuity rates through his or her pension plan (for example, their account balance in an employer-sponsored 401(k) plan).

Many observers find the Chilean experiment to be successful. The Chileans' savings rate has surged to a whopping 26 percent of GDP in 1995. In contrast, the U.S. savings rate ran about 5 percent of GDP in 1995.

But there are glitches in the Chilean plan. Benefits at retirement are not guaranteed, and may wane based on the country's investment experience and prevailing market conditions. In addition, there are significant current unfunded liabilities associated with the current Social Security system that must be addressed. These are currently estimated at $7–8 trillion. That's real money in anyone's terms and Medicare's unfunded liabilities are much higher.

The current call for privatization comes from in part those who question whether people get their money's worth from the current Social Security program. Specifically, are they receiving their due—a reasonable retirement benefit based on the contributions that they and their employers make during their working lives? What about the earnings attributable to those contributions?

No doubt about it, the first retirees under the Social Security program got a great deal because they paid little or nothing for their retirement benefits. In addition, lower-wage earners get a better deal than higher-wage earners due to the regressivity of Social Security's benefit formula. Furthermore, as time goes, successive generations get less return on their investment because more of their contributions have been used to pay for the benefits of prior retirees.

Exhibit 2-9 summarizes the average past and projected benefit to tax ratio for retirees at different normal retirement dates. Despite the projections, the benefit to tax ratio is likely to continue to decline in the future given the wobbly financial stance of the current Social Security retirement program.

Irrespective of the Chilean experience, I doubt this country will adopt the Chilean approach in toto because it would represent a more dramatic change than our current political system would likely tolerate. I also do not think the American public or most government leaders want to fully privatize OASI. Many like the defined-benefit element of the current program. In addition, any changes will involve great

OASDI Benefit-Tax Ratios for Selected Workers
Based on the Intermediate Assumptions
of the 1995 OASDI Trustees Report

Year of Birth	NRA	Year of Attainment of NRA	Low Earnings	Average Earnings	Maximum Earnings
			Single Male Worker		
1920	65.0	1985	397%	266%	227%
1931	65.0	1996	219	161	127
1940	65.5	2006	178	132	102
1950	66.0	2016	160	119	86
1960	67.0	2027	172	128	85
1970	67.0	2037	202	150	99
1980	67.0	2047	216	161	106
1990	67.0	2057	222	165	109
2000	67.0	2067	227	169	112
			Single Female Worker		
1920	65.0	1985	492	330	279
1931	65.0	1996	262	194	152
1940	65.5	2006	210	156	120
1950	66.0	2016	189	141	102
1960	67.0	2027	201	150	100
1970	67.0	2037	234	174	115
1980	67.0	2047	249	185	122
1990	67.0	2057	254	189	125
2000	67.0	2067	259	193	128
			Married Male Worker		
1920	65.0	1985	985	671	564
1931	65.0	1996	476	356	276
1940	65.5	2006	380	287	217
1950	66.0	2016	338	254	182
1960	67.0	2027	357	268	177
1970	67.0	2037	413	309	204
1980	67.0	2047	435	326	215
1990	67.0	2057	443	332	219
2000	67.0	2067	449	336	222

(Continued)

Exhibit 2-9 Average return on investment (money's worth) (*Source: 1995 Social Security Administration, Office of the Chief Actuary.*)

Year of Birth	NRA	Year of Attainment of NRA	Low Earnings	Average Earnings	Maximum Earnings
			Married Female Worker		
1920	65.0	1985	811%	549%	460%
1931	65.0	1996	410	306	237
1940	65.5	2006	330	248	189
1950	66.0	2016	294	220	158
1960	67.0	2027	310	232	154
1970	67.0	2037	358	267	176
1980	67.0	2047	380	284	187
1990	67.0	2057	388	289	191
2000	67.0	2067	384	294	194

Notes:
1. The OASDI benefit-tax ratio is the ratio of the present value of expected OASDI benefits to the present value of expected OASDI employee payroll taxes; if both employer and employee taxes are used, the resulting ratios are one-half of those shown here.
2. The selected workers are assumed to enter employment covered by the Social Security program at age 22 and to have steady earnings at the specified level (low, average, or maximum) in such employment until death, disability, or retirement at the Normal Retirement Age ("NRA") for the program
3. Low earnings are 45 percent of average earnings.
4. Average earnings are equal to the National Average Wage Index.
5. Maximum earnings are equal to the OASDI maximum taxable earnings (that is, the contribution and benefit wage base cap).

Social Security Administration
Office of the Actuary
March 8, 1996

Exhibit 2-9   *(Continued)*

political risk when one considers the rapid growth in the seniors population, their higher degree of voter turnout and political activism.

I have been suggesting a middle-of-the road, two-tiered approach similar to what many employers now use in employer-sponsored programs since early in 1995. Specifically, we would maintain a lower defined benefit than the current law, at least for lower-income workers, with a forced savings account for all. The savings would be funded by a portion of the employer and employee payroll tax contributions, and each person would be able to invest his or her account in several passive, pooled investment options. A base defined benefit element would be maintained, at least for middle and lower income individuals. In addition, people would be required to take their individual account benefits in annuity form to prevent premature consumption.

Interestingly, the Social Security Advisory Council's report scheduled to be issued during the summer of 1996 is expected to include three possible means of reforming the Social Security program for the twenty-first century. Two of the three approaches involve a two-tiered and partial privatization approach. Of those two, one would retain the new "privatized portion" as a government program (both investment and program administration) while the other would have private sector entities (e.g., banks, insurance companies, mutual funds) handle these matters. While two of the three approaches represented a major change from the current benefit structure, 6 of the 13 council members evidently support maintaining the present structure approach with higher payroll taxes and a change in the current OASI Trust Fund investment policy to allow a portion of its assets to be invested in stocks. The final report of this bipartisan group of Social Security advisers will likely mark the official beginning of a major policy debate, which is likely to be a long and heated one.

Let me also emphasize that I believe OASI should be saved now rather than when it's at a crisis stage. We must also view the OASI program in the context of other government programs and set clearly defined and consistently applied priorities.

Let's be realistic: There is a limit on how many resources our country can dedicate to social insurance programs if we expect to maintain and improve our competitive posture and the standard of living for all of our citizens in the twenty-first century. As a result, some changes are necessary, appropriate and inevitable.

When it comes to your retirement security, it is also inevitable that the effect of any OASI changes will vary, based on what changes are made and according to your age, earnings history and economic status.

As hard-pressed Americans know all too well, there are two options when income won't meet obligations. There must be new income in the form of increased OASI payroll or other taxes before they retire, which will decrease the amount of their discretionary income for personal savings, and/or there must be reduced OASI spending. This could be a double whammy for many and will require great personal discipline.

The bottom line? If we don't fine-tune the engine now—look at other retirement options such as more personal savings and wiser investments—we should not be surprised if our car breaks down before the end of the trip.

We need to take steps to ensure that we will have enough assets to last throughout our retirement years. Speaking of the need for additional assets, let's move on to Medicare, a much greater candidate for bankruptcy.

CHAPTER THREE

Medicare

MYTH 3

The Medicare system can be saved by enacting the $270 billion in spending reductions proposed by the GOP as part of the fiscal 1996 budget process.

False. While the proposed reductions in Medicare spending and the related reforms are controversial, they are immaterial to the long-range financial challenge facing the Medicare program. Enactment of the proposed reductions and reforms will only have extended the projected HI Trust Fund insolvency date for three to four years at best, or from 2002 to 2005 or 2006, which is five to six years before the first baby boomer is eligible for Medicare benefits.

As a result, the current Medicare debate represents just the tip of the iceberg. To put it bluntly, Medicare HI and SMI programs are unsustainable in their present form. They require fundamental and dramatic reform before the next decade begins, which translates to significant reductions in current benefit levels and additional cost burdens over time.

MYTH 4

All individuals pay for their Medicare benefits.

False. In the past, no individual has paid fair value for his Medicare benefits. A new retiree who's 65 in 1996 paid for only about 25 percent of the value of his HI benefits through payroll taxes. In addition, the individual SMI premium in 1996 will pay for only about 25 percent of the estimated cost of the program. The balance comes from general revenues (income and other federal taxes). In addition, because the wage cap on the HI payroll tax has been eliminated, some higher-income individuals will likely be faced with the double hit of excessive tax burdens during their working lives and significant benefit reductions during their retirement years.

Escalating medical costs pose the biggest threat to the economic security of retirees and the nation, much greater than the risks related to the Social Security program. Since 1965, Medicare, the nation's health insurance program for senior citizens and the disabled, has paid the bill. But this is likely to change. Congress is trying to pare ballooning Medicare/Medicaid expenditures as a part of its effort to balance the federal budget.

41

In late 1995 and early 1996, the Republicans made Medicare reform a major part of their initiative to balance the federal budget by proposing legislation to reduce projected Medicare spending by $270 billion over the seven-year period from 1996 to 2002. These proposed reductions would be achieved by cutting reimbursements to providers, increasing premiums for Part B (SMI) insurance coverage, especially for the wealthy elderly, as well as expanding and reforming the use of managed-care approaches under the Medicare programs.

The Democrats, too, had their say in this mudslinging contest. They proposed reducing future Medicare expenditures by approximately $127 billion over the coming seven years based primarily on the historical approach of reducing payments to providers.

Importantly, under both parties' proposals, total Medicare expenditures would have risen faster than any type of federal spending in overall and per-beneficiary terms during the next seven years.

Medicare, like Social Security, is one of the nation's most misunderstood, misrepresented, and hotly debated entitlement programs. It suggests various connotations to different groups. This chapter will discuss the retirement portions of the Medicare programs: what they are and aren't, their current and projected financial conditions, what may happen to them in coming years and what changes in the programs may mean to your retirement security.

Medicare refers to the two federal health-care programs for senior citizens (individuals 65 and over): the Hospital Insurance (HI) program, known as Part A, and the Supplementay Medical Insurance (SMI) program, known as Part B. The HI program is designed primarily to cover medically necessary inpatient hospital and certain nursing facility charges as well as certain home health care and medical equipment supplied as part of the home health benefit. The SMI program covers doctors' fees and outpatient charges.

It is crucial not to confuse Medicare with Medicaid. Medicaid is the nation's federally funded health insurance program for people with low income and limited assets. In 1995, Medicaid covered 36.1 million individuals of which close to half were children. Medicaid is administered by each state, though the costs are shared by the federal government and states.

BACKGROUND/HISTORY

Harry S Truman was the first U.S. president to propose enactment of a comprehensive health insurance program for Americans, including the elderly in the late 1940's. Medicare programs weren't enacted into law, however, until 1965 as part of President Johnson's Great Society. The programs were intended to offer seniors access to and financing for health care in their retirement years to help reduce the growing poverty rate among the elderly.

The program initially was structured to provide access to health care at group rates. Financing of the HI program via a payroll tax approach paralleled the Social Security's OASI program. SMI was designed to be a voluntary term insurance program, which would be financed partially by premiums paid by beneficiaries and partially through general income revenues and other taxes.

Although Medicare programs are only 30 years old, a number of dramatic external and internal factors have affected these programs since their creation. In fact, these changes, many of which are similar to those affecting OASI over the last 60 years, have had a greater impact on the Medicare programs than those affecting the OASI program. More changes loom on the horizon. In addition to an aging population

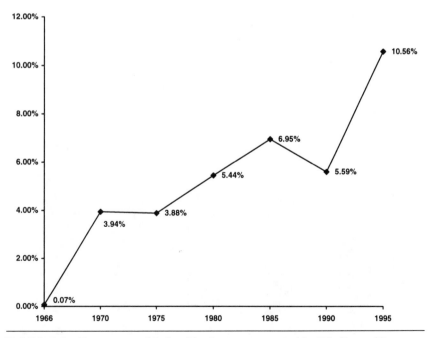

Exhibit 3-1 Percentage of federal budget represented by Medicare (*Source: Economic Report of the President,* February 1996.)

and a longer life expectancy (see Introduction and Chapter 1), the following represent the most significant changes since 1966:

- The percentage of the federal budget represented by the Medicare program increased from less than 1 percent to over 10 percent (Exhibit 3-1).

- The percentage of the federal budget represented by entitlement programs, including the Social Security and Medicare programs, grew from a little over 30 percent to approximately 50 percent (Exhibit 3-2).

- The percentage of SMI annual program costs funded by SMI premiums declined from 50 percent to 29 percent in 1995 and 25 percent in 1996.

- The percentage of the U.S. economy, as measured by gross domestic product (GDP), dedicated to health care increased from about 6 percent to over 14 percent (Exhibit 3-3).

- The overall health-care price index increased from about 30 to about 220 (with 1983 being 100).

- The poverty rate among seniors decreased from 28.5 percent to about 11.7 percent.

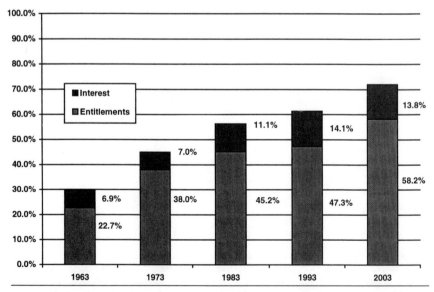

Exhibit 3-2   Percentage of federal budget represented by entitlement programs and interest on the federal debt (*Source: Bipartisan Commission on Entitlement and Tax Reform, Final Report to the President,* January 1995.)

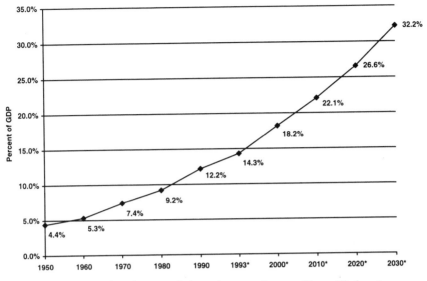

*Projections assume that the growth in real per capita spending will slow to a pace only two-thirds as fast as its actual historical rate between 1965 and 1990.

Exhibit 3-3 Percentage of U.S. economy dedicated to health care (*Source:* U.S. Department of Health and Human Services.)

- The federal budget deficit increased from $1.4 billion to $234.8 billion in 1994.
- The total national debt grew from about $329 billion to $5.1 trillion today.

Some of these numbers are staggering. While many of the factors just listed also affect the OASI program, particularly those relating to demographic trends, there is a major difference between the Medicare and OASI programs. OASI promises a defined dollar benefit that can be calculated. Current Medicare programs promise a specified level of health care for all covered individuals, which must be provided and paid for by the government, regardless of the recipient's income level and net worth. In addition, recent changes in the reimbursement system allow providers to get reimbursed directly by the government without providing a detailed statement of charges to the Medicare beneficiary. This procedure can serve to facilitate fraud and further disconnects the beneficiary from the rest of the Medicare program.

Compared to OASI, trying to calculate the long-term projected cost of Medicare is a stab in the dark. This is due to the current structuring of HI and SMI, which does not separate the issues of access to health care at group rates from the issue of who pays. As a result, when projecting Medicare expenditures, the trustees must estimate future health-care utilization (the number of services used), intensity (the type of procedures performed), and inflation for the Medicare population over the next 75 years.

ELIGIBILITY, LEVEL OF BENEFITS, AND TAXES

General

The HI and SMI programs are like fraternal twins, born at the same time, but different in appearance and emotional makeup. HI is somewhat regressive since higher-income individuals pay more payroll taxes during their working lives for the same level of benefit coverage in retirement. This is even more true after elimination of the wage base cap. Like OASI, HI is financed primarily by a payroll tax imposed on employers and employees and certain income tax revenues that relate to the taxation of OASI benefits. The current HI payroll tax, 1.45 percent, is imposed on both employers and employees. Self-employed individuals pay both taxes.

Effective in 1994, there is no taxable wage base cap for HI, and some people end up paying more in HI payroll taxes than OASI taxes. Specifically, due to the $62,700 OASI wage base tax cap in 1996, individuals who make over $268,096 in 1996 will pay more in HI payroll taxes than OASI taxes. As is true for OASI taxes, HI taxes are not levied on passive income like interest, dividends, rents, and capital gains.

As a result, individuals with greater overall wealth may have considerably lower relative social insurance tax burdens than middle- and upper-income workers. For example, many millionaires didn't pay social insurance taxes on a vast majority of their accumulated net worth.

While Washington historically has generally paid little attention to the imposition of much higher tax burdens on those with higher incomes, this view has been questioned by some politicians in recent years. The elimination of the HI wage base cap will be an issue of growing attention and concern because it is highly likely that those who pay such higher payroll taxes will become aware that they are paying taxes—or, as some politicians say, premiums—that are wholly unreasonable compared to the benefits they receive. Furthermore, these people are likely to have their benefits reduced or SMI premiums increased to a much greater extent as a result of the eventual reengineering of the Medicare program. This so-called double whammy will be particularly acute for the self-employed, who are required to pay both the employer and employee portion of HI taxes.

In contrast to HI, SMI is not regressive. People currently pay the same monthly premiums, generally starting at age 65 as described later, regardless of their income or net worth. SMI is financed partially by general federal government revenues and partially by individual contributions (SMI premiums). In 1995, individual premiums paid approximately 29 percent of the cost of the SMI program, compared to approximately 50 percent of the average cost of the program in 1965, when the program began. The individual percentage is projected to decline to 25 percent in 1996, which just happens to be an election year!

Eligibility for both HI and SMI programs begins from the first of the month after a person turns age 65. Those who continue working past age 65 and don't apply for OASI coverage are still eligible for HI and SMI coverage, though both programs then pay only for claims after the person's employer-provided health-care coverage kicks in. In other words, Medicare is the secondary payer after any employer-provided insurance (for active employees versus retirees), but the primary payer in connection with certain personal health insurance policies such as Medigap policies, private health insurance policies designed to fill the gap not paid for by Medicare.

Medicare has begun to experiment with managed care options as an alternative to the traditional fee for service arrangements. These programs are designed to improve beneficiary choice while controlling initial Medicare program costs through the use of HMO, PRO, and other managed care options.

The jury is out as to whether the current managed care programs achieve their intended objectives. Most seniors who chose managed care stay in the program despite some concerns regarding program flexibility and responsiveness to complaints. Medicare may not save as much as the government would like due to efforts by providers to target their marketing to healthier seniors. Despite some problems in the past, managed care clearly will play a greater role in Medicare's future.

Both Medicare programs are administered by the Health Care Financing Administration (HCFA), with the Social Security Administration providing some administrative assistance, particularly in connection with enrollment. Regional independent contractors process claims.

The HI Program (Part A)

HI (Part A) pays for medically necessary hospitalization, inpatient care, skilled nursing facility care, and home health services limiting reimbursement to stated amounts based on the specific service or procedure.

The HI program automatically covers those who are eligible for either OASI benefits or Railroad Retirement Benefits. Certain government employees not covered by OASI may qualify for the Part A program because they are required to pay the HI portion of the FICA tax. Their state may not be covered under the OASI program, but they, along with their employer, may have paid the 1.45 percent HI tax for long enough to qualify for HI benefits. Spouses of those eligible, including people who've been divorced, may qualify based on the eligible person's record. Those who receive Social Security disability benefits for at least 24 months, those with permanent kidney failure, and an overwhelming majority of all who are age 65 and over also qualify.

The few individuals over 65 who don't otherwise qualify can purchase Part A coverage for about $289 for those with fewer than 30 quarters of Medicare covered employment per month (1996 figures). These rates are adjusted annually. But there's a catch. Anyone who purchases HI coverage must purchase SMI coverage for an additional $42.50 per month. As of the end of last year, over 33 million seniors were covered by the HI program.

While those with 40 quarters of Medicare covered employment do not pay a separate HI premium other than the payroll taxes that are based on their wages, even after they retire, they incur certain costs. Generally, in 1996 those covered pay an initial deductible of $736 per benefit period for hospital charges. After 60 days, they pay $184 for insurance per day for their hospital stay. After 90 days, they can choose to pay $368 for insurance per day for up to 60 additional lifetime reserve days of hospitalization rather than the actual hospital charges. If they're readmitted within 60 days of their original admittance, they do not face an additional deductible charge. Certain appliances permanently installed at the hospital such as pacemakers continue to be covered without further cost-sharing by the patient. In addition to hospital-related expenses, HI covers certain skilled nursing home, home health, hospice, and other services. Skilled nursing and hospice benefits are subject to some conditions and limits. Certain home health benefits may be paid for in full by HI if the services are prescribed by a doctor and the home health agency that has been approved by HCFA.

The SMI Program (Part B)

SMI (Part B) is a voluntary program designed to cover certain physician charges. Specifically, persons who are fully insured for Medicare (HI) do not have to purchase SMI coverage. However, since the cost of the SMI program is heavily subsidized by general revenues from the federal budget, an overwhelming majority of eligible people do purchase it. Simply stated, it's a great buy.

The current monthly premium for the SMI program is $42.50 versus $3 per month in 1966. This amount is typically adjusted annually, the politician's euphemism for raised (see Exhibit 3-4). In fact, the SMI monthly premium increased from $29.90 in 1991 to $46.10 in 1995. However, in 1996 the SMI monthly premium was actually reduced from $46.10 to $42.50. While this made little to no policy sense given escalating SMI program costs and the original 50/50 cost split, 1996 is an election year and seniors tend to have higher voter turnout rates!

While the SMI program is independent of OASI, in most cases, the SMI premium is deducted from a person's Social Security (OASI) check as a matter of convenience. This has caused some to decry that raising SMI premiums is analogous to cutting Social Security benefits. I don't share this view and believe that it adds to the misinformation being disseminated by some in Washington. By the end of last year, over 32 million seniors were covered by the SMI program.

Those who voluntarily enroll in SMI will have different services covered, including certain doctors' fees, hospital outpatient expenses, and other related expenses. Generally, SMI pays for 80 percent of eligible expenses after a $100 annual deductible. As a result, individuals pay the $100 annual deductible plus 20 percent of the approved amount of Medicare reimbursable costs (50 percent for certain mental health services). The deductible and coinsurance provisions apply to most doctors' fees, outpatient hospital treatment, mental health services,

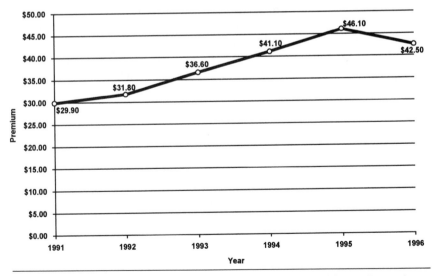

Exhibit 3-4   SMI premium adjusted annually (*Source:* Healthcare Financing Administration.)

physical and speech therapy, screenings, certain drugs that can't be self-administered, ambulance services, and durable medical equipment such as wheelchairs and oxygen tanks.

Some SMI-related items are not subject to the $100 deductible of co-insurance provisions, including some vaccines, diagnostic laboratory tests, and home health services. SMI also covers certain chiropractic, podiatrist, dental, optometrist and certain specifically qualified non-practitioner services, subject to certain conditions and benefit limits.

Limitations on HI and SMI

While HI and SMI cover a wide variety of medical services and equipment, they do not cover routine physical exams, eyeglasses, hearing aids, dental services, cosmetic surgery, outpatient prescription drugs, private rooms and nurses, and certain services paid for by the government, workers' compensation, or automobile insurance policies or long-term care that is strictly custodial.

Both the HI and SMI programs also have certain deductible and co-insurance provisions. Many retirees buy Medigap insurance policies offered by AARP or others to fill in on medical expenses not covered by Medicare.

There are 10 varieties of Medigap policies designed by the National Association of Insurance Commissioners (NAIC). A typical Medigap basic benefits policy would cover such items as the co-payment for hospital days 61–150 and up to 100 percent of up to 365 additional days per lifetime (Part A) and the 20 percent co-payment for allowed physician charges (Part B). Importantly, Medicare would pay nothing after the 151st day and would only pay once for days 91–150. In 1996, the typical cost of an individual Medigap policy ranged from $50 to $125 per month, excluding prescription drug coverage, depending on age and the level of Medigap coverage desired.

Pre-Medicare-Eligible Retiree Issues

People who retire before age 65 are not eligible for Medicare coverage. They might have to purchase health-care coverage on their own if they're not covered by their last employer's health plan. Many who fall into this category may be eligible to purchase so-called COBRA health insurance coverage, which stands for the Consolidated Omnibus Budget Reconciliation Act of 1987, which included this provision. Under this federal law, a retiree under 65 is generally entitled to buy insurance at the spouse's former employer's specified group rates for 18 months (see Chapter 5).

MEDICARE FINANCING AND PROGRAM DEFICITS

What's in the cards for these twin programs? Due to the failure of Congress, the administration, and the press to publicize the real nature and extent of the financial imbalance in the Medicare programs beyond the next decade, there will be a large gap between what Americans expect to receive and what they will likely receive. This expectation gap is significant and needs to be addressed.

Like the OASI program, the HI and SMI programs have separate trust funds that collect related program revenues and pay covered benefits and administrative expenses. Based on the 1996 Annual Trustees' Reports, the HI and SMI programs were projected to have $136.3 billion and $17.9 billion in assets in their trust funds at the end of 1995, respectively.

Unlike the OASI program, which currently has an annual surplus, the combined Medicare Trust Funds have been operating in a negative cash flow position since 1992, excluding interest on the government securities in the trust funds. While total HI Trust Fund assets have grown somewhat until 1995 due to accrued interest on the government securities held by the Trust Fund, the HI Trust Fund ratio—the ratio of assets at the end of the year to projected expenditures for the next year—peaked financially in 1992 and has been declining ever since (Exhibit 3-5). The 1996 Annual Trustees' Report showed that the Medicare programs experienced a net decline in assets of $8.9 billion in 1995. Simply stated, the HI Trust Fund ratio is in free fall, and the program is headed for insolvency unless needed reforms are enacted.

If the trend is not reversed, according to the Bipartisan Commission on Entitlement and Trust Reform, the projected annual deficit in the year 2025 for the HI program alone will be $758 billion (Exhibit 3-6), almost $300 billion more than OASI's annual deficit in the same year (Exhibit 2-1).

Both Medicare programs will be affected by social changes—the aging of our society and other demographic trends noted earlier. They also both experience annual growth in program costs far in excess of the general inflation rate. The combined annual spending gap for both in the year 2020 is likely to approximate $1.5 trillion. Yes, I said trillion!

Taking a broader perspective, the overall percentage of our economy, as represented by the percentage of our GDP dedicated to health-care increases and the federal budget dedicated to entitlement programs, including Social Security and Medicare, continues to escalate annually, with no sign of stopping.

Will the cupboard soon be bare? Yes. Without significant program reforms and/or tax or fee increases, there may be no money available for other expenditures such as national defense, law enforcement and

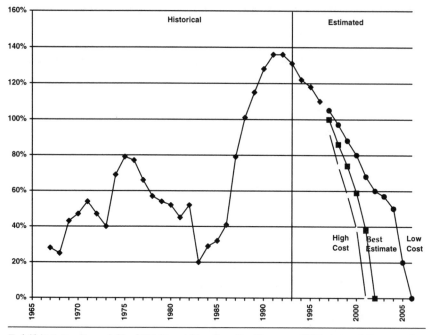

Exhibit 3-5   Free fall of HI Trust Fund ratio (*Source: 1995 Annual Report of the Board of Trustees of the Federal Hospital Insurance Trust Fund.*)

foreign relations. They will be crowded out by soaring entitlement spending and debt service costs. Ironically, many of the items that are in danger of being squeezed such as national defense, foreign relations and law enforcement are expressly provided for in the Constitution. The entitlement programs are not, even though they are important.

The 1995 Trustees' Annual Report, which was the last one which I signed as a Public Trustee, noted that the HI Trust Fund, which pays inpatient expenses, would only be able to pay full benefits for seven years, or until 2002. The 1996 Trustees' Annual Report noted that the HI program is now estimated to become insolvent in 2001.

Given the shortfall in the HI program, the 1995 Trustees' Annual Report called for timely congressional action to take steps and curb the rate of increase in Medicare (both HI and SMI) program costs. The trustees' outcry was not new. Beginning in 1990, the trustees had urged Congress to address this and control HI program costs for the short and long run through broad-based or Medicare-specific health-care reform legislation. To illustrate the severity of this imbalance, when Congress eliminated the wage base cap on HI payroll taxes in 1994 and allocated

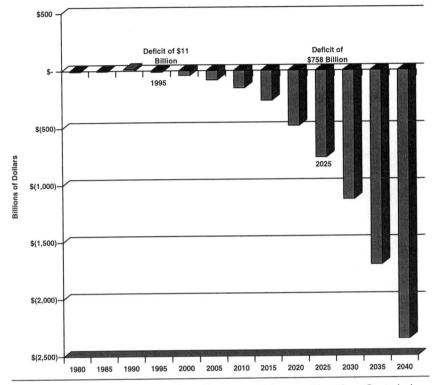

Exhibit 3-6 Projected deficit for HI program (*Source: Bipartisan Commission on Entitlement and Tax Reform, Final Report to the President,* January 1996.)

additional taxes from subjecting 85 percent of certain individuals' Social Security benefits to income tax, the additional revenues only extended the trustees' estimated date of HI Trust Fund insolvency by one year.

The 1995 Trustees' Annual Report received much greater attention in the press and in Congress than in prior years due in large part to the change in the political balance in Congress, which resulted from the Republican sweep of both houses in the November 1994 congressional elections.

That season, many House Republican candidates campaigned on the basis of a Contract with America, which called for a balanced federal budget and individual income tax cuts. But when faced with how to balance the federal budget deficit, most economists and politicians zeroed in on the fact that growth should be slowed in federal entitlement programs of Social Security and Medicare. It seems unlikely, however, that Social Security will be tampered with in the near term. It represents political dynamite, which leaves Medicare and the various federal welfare programs as the more likely targets. In fact, both major parties have taken Social Security reforms off the table, at least until after the 1996 elections.

When the 1995 HI Trustees Annual Report was issued, which calling for Congress to take steps to strengthen the financial condition of the HI program and slow the growth in HI and SMI program spending, Haley Barbour, chairman of the Republican National Committee, declared it "manna from heaven."

Why? Because the report was signed by four Clinton administration trustees as well as the two public trustees. This included three members of the President's Cabinet (Secretary of the Treasury Robert Rubin, Secretary of Labor Robert Reich, and Secretary of Health and Human Services Donna Shalala) and Commissioner of Social Security Shirley Chader, in addition to the public trustees (Stanford Ross and myself). The signatures of the Clinton administration trustees gave the Republicans in Congress the credence and ammunition to call for reductions in the rate of Medicare spending growth.

Stan and my final public trustees' statement in the 1995 Summary of the Social Security and Medicare Annual Reports went even further by noting, among other things, that the Medicare program is "unsustainable in its present form" and that "Medicare needs to be addressed urgently as a distinct legislative initiative." This should include a review of the program's financing methods, benefit provisions, and delivery mechanisms.

Once this grabbed the attention of Congress and the press, it seemed the propitious time to correct some distorted information. However, most of the debate has focused on the inadequacies of the HI program because of its projected insolvency date. This was misleading and another reflection of the flat-earth theory, the tendency of many politicians and the overall federal budget process to consider the impact of proposed changes only over the next several years in balancing the federal budget rather than over the longer haul. The program is headed down the tubes with rapidly escalating deficits and a sea of red ink (Exhibit 3-6).

While politicians' messages differ, both parties and virtually all major economists and program experts recognize that some reduction in projected Medicare costs is in order. To state otherwise ignores reality.

The Republicans' proposed $270 billion spending reduction in late 1995 and early 1996 would not have come close to "saving the Medicare program." However, it would have served to strengthen it over the near term and would stave off insolvency in 2002. Realistically, the proposed spending reductions represents only a drop in the bucket and a small down payment as compared with the size of the spending reductions and/or tax increases that would be necessary to restore the financial integrity of the HI program over the next 25 years, much less the next 75 years. In fact, it wouldn't maintain the financial integrity of the HI program until the year that the first baby boomer reaches age 65 in 2011.

The cold hard facts are these: Somewhat ironically, the Democrats' unwillingness to make more than cursory spending reductions may represent a much greater threat to the future survival of the Medicare program than the Republicans' larger current cuts since once the HI Trust Fund runs out of assets the related Medicare benefits cannot be paid. In addition, lower current spending reductions and further delays will only serve to increase the severity of future changes and the degree of difficulty in achieving them.

Politics aside, the need to strengthen the financial condition of the HI program and reduce the rate of growth in Medicare expenses exists whether or not income tax cuts are enacted. The ability to strengthen the financial condition of HI will not be affected by any income tax increase or decrease because Medicare benefits can be paid only with HI Trust Fund assets. HI tax receipts must increase and/or HI program costs must decrease to improve the program's financial condition.

Many of the current proposed spending reductions reflect more of the same past cost-shifting policies—reduction in cost reimbursements to doctors and hospitals and increases in Medicare premiums, deductibles, and co-pays. These approaches are old, tired, and almost played out. We must get beyond the past and toward more comprehensive and innovative approaches. In the end, effectively controlling care costs will require a fundamental change in the current incentives affecting both providers and consumers of health care services. Providers will need to focus on providing quality and cost effective care and individuals will need to become smarter and more cost conscious health care consumers.

While a handful of additional approaches have been proposed and are being pursued, including some contained in the Republicans' legislative reform proposal, such as expansion of managed-care arrangements and a crackdown on waste, fraud, and abuse, most lack adequate safeguards or enough specifics. At least Washington is beginning to think outside the historical box.

Possible Future Medicare Program Reforms

The projected deficit in the HI program is so monumental, and HI and SMI program costs are projected to grow so rapidly, that I believe the Medicare programs are unsustainable in their present form. They must be fundamentally reformed. While such programs may have been affordable 30 years ago, they no longer make sense today and will make even less sense in the twenty-first century since our top priority should be to save OASI.

To make sweeping reforms is precarious. As one U.S. Senator from California said to me during one of my many Congressional appearances in 1995, "we want to be fair to our seniors." But what's fair? I believe that the concept of fairness requires that the interests of different generations should be weighed. Namely, we need to balance the interests of today's seniors with those of the baby boomers and Generation Xers who are being asked to finance a vast majority of ballooning Medicare costs. To do so, Congress must consider more severe reform proposals than it has in the past.

What Medicare reforms can be expected? In addition to cracking down on fraud, waste, and abuse, the following represent the more likely reforms that will pop up over the next several years:

- Change existing managed-care options under Medicare to increase competition. Introduce more competitive bidding in the process and reduce adverse selection, or cherry picking, to cover lower-risk individuals at an average premium level, which translates into more profits for the insurer and more cost for the payer—in this case Medicare, or you, your children, and grandchildren.
- Expand the use of managed-care approaches under Medicare such as second surgical opinions, HMOs, PPOs, while reserving patients' freedom to choose their own physicians and remain under a traditional fee-for-service arrangement, but at a significantly greater cost than under the managed-care options.
- Eliminate medical education subsidies to teaching hospitals from Medicare cost reimbursements.
- Raise the eligibility age from 65 to 67 or 70 on a gradual basis.
- Reduce benefit coverage by raising deductibles and co-pays and freezing or lowering overall benefit caps.
- Broaden the HI payroll tax base by including the value of certain employer-provided fringe benefits such as health care.
- Increase the HI payroll tax rate from the current rate of 1.45 percent of wages and earnings from self-employment and/or impose a national consumption or sales tax to finance the ballooning deficit.
- Increase the percentage of cost that individuals pay for SMI coverage from the current 25 percent in 1996 through increasing SMI

premiums to 50 percent or more of the average cost on a progressive basis.

- Revise the investment restrictions applicable to the HI Trust Fund to allow for a portion of trust fund assets to be invested in higher-yielding but passive investment vehicles such as stock index funds.

While the above represent the reforms which, in my view, are more likely, their listing herein does not mean that I personally support all of these potential changes.

Accomplishing significant and more fundamental Medicare reforms will require Congress to take the following three-step approach:

1. Take steps to enact necessary program reforms, such as some of the above, to assure the financial integrity of the HI program and slow the growth in Medicare program costs over the next 10 years.
2. Educate the American people on the nature, extent, and magnitude of our Medicare, Social Security, and other entitlement challenges in the twenty-first century to help them understand the need for dramatic reform and help Congress set appropriate priorities.
3. Enact more dramatic and fundamental Medicare program reforms within the next five to 10 years and periodic incremental reforms thereafter, as necessary, to assure the longer-term viability, sustainability, and equity of the Medicare programs.

While the preceding list represents the most likely approach to Medicare reform, I believe there is a better and more comprehensive strategy that would take into consideration not only our aging population, the incremental cost associated with providing disproportionately expensive health care to seniors, but also the need to address the growing health-care coverage gap among Americans and the special needs of children. Specifically, more than 37 million Americans currently lack any health-care coverage, and that number is growing. In addition, too many children also lack access to basic preventative care programs that more than pay for themselves in reduced health care expenses over time.

Such an alternative strategy could involve the federal government phasing out the current Medicare and Medicaid programs and transitioning to a single health insurance program that would finance catastrophic coverage (for which the related coverage or premiums would vary based on the financial circumstances of the individual) for all Americans, though avoiding heroic medical measures at general tax-payer expense—expensive procedures that are not expected to extend or improve a person's life long term. They would be paid for by individuals, if they so choose.

The government could also facilitate the creation of appropriate risk pools to assure that people could purchase additional coverage at group rates. Finally, the government could take steps to assure that selected preventive care is provided to certain segments of the population, those needing prenatal care or childhood inoculations, for example.

Reforming the existing Medicare program in this fashion would meet several needs and circumvent numerous problems. Employers and employees would be free to determine the level of coverage to pro-vide or purchase the degree of risk to assume and the amount of their resources to dedicate to health-care coverage. Furthermore, the new catastrophic program would provide individuals with the option to purchase broader health-care coverage at group rates. Any coverage be-yond the basic catastrophic benefit would be paid for by an employee and employer and not by taxpayers. This would separate health-care access from health-care financing. It also provides a much needed real-ity check for the general public in connection with health-care costs.

The impact of Medicare and OASI reform will vary based on when and which programs, if any, are altered. In general, most people would face more severe changes in their Medicare benefits than in their re-formed OASI benefits because the Medicare programs are in much worse long-term financial shape.

Adding fuel to the fire, the expectation gap will be greater because many people, especially baby boomers, overdiscount their future Social Security benefits and underdiscount future Medicare benefits. Part of the reason relates to political rhetoric. Many politicians suggested that their proposed $270 billion spending reduction over the next seven years to be enacted as part of the 1995 budget deal would have saved Medicare from bankruptcy. But the proposed changes fall far short of what it will really take to save the current Medicare programs. That assumes that we can and should save the existing programs in their present form. As noted earlier, we need to think more in terms of real reforms and com-prehensive reengineering of these programs. Times change, and we must, too.

If needed changes aren't forthcoming, the burden will fall on individ-ual taxpayers. They will have to dedicate more retirement income to health-care expenditures than they now do to compensate for higher Medicare premiums and lower Medicare benefits, and purchase addi-tional private insurance premiums to fill all or part of an expanding health-care coverage gap in their retirement years. This gap is inevitable as we focus on how much health care coverage we can afford rather than how much we want.

What are the chances Congress will make the fundamental changes necessary to address the long-term financial shortfall in the Medicare programs? It is not very likely without the creation of a Greenspan-type commission and additional public education within the next two to three years under ideal circumstances. Importantly, the 1996 Trustees' Annual Report called for the creation of an advisory group to develop long-term options for both the HI and SMI programs. This is a positive step which, if acted on and implemented properly, will help to break the Medicare reform stalemate.

In summary, while there are no magic bullets, dramatic and fundamental changes in the Medicare programs are essential, not only to assure the financial integrity of the reengineered Medicare programs and intergenerational equality but also to guarantee the economic security and the continued improvement of our standard of living in the twenty-first century. This will require the employment of sound policy as opposed to strident politics. Stated differently, we need to explore non-partisan policy options and adopt bi-partisan solutions to be successful. This will require some statesmanship and stewardship, but it is essential and we as citizens should demand it of our political and government leaders.

Over time, significant changes in the Medicare program are inevitable. The longer the wait the more dramatic the changes will need to be. As time passes, additional support will grow to transform Medicare into the type of program I noted previously. In the alternative, it is likely to change to a defined contribution type program to guarantee access to health care while stopping the drain on the budget. Guess who will pick up the difference, we will.

Nonetheless, the clock is ticking. It's time to get on with it.

CHAPTER FOUR

Employer-Sponsored Pension and Savings Plans

MYTH 5

Defined-contribution plans are better than defined-benefit plans.

Yes and no. Defined-contribution plans are more portable than defined-benefit plans and easier to understand because of their individual account feature. Some defined-contributions plans also give people the ability to decide how all or part of their individual accounts will be invested. On the flip side, individuals bear all of the investment risk, and their account balances are not insured. Some defined-contribution plans require people to save money before they receive any employer contributions. Furthermore, individual account balances can fluctuate significantly, and most "amateur" investors can't beat the pros in getting their money to grow.

MYTH 6

The benefits of defined-benefit plans are safe.

Not always. Between 1988 and 1991, 30,000 company pension plans terminated. Employers bear the investment risk associated with defined-benefit plans and are required to meet certain minimum funding standards. Also, most private sector defined-benefit plans are insured by the Pension Benefit Guaranty Corporation (PBGC). Not all defined-benefit plans are well funded and not all companies are financially sound. As a result, if your defined-benefit plan terminates in an underfunded position and your employer goes out of business, the funds in the trust may be insufficient to pay your promised benefit. Importantly, the PBGC does not insure all defined-benefit plans and has limits on the amounts that it will insure. In addition, it does not insure any defined contribution plans. Furthermore, the PBGC, like most government corporations, is also not in great financial shape.

Employer-sponsored pension and savings plans and individual savings efforts have played an important role in helping Americans achieve a reasonable standard of living during retirement. As retirement security becomes more illusory, however, the only way most people will retire comfortably is to rely more on these plans and their other personal savings efforts. That means Americans need to have a better handle on how these plans work.

Today, people must be their own watchdog because many companies are cutting back or fundamentally changing the nature of their plans. Occasionally, in fact, employers will use plan assets, particularly from 401(k) plans, to pay for company needs. Employees and retirees are well advised to check periodically on their retirement plans.

They should know who oversees them, how often contributions are made, and how those contributions are invested. If they are covered under a traditional defined-benefit pension plan (a plan that provides a retiree a stated level of monthly income in retirement typically based on their age, years of service, and compensation level), they need to know how well the plan is funded, especially if their employer experiences financial difficulties.

People also need to know whether retirement benefits are paid to a surviving family member and what happens in the case of a divorce. Finally, they need to know how the payment can and should be made—in a lump sum or periodic installments.

BACKGROUND/HISTORY

Employer-sponsored retirement plans have come a long way and undergone several incarnations since the American Express Company created the first private sector pension plan for its employees in the 1870s. In the beginning, most plans did not require employees to get involved. Instead, they simply promised to pay some of their employees a retirement benefit if they made it to retirement, and funded those benefits from the company's general assets.

Today, many employers, especially small businesses, are switching to plans that typically require workers to kick in some money and to select how that portion of their pension account should be invested.

But let's back up. The most dramatic growth in employer-sponsored pension and savings plans came after World War II. Much of the growth was related directly or indirectly to the emphasis that organized labor put on these plans through collective bargaining (the process by which labor and management negotiate wages, benefits, work rules, and working conditions).

While labor union support for these programs was historically important, it is less significant today as the percentage of workers represented by unions continues to decline. In addition, most private sector pension and savings plans cover non-union employees. Employers now have a much greater ability to unilaterally create, terminate, and change future benefits under their current plans while preserving amounts their employees have already earned. Organized labor does, however, still play a role in major pension and savings plan legislation and regulation.

In fact, employer-sponsored pension and savings plans have grown to the point that they not only represent a crucial element in our country's retirement security model but are major players in the capital markets and in corporate governance. They represent the single largest pool of capital in the world—total private sector pension and savings plan assets grew to over $4.0 trillion at the end of 1995. Ironically, one of the few larger financial numbers is the federal debt, which now exceeds $5 trillion and is growing.

These plans are not designed to stand alone. They are intended to be augmented by Social Security retirement (OASI) benefits and personal savings arrangements. After OASI is reformed, however, the importance of employer-sponsored retirements plans and personal savings will rise like the Dow Jones industrial average on a good day.

WHO PARTICIPATES

Not everyone receives the benefit of employer-sponsored retirement plans. Reasons vary. Employer-sponsored retirement programs are voluntary. Not all employers offer a plan, and those that do may not cover all employees. Typically, participants must be 21 years old and work at least 1,000 hours in a plan year to be covered. In addition, employers have some discretion to exclude some employees or groups of employees without running afoul of federal tax and labor laws.

Some small-business owners may forgo the opportunity to set up one of these plans to contribute on behalf of themselves because to do so they may have to contribute more than they want to on behalf of their employees. Even if an employee is covered, the employee may not work a sufficient number of years to become vested or earn a nonforfeitable right to their arrived benefits. Most private sector companies require no more than five years of work before an employee is fully vested in any contributions made by the employer.

Governmental employers and certain union plans (multiemployer plans) typically require longer periods of service to become fully vested in a benefit. Individuals are always fully vested in any contributions that they make through salary reduction arrangements (Section 401(k)), employee contributions, and after-tax employee contributions.

TYPES OF PLAN SPONSORS

Several entities sponsor pension and savings plans, such as private sector companies; federal, state, and local governments; unions; and not-for-profit entities. Plans vary. This book will focus on private sector pension and savings plans, the largest segment in the pension and savings plan universe, typically referred to as *single-employer, multiple-employer,* and *multiemployer plans.*

A *single-employer plan* is simply that, one maintained by one or several companies within a single controlled group of companies. For example, the Southern Company based in Atlanta owns a controlling interest in several major utilities, including Georgia Power, Alabama Power, Mississippi Power, Gulf States Power, and Savannah Electric. Southern Company could have one pension plan that would cover employees of all these entities if it chose. Not-for-profit entities also sponsor single-employer plans. *Multiple-employer plans* represent pooled retirement plan arrangements sponsored by several unrelated employers, usually covering non-union employees. Specifically, two or more unrelated employers combine their asset management and benefit administration activities to gain economies of scale. Professional or trade associations often administer these plans for member companies. Two examples are the National Automobile Dealers Association, in McLean, Virginia, and the Iowa Bankers Association, in Des Moines, Iowa.

Certain unions sponsor so-called *multiemployer* plans for their members. Under these plans a number of unrelated employers contribute to a collective trust fund covering union members who work for various employers but belong to a particular union such as the Teamsters or Boilermakers. According to the Taft-Hartley Act, these union-sponsored plans must be governed by a joint board of trustees comprised of an equal number of union and management officials. Management trustees are selected from the companies whose union employees are covered under the plan. Union trustees are chosen from union members who are covered under the plan.

While multiemployer plans are the only type administered by a union, single- or multiple-employer plans can also cover union members. Specifically, while the union may not administer the plan, the benefits provided under these plans may relate to union employees. For example, each of the major U.S. auto companies sponsors a single employer defined benefit pension plan for its employees who belong to the United Auto Workers (UAW).

By the end of 1992, there were approximately 700,000 private sector pension and savings plans covering approximately 63 million individuals and holding approximately $2.2 trillion in assets (see Exhibits 4-1, 4-2, and 4-3). By the end of 1995, they held over $3.0 trillion in assets. Of these, approximately 3,000 were multiemployer plans, which covered approximately 10 million individuals and held approximately $215 billion in assets.

There is also the assortment of federal, state, and local *government plans* that covered approximately 14 million individuals and held about $1.5 trillion in assets at the end of 1995.

TYPES OF PLANS

The two primary types of employer-sponsored pension and savings plans are *defined-benefit* and *defined-contribution plans.* Both can qualify for favorable tax treatment under the Internal Revenue Code (IRC), as long as they meet a broad range of complex plan design and operating parameters. Favorable tax treatment means that employer contributions are deductible currently, within limits; the plan's income and earnings are generally tax-exempt; and participants are not taxed on the benefits until they are paid.

These plans must not discriminate in favor of so-called highly compensated employees. This means the group of employees who earn more

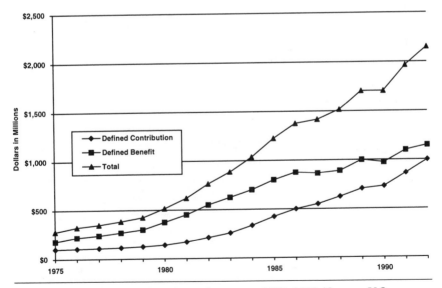

Exhibit 4-1   Pension and savings plan assets 1975–1992 (*Source:* U.S. Department of Labor [DOL].)

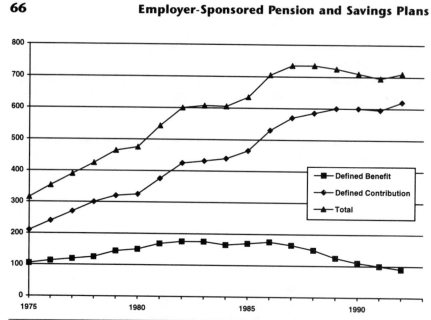

Exhibit 4-2   Number of private pension plans 1975–1992 (*Source:* U.S. Department of Labor [DOL].)

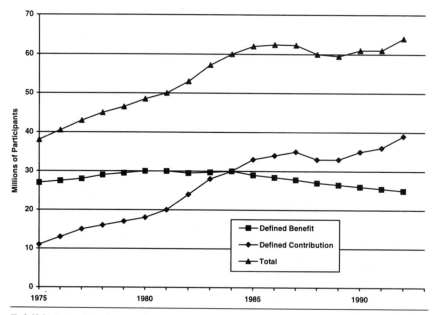

Exhibit 4-3   Pension and savings plan participants 1975–1992 (*Source:* U.S. Department of Labor [DOL].)

than $100,000, or the top 20 percent of an employer's workforce who earn above $66,000. In addition, all officers of the employer who make $60,000 or more must be counted.

All plans must cover a minimum percentage of the workforce, generally the lesser of 50 individuals or 40 percent of the eligible workforce. A minimum percentage of the covered workforce must actually participate under the plan, typically 70 percent or a ratio of non-highly compensated employees that is at least 80 percent of the ratio of highly compensated employees covered under the plan.

The maximum annual compensation that can be considered for contribution and benefit purposes is $150,000. As a result, many employers will turn to supplemental nonqualified plans for their executives and other select groups of management or highly compensated employees. These plans typically provide benefits in excess of allowable limits under tax qualified plans. Participants and beneficiaries in these plans are not afforded many of the protections under the Employee Retirement Income Security Act (ERISA). This chapter will concentrate on tax-qualified plans protected by ERISA that cover the majority of Americans who are covered under employer-sponsored pension and savings plans.

Defined-Benefit Plans

Defined-benefit plans are the traditional pension plans. As a rule, these promise workers a specific monthly payment, based on the workers' wages and/or years of service, when they retire. There is also a new kid on the block, a defined-benefit plan known as a *cash balance plan*. Here the employer promises to make a stated contribution—a percentage of pay—and to pay a stated rate of return on all contributions.

Both types of defined-benefit plans have an annual cap on the benefit paid to an individual on retirement, typically at age 65. The current annual benefit limit under a tax-qualified defined-benefit pension plan is $120,000. This benefit limit is another reason for the proliferation of supplemental plans. After all, many owners and top management feel that they should receive a similar level of benefits (as a percentage of their preretirement income) as their rank-and-file employees. In addition, owners of closely held companies generally want to feel that they can receive meaningful benefits under a tax-qualified plan before they are willing to share the wealth with their employees.

Under defined-benefit plans, the plan sponsor (the employer) is responsible for making the necessary contributions to pay the promised benefit. These contributions are subject to certain federal minimum funding standards. The sponsoring employer also bears the primary risk of making sufficient contributions to fund the benefit and all the related investment risk.

In single-employer and multiple-employer plans, the employer usually appoints one or more trustees to manage related plan assets, and, in turn, the trustees usually hire one or more professional money managers to invest the plan's assets.

To provide some protection against the termination of a pension plan that does not have adequate assets to pay accrued benefits (such as when an employer goes out of business), most private sector defined-benefit plans are required to purchase insurance from the PBGC. Similar plans sponsored by church and related religious organizations have the option of doing so. Certain defined-benefit plans, such as governmental plans, are not covered by the PBGC program. In addition, the PBGC does not insure any defined-contribution plans.

Defined-Contribution Plans

Defined-contribution plans relieve the employer of some financial, accounting, and regulatory burdens associated with defined-benefit plans. Under them, the employer promises to make a stated contribution, versus providing a stated benefit or guaranteeing a stated rate of return on its contributions. Annual employer contributions will generally be limited to the lesser of 15 percent of an employee's annual compensation or $30,000. All employer contributions are allocated to individual accounts for each participating employee. Assets can be managed by one or more trustees with the assistance of professional money managers.

Alternatively, an increasing number of participants in defined-contribution plans now bear the responsibility for how some or all of their account will be invested. These are known as *participant-directed plans*. Most defined-contribution plans are not subject to federal minimum funding standards. None is covered by PBGC insurance.

There is a potpourri of different defined-contribution plans. The most common ones used by for-profit employers include profit sharing, money purchase, stock bonus, employee stock ownership, thrift/savings, and Section 401(k) plans. Not-for-profit employers can sponsor defined-benefit pension and certain-defined contribution plans under Section 401(a) of the IRC and can also sponsor Section 403(b) and Section 457 plans. Both not-for-profit and government employers are currently prohibited from sponsoring 401(k) plans.

401(k) Plans   This type plan is named after the related Internal Revenue Code section that allows for salary deferrals under certain types of defined-contribution plans (e.g., profit sharing). It is the fastest-growing type of retirement-savings plan in the United States. Millions of employees use them to put part of their salaries before taxes into investment vehicles. So far, more than $525 billion has been stockpiled in these plans.

There is some risk associated with these plans. In recent months, it has come to light that employers may be responsible if the investment vehicle for the 401(k) loses money. Employees of Unisys Corporation filed suit in 1991 for an alleged breach of fiduciary duty in connection with the purchase of a guaranteed investment contract (GIC) from First Executive Life Insurance Company of California after First Executive filed for insolvency protection. The case was among the first of its kind and currently is pending (Meinhardt vs. Unisys Corp., Third U.S. Circuit Court of Appeals, Nos. 95-1156, 95-1157, and 95-1186).

The following represents a listing of several other types of defined-contribution plans:

- *Profit-sharing plans.* Employers usually contribute a discretionary stated amount or stated percentage of their profits to the plan each year. Ironically, under applicable tax laws, an employer does not have to have current year profits to make a contribution under these plans. Typically, however, employers will make contributions under these plans based on a percentage of their profits.

- *Money purchase plans.* The employer promises to make a stated contribution based on a formula in the plan document. Federal law mandates certain minimum funding standards.

- *Stock bonus plans.* These represent a defined contribution in which all or a part of a plan's assets are invested in securities—stock—of the employer sponsoring the plan. Contributions are outlined in the plan document. Plan participants receive securities allocated to their account when they are eligible upon either retirement, separation from service, death, or disability. The employer may, however, stipulate that the employee has a right of first refusal (ROFR) to purchase employer securities that are not readily tradable on an established securities exchange before the plan participant sells them to anyone else.

- *Employee stock ownership plans (ESOPs).* These are a cousin of the stock bonus plan that under the IRC must have more than 50 percent of the assets invested in certain kinds of employer securities (common stock with the highest dividend and voting rights, or preferred stock that is convertible into the highest class of common stock). ESOPs are eligible for a special tax preferences and subject to a number of additional requirements.

Certain leveraged ESOPs can provide annual benefits of up to 25 percent, versus 15 percent, of an employee's pay. There is still a $30,000 annual contribution cap. However, if the ESOP is deemed to be broadly based—not more than one-third of annual allocations go to so-called highly compensated employees—then interest and forfeiture amounts (amounts lost due to failure of individuals to fully vest in their employer contributions) are excluded from the 25 percent and $30,000 limit. In addition, dividends on stock held in the plan are not counted for purposes of this limit if the dividends are used to pay down ESOP loans or are distributed to the respective employees. Finally, this limit is based on the cost of the stock rather than its fair market value, which can also allow significantly higher real benefits if the stock has appreciated greatly since its initial acquisition by the plan.

ESOPs generate pros and cons. On the plus side, individuals can receive significantly more benefits through a tax-qualified ESOP than under other types of tax-qualified plans, especially if the employer's stock increases in value.

The primary downside is that ESOPs do not offer a diversified investment portfolio, because almost all plan assets are placed in one basket—the employer's stock. You could be stuck with nothing if your employer goes belly-up. To provide some hedge against this possibility, ESOPs are subject to a number of additional tax and labor laws and regulations that must be met.

ESOPs can borrow funds to purchase employer securities, adhering to certain guidelines. Under the so-called leveraged ESOP, the acquired stock usually serves as collateral for a loan to the plan, which the employer usually guarantees. The ESOP debt, interest, and principal is then paid off via periodic contributions from the employer to the plan. As contributions are made, and the related ESOP debt is reduced, certain shares of stock are released from any related bank lien. They are then allocated to accounts of individual participants based on the formula in the plan (typically, compensation subject to the overall $150,000 cap) and are subject to certain federal annual benefit limits. Stock not released and subject to a bank lien is referred to as *unallocated shares.*

ESOP plan participants are generally eligible to receive their account balance on their retirement or separation from service or to pass it on to their survivors upon their death. However, employers with leveraged ESOPs, which hold stock that is not publicly traded, can be allowed to delay certain stock distributions. Specifically, they can delay such distributions until the ESOP debt has been retired. Otherwise, participants with account balances of $690,000 or less usually must be able to receive their entire account balances within five years. Employers can extend this five-year period one year for each $135,000 in additional account balances above the $690,000 threshold.

As in stock bonus plans, ESOP participants are entitled to receive employer stock, when they are eligible, under the terms of the plan. Employers who do not have publicly traded stock must allow ESOP participants to sell their stock to the employer of the plan at fair market value (a "put option"). Fair market value typically is determined by an independent appraisal. Such independent appraisals are required in connection with stock purchased by an ESOP after 1986. Under ESOPs, employers can also have a ROFR.

- *Thrift/savings plans.* These plans enable employees to save for retirement on a pretax or after-tax basis. Pretax means the employee's contribution is not subject to income taxes until paid from the plan. After-tax means that employee contributions are subject to current taxation and are not taxed when they are distributed. In any event, all employee contributions, whether pretax or after-tax, grow tax-free in the plan, but the tax is due on these earnings when the benefits are paid. In addition, both pretax and after-tax contributions are subject to FICA (Social Security and Medicare) payroll taxes.

- *Section 401(k) plans.* These plans, which will be a key retirement vehicle in the future, represent a kind of thrift/savings plan that allows workers to save the lesser of 15 percent of their pay or $9,500 on a pretax basis in 1996. This is a dynamite individual savings vehicle. With this plan, employees save money for retirement by contributing pretax income from their paycheck, reducing gross income, which, in turn, cuts the amount owed to Uncle Sam. In addition, many employers kick in from 25 cents to one dollar for each dollar that an employee contributes, subject to certain limits and restrictions. Importantly, Congress recently created inhanced "SIMPLE 401(k) plans and SIMPLE IRAs" for employers with 100 or fewer employees (Appendix B).

Today, fewer employers offer totally employer-funded retirement plans. A majority are attempting to reduce related costs given increasing competitive pressures and shareholder activism. Most retirement-savings plans are designed to retain a participant's benefit in the related trust until the person's death, disability, retirement, or separation from service.

Defined-contribution plans generally provide for significant asset portability because employees can take the value of their account with them or roll it over into an IRA of a qualified plan maintained by their new employer when they leave. Defined-benefit plans generally provide limited portability of pension assets. Specifically, most defined-benefit plans do not provide lump-sum options when employees leave, except for those with accrued benefits of $3,500 or less.

Some defined-contribution plans and a few defined-benefit plans allow employees to borrow a portion of their accrued benefits. These loans are generally secured by a portion of their account balance (e.g., up to 50 percent of their 401(k) balance), bear a market rate of interest, and are repaid via payroll deduction. Loans can provide a release valve to give employees temporary access to a portion of their retirement benefits prior to retirement. In addition to loans, many 401(k) plans allow employees to access up to 50 percent of their account balances even when they have a loan for the balance of the account for certain hardships such as a catastrophic illness. Any withdrawal must be consistent with applicable tax law provisions and is subject to both income and excise taxes.

Annual benefit and lump-sum payments, at or after retirement, are subject to income taxation based in part on whether the individual contributed on a pretax or after-tax basis. Employer contributions and earnings on all contributions are subject to income tax. Annual benefit and lump-sum payments are not subject to payroll taxes.

Plan benefit payments in excess of stated amounts—$155,000 and $750,000, respectively, in 1996—may be subject to a 15 percent excise tax, payable by the recipient, in addition to applicable income taxes. Importantly, the Small Business Job Protection Act of 1996 (SBJPA) included a provision that would suspend the imposition of this 15 percent excise tax for the years 1997–1999. Furthermore, benefit distributions before age 59½ are subject to a 10 percent early distribution tax in addition to otherwise applicable income taxes. However, plan loans are not subject to income or excise taxes unless they aren't repaid within prescribed time frames. Under SBJPA, plan participants who do not continue to work or who are 5 percent or more shareholders must begin receiving payments of a portion of their benefits by April 1 after they reach age 70½.

Not-for-profit entities, such as museums, often sponsor Section 403(b) plans, which have been viewed as the stepchild of the 401(k). Options are more limited, employer-matching contributions are nonexistent, and the plans tend to be heavily invested in annuities. On the plus side, these plans let workers contribute a stated amount or percentage of their pay on a pretax basis to an individual retirement arrangement subject to certain annual limits—$9,500 this year. Employees can invest these amounts in certain tax-deferred annuity arrangements or tax-deferred custodial accounts such as mutual funds.

Section 457 plans, a cousin of Section 403(b) plans, are available only to state or local government employees. Section 457 also has various provisions and limits. The maximum annual amount that can be contributed to an employee's Section 457 now is $7,500.

FEDERAL LAW PROTECTIONS—ERISA

As the largest pool of capital in the world, employer-sponsored pension and savings plan assets need to be protected. Unlike the Social Security and Medicare Trust Funds that are required by law to invest in government securities, pension and savings plans have a variety of types of assets—stocks, bonds, and U.S. treasury instruments and sometimes more exotic investments like real estate, futures, options, and other derivatives.

Participants' savings are protected by several federal labor and tax laws, with the primary federal law ERISA. That was signed into law by former President Gerald Ford in 1974 as a result of two issues: the widely publicized losses incurred by employees whose employers had shut down their businesses, and the increasing concerns over the unrestricted investment of pension assets. When Gerald Ford signed ERISA into law, it was championed by a small group of senators and congresspersons on both sides of the political aisle. While a number made significant contributions, the primary champions were Senators Jacob Javits (R-NY) and Harrison Williams (D-NJ) and Congressmen John Dent (D-MO) and John Erlenborn (R-IL).

ERISA does not mandate the kinds or level of benefits that an employer must provide its employees. Rather, like a doctor recommending a prescription for a healthy diet, it dispenses a set of rules to be followed if the employer or union voluntarily decides to offer a plan to its employees. Under ERISA, the pension or savings plan provide retirement income to employees, or result in the deferral of income by employees for periods that extend to the termination of covered employment or beyond.

Like a pie, ERISA is divided into four separate sections, called titles:

- Title I contains the fiduciary, reporting, and disclosure standards, which are administered by the Department of Labor's (DOL's) Pension and Welfare Benefits Administration (PWBA).

- Title II contains amendments to the Internal Revenue Code (IRC) and is administered by the IRS.

- Title III, basically an administrative section, divides responsibility between the DOL and IRS in connection with certain provisions contained in Titles I and II.

- Title IV establishes the program of federal insurance for most private sector defined-benefit pension plans and is administered by the Pension Benefit Guaranty Corporation (PBGC).

ERISA does not cover government plans, but many states have passed statutes that adopt or parallel ERISA's fiduciary provisions. Unfortunately, most state and local government plans are not subject to the same safeguards, such as the reporting and disclosure provisions or the independent audit requirement.

ERISA enumerates a number of provisions designed to protect participants. Employee benefit plans, including pension and savings plans, must be governed by a written plan document and trust instrument. Also, most employee benefit plan assets (pension and savings plan assets not held by insurance companies, including employee contributions under a 401(k) plan) must be held in trust and separated from the general assets of the plan sponsor on a timely basis.

Generally, employee contributions (such as 401(k) salary reduction contributions by employees) must be placed in the respective plan trust as soon as feasible but no later than three days after the applicable payroll period. Employer contributions must also be placed in trust on a timely basis.

In August 1996 the DOL issued regulations relating to the placement of employee pension and savings plan salary reduction and other contributions in trust because of increasing concern that employers may attempt to use these monies. The new final regulations generally call for such contributions to be placed in trust no later than 15 business days after the month in which they are withheld or received. This compares with the 90-day-maximum mandate of the prior regulations.

ERISA also includes a range of reporting and disclosure provisions. For example, plan sponsors must submit an annual report to the IRS. These reports are used by the IRS, DOL, and PBGC for enforcement, research, and other purposes. Most ERISA plans with more than 100 participants are subject to an annual audit by an independent accounting firm.

Title I

The cornerstone of ERISA's protections are the fiduciary standards in Title I. These are like a built-in security system. These provisions require that all plan assets be managed prudently, in the interest of plan benefits and beneficiaries, and for the purpose of paying plan benefits and reasonable administrative expenses. Many plan fiduciaries hire outside experts to handle or to advise them on certain plan matters beyond their individual areas of expertise.

Title I also clamps down on plan fiduciaries to manage the plan in accordance with applicable documents and instruments, to diversify the plan's assets and to avoid conflicts of interest and so-called prohibited transactions. These represent certain transactions such as purchases, sales, exchanges, loans, leases, and use of plan assets between the plan and certain parties in interest such as an employer, union, fiduciaries, and plan service providers unless they are exempted by law or by DOL administrative exemption.

Title I places limits on the amount of plan assets that may be invested in an employer's stocks or bonds. The maximum is 10 percent of the plan's assets as of the date of the applicable purchase. Title I exempts certain defined-contribution plans, like stock bonus plans and ESOPs from these limits and from ERISA's general diversification requirements, if certain conditions are met.

ERISA mandates that certain reporting and disclosure requirements be met. Plan participants must receive a summary of their plan document in plain written English, a summary of the plan's annual report, and advance notice of any proposed benefit reductions. In addition, most plan participants, other than participants in multiemployer plans sponsored by a union, have the right to request a summary of their benefits under the plan once a year without charge. They may also request copies of other plan documents and reports for a nominal charge. Participants in defined-benefit plans must also be notified on a timely basis if their plan's assets are less than 90 percent of their accumulated benefit obligations—the discounted present value of promised benefits based on service rendered to date.

To help participants exercise individual rights under ERISA, these disclosures are an additional safety net and must be made within prescribed time frames. Specifically, ERISA allows plan participants, beneficiaries, and other interested parties to sue through the federal district courts if they feel their rights have been violated. This could happen if they find that the responsible plan fiduciaries have mismanaged the plan's assets, engaged in prohibited transactions, or denied them benefits.

Title II

Title II, which concerns a plan's qualifications for favorable tax treatment, amended the IRC and includes a number of requirements that must be met. These provisions include certain minimum coverage, participation, funding, vesting and plan merger/spin-off, and transfer requirements. Many of these provisions are also contained in Title I of ERISA.

In addition to the coverage, participation, and vesting rules, which have already been discussed, the IRC subjects defined-benefit and money purchase plans to certain minimum funding requirements. These requirements are designed to assure that defined-benefit plans fund their promised benefits over a reasonable period of time, and place more stringent funding requirements on plans that are deemed to be underfunded or whose assets are less than their accumulated benefit obligations.

Title II and the IRC also contain certain "bad-boy" provisos. These govern how forfeitures are handled and prohibit the denial of benefit accruals based on age alone. They also forbid employers from denying former employees their accrued benefits under the plan, if they enter into competition with their former employer. However, employers can defer the payment of any accrued benefits until the person's normal retirement age, if the plan so provides. ERISA also sets out certain asset transfer rules that must be fulfilled in connection with any plan mergers, spin-offs, transfers, or terminations. These rules are designed to prevent the skimming of assets from one plan to benefit another. They also prevent the employer from obtaining a reversion of any plan assets prior to termination of the plan and satisfaction of all accumulated benefit obligations, including fully vesting all participants in their accrued benefits on termination. These so-called asset reversions, or "asset perversions" in the words of former Senator Howard Metzenbaum (D-OH), are a subject of continuing controversy.

The IRC also spells out the tax-qualifying parameters. For a pension or savings plan to achieve this status, it must meet the provisions under Title II of ERISA and a number of additional IRC requirements.

Like a benevolent parent, the IRC tries to be fair to all employees. That's why it contains a number of nondiscrimination rules that are intended to insure that tax-qualified plans benefit an appropriate number of non-highly compensated employees and that highly compensated employees are not given better treatment—higher relative benefit levels or additional benefit options.

Violating tax provisions can result in more than just a slap on the hand. It may mean loss of the tax-favored treatment that typically includes employer deductions for contributions to the plan, tax-free buildup of trust assets, and deferral of any individual taxation of benefits accrued under the plan until they are paid. In addition, participants may lose the ability to make contributions to the plan on a pretax versus after-tax basis.

The preceding rules provide a number of important protections, but are not perfect. Holes from an individual's perspective include the fact that employers do not have to cover all employees under their plans, that they have some opportunity to affect the amount and timing of contributions to defined-benefit plans by changing the assumptions they use, and that employers and union plan trustees have the unilateral right to create, amend, or terminate a plan without violating applicable labor and tax laws as long as certain conditions are met. For example, ERISA and the IRC prohibit the reduction of any pension benefit that has already accrued under the plan, including amounts and form of benefits, be it a lump sum or an annuity. They do not, however, prohibit the reduction or elimination of future benefit accruals.

Title III

Title III is an administrative provision that outlines how the responsibilities for administering ERISA should be divided between the IRS and the DOL. This division was modified by the Reorganization Act of 1978. The DOL administers the fiduciary, reporting and disclosure, and prohibited transaction provisions of ERISA. The IRS administers the tax qualification requirements and imposes any excise taxes applicable to pension and savings plans.

Title IV

Title IV establishes the federal pension insurance program and the PBGC. Self-funded plans represent those funded by the employer and/or employee where benefits are paid from a separate trust fund, so called self-funded plans. In self-funded plans, a participant's benefit security risk is related to the funding status of the plan/trust and the financial strength of the employer. Plans for which the employer or union purchases insurance contracts from an insurance company to pay the benefits promised under the plan are called *insured plans*. In insured plans, the participant's benefit security risk is related directly to the financial strength of the insurance company that issued the policy.

The perception that insurance contracts are as solid as a rock no longer holds true. Several insurance companies have filed for bankruptcy under various state insolvency laws in the past few years, including First Executive Life and Mutual Benefit Life.

PBGC insures single employer plans which terminate and are deemed to be underfunded on a termination basis as of the date-of-plan termination. The event triggering payment of insurance for multi-employer plans is insolvency or when the plan has insufficient assets to meet its current obligations.

Like most insurance policies, the PBGC's coverage is bought and funded by premiums. PBGC's premiums are paid by companies that sponsor defined-benefit pension plans covered by ERISA or the related plan which is insured.

In the case of single-employer plans, the PBGC base premium is $19 per plan participant per annum. Certain underfunded plans pay an additional annual premium, known as a *risk-related premium*, based on the degree of underfunding. Effective in 1994, the previous cap on the PBGC risk premium of $53 per person began to phase out and will be eliminated (for plan years beginning after 7/1/96). Premiums for multi-employer plans do not vary based on the funding status of the plan and are $2.60 per plan participant per year.

Of course, PBGC guarantees are subject to certain limits and conditions. The PBGC guarantees only certain vested benefits up to a stated limit ($2,642.05 per month in 1996). PBGC does not guarantee all types of ancillary benefits such as severance pay in nonannuity form that may be promised in connection with the defined-benefit plan. Also, benefit increases during the five years prior to plan termination are not fully insured. These limits can result in significant reductions in benefits for certain types of nonmanagement personnel such as airline pilots. Why? Because these people typically earn pension benefits exceeding applicable PBGC insurance limits. This was dramatically illustrated when a number of airlines shut down in the 1980s, including Braniff, Eastern, and Pan Am.

As for most government corporations, PBGC liabilities exceed its assets, though there is no immediate threat to its solvency. Various reforms have been enacted since the mid-1980s to strengthen the PBGC insurance system and avoid a repeat of anything similar to the savings and loan crisis of the 1980s.

In summary, while ERISA is far from perfect, it has made a real difference in enhancing the integrity and security of the private pension system. Clearly, more will and should be done to expand coverage, improve portability, enhance the security of pension benefits, and eliminate unnecessary tax-related regulatory burdens. Certain related proposals by both Republicans and Democrats alike are included in the proposed Pension Savings and Security Act of 1996. Many of these proposals are likely to be enacted if the President and the Congress can focus on policy versus politics.

DISTURBING TRENDS

While the growth in pension and savings plan assets since ERISA's enactment has been impressive, clouds are gathering on the horizon. Let's first examine the least ominous signs, which *could* lead to severe thunderstorms if not checked.

Overall private sector coverage rates—the percentage of full-time workers employed by an entity that offers a pension or savings plan— hit a peak in the late 1980s and have declined somewhat since then.

This is a matter of concern because of the deteriorating financial condition of the Social Security and Medicare programs and anemic personal savings rates.

Real contribution rates to defined benefit plans, adjusted for the effects of inflation, for both employers and employees, have declined significantly since 1980. Between 1981 and 1991, such employer and employee contributions dropped a whopping 51 and 22 percent in real terms (adjusted for inflation), respectively (Exhibit 4-4). While some of the decline in employer contributions was due to favorable investment experience that served to reduce the amount of required contributions under defined-benefit plans, much was related to increasing

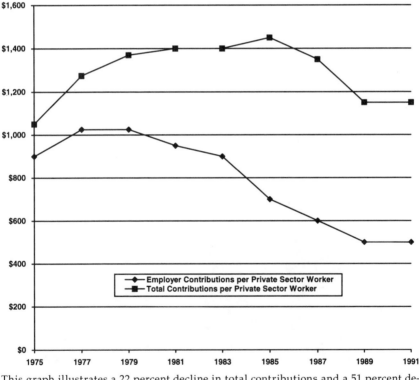

This graph illustrates a 22 percent decline in total contributions and a 51 percent decline in employer contributions since 1981.

Exhibit 4-4 Contributions to private defined benefit pension plans 1975–1991 (in 1987 Dollars) (*Source:* The Brookings Institution, Bureau of Labor Statistics, Bureau of Economic Analysis.)

business competition and reductions in applicable tax-favored contribution and benefit limits. These trends, when coupled with additional
government regulation, have put us in the position we are in today.

This increased government regulation, which is particularly applicable in the case of defined-benefit plans, has resulted in a significant
decline in the number of defined-benefit plans and the relative amount
of assets in these versus defined-contribution plans. This also included
several reductions in the level of contributions and benefits relating to
tax-favored pension and savings plans.

Concurrent with these declines, administrative costs relating to pension and savings plans have soared since 1981, especially in connection
with smaller plans (Exhibit 4-5). These increased administrative costs
are adjusted for inflation so we are comparing similar numbers. Such
soaring costs at a time of greater competitive pressures undermine the
creation and maintenance of these plans, particularly defined-benefit
plans, which are also subject to greater regulatory burdens.

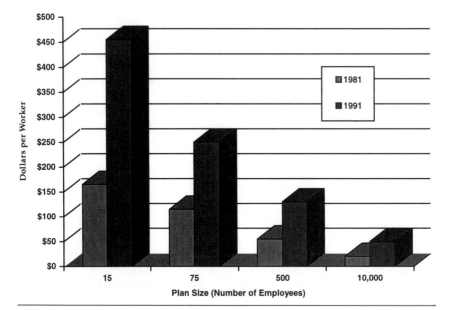

Exhibit 4-5   Administrative costs of pension and savings plans (in 1990 dollars) (*Source:* Hay/Huggins Company, Inc.)

Recent Governmental Changes

ERISA, too, keeps changing. Since its enactment more than 20 years ago, Congress has legislated over 15 major changes, with the latest to be signed into law being the Small Business Job Protection Act of 1996 (Appendix B). This compares with only 5 major changes during the period between 1920 and 1974. While some of the changes since 1974 have served to enhance benefit security and improve the financial integrity of the PBGC insurance system, many simply propagated the complexity and related administrative burdens and were designed to raise revenue by reducing related tax preferences. Even some of the changes that were merited at the time have weakened the stability of the private pension and savings system.

One of the most disturbing trends has been the government's efforts to raise revenue by reducing tax preferences accorded to private pension and savings plans. Congress has taken such steps almost annually since the early 1980s.

An example of this approach was the reduction in the so-called full-funding limit, applicable to defined-benefit pension plans in 1988. That limit serves to restrict the amount of contributions that an employer can make on a tax-deductible basis. This is important because employers are not likely to make nondeductible contributions to their pension plans, especially since such contributions face a 10 percent nondeductible excise tax. Pundits contend that this action further mortgaged our already mortgaged future.

What prompted Congress to make this decision? It seems a spurious move to raise revenue for federal budget purposes. The new limit, based on an arbitrary 150 percent of the current accrued benefit liabilities, regardless of how much money the plan's actuary said is needed to properly fund the plan, served to raise short-term revenues at the expense of longer-term benefit security. Although designed solely to raise revenue, it backloaded future pension contributions at a time when employers face increasingly competitive pressures and a sharp decline in their number of workers per retiree.

It is understandable that Congress has taken steps to toughen funding standards of underfunded plans and that it strived to place some reasonable controls on the ability of employers to make pension contributions on a tax-favored basis given existing budget deficits. Nevertheless, in many cases, these changes have been shortsighted, poorly timed, and should be reversed. Given the ups and downs in business cycles and increasing competitive pressures, Congress needs to give employers the flexibility to adequately fund their plans for arranged increases in employee compensation, while they have the ability and willingness to do so. Congress should allow employers to take into account the nature of their workforce and any likely increases in employee compensation, especially when a plan promises a benefit that is based on the final year(s) of employee compensation prior to retirement.

Congress has also taken steps to reduce the amount of contributions and benefits that can be provided under tax-qualified pension and savings plans. These reductions should be revoked. In addition, Congress should allow base individual limits on a rolling lifetime limit rather than individual annual limits. This would permit people to make up some of their missed contributions, when they have a greater economic ability to do so, such as after their children have graduated from college.

Unfortunately, it seems that Congress is unlikely to favor change without significant additional pressure from its constituents and other interested parties. While these issues are important to the nation's and your economic security, they are complex. Let's face it, such decisions don't generate many votes.

But let us not get too far afield of more recent and disturbing trends. Already, this shortsightedness is backfiring. One indication is the increase in the overall level of underfunding in defined-benefit plans between 1984 and 1993 (Exhibit 4-6) and the reduction in the number of

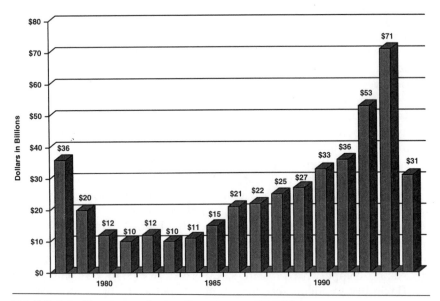

Exhibit 4-6   Pension underfunding (*Source:* PBGC.)

defined benefit plans since the early 1980s (Exhibit 4-2). Importantly, while the overall level of pension underfunding declined significantly in 1994, it is estimated to have risen significantly in 1995. Why? Because the decline in interest rates and the resulting effect on plan obligations more than offset the favorable investment returns for the year. At the same time, most underfunding is concentrated in a relatively few large pension funds.

Another potentially disconcerting trend is the shift by employers from benefit plans to defined-contribution plans (Exhibit 4-2) due to a variety of factors:

- The greater regulatory burdens and administrative costs associated with defined-benefit plans.
- Increasing competitive pressures to cut costs and a desire by employers to exercise greater control over the timing, amount, and form of the contributions they do make.
- A desire by employers to avoid any adverse accounting statement implications associated with underfunded defined-benefit pension plans.
- Increasing interest on behalf of employees in defined-contribution plans as compared to defined-benefit plans. Employees can better understand and identify with defined-contribution plans given their individual account structure and the increase in the trend to allow participants to control their own investments. Defined-contribution plans have greater asset portability than defined-benefit plans, which appeals to a younger and more mobile workforce. They also typically have shorter vesting schedules for employer contributions although they are not required to by law.

While this shift from defined-benefit to defined-contribution plans is real, it is important to note that a number of larger employers offer both defined-contribution and defined-benefit plans. Defined-contribution plans seem to be the preferred choice for most small to medium-sized employers, which represent the largest and fastest-growing segment of the economy.

Many in the workplace, however, are concerned about the longer-term ramifications of this shift on their retirement security. One reason is that under certain defined-contribution plans, employees may not receive employer contributions unless they make their own contributions that employers match. Unfortunately, many Americans do not have the ability or the discipline to save. Therefore, many who are eligible do not participate in their company's 401(k) plan, particularly if the company does not match their contributions.

Some are also worried because defined-contribution plans do not provide a specific monthly benefit during retirement, and they're not insured by the PBGC. As fewer employees participate, a shrinking pool of employers may be left to pay premiums for PBGC's past and future obligations. Furthermore, employees covered by defined contribution plans may choose to receive their benefits in one lump sum if they change jobs. This may tempt them to spend their nest egg rather than rolling it over. This type of action serves to further mortgage the employee's retirement security while giving an additional amount to Uncle Sam at the same time. Trust-to-trust transfers or annuity form payments are an alternative in such cases.

Many observers, too, are distressed about the switch within defined-contribution plans, in particular 401(k) plans, from professionally managed to participant-directed investment arrangements. Under participant-directed plans, workers may choose from a menu of investment options, typically at least three pooled investments—mutual funds—with different investment objectives and the ability to change investment directions at least quarterly. The problem is that most participants are not investment professionals and tend to be risk-averse, so they are not likely to achieve investment returns as high as those of professional investment managers. Given this trend, additional steps need to be taken by employers and others to assure that employees make informed judgments in connection with their retirement savings and investments.

Many workers also worry that the shift to defined-contribution plans will mean a significant reduction in the average amount of income they receive from employer-sponsored plans in retirement. Typically, these plans tend to attract fewer employer contributions, lower investment returns, and higher lump-sum consumption rates than defined-benefit plans.

Needed Reforms

While we need to curb the pace of change in the pension laws, current laws also need to be reformed. These reforms should achieve the objectives listed on page 85.

Certain groups are working to effect change. The Committee for Economic Development, the Association of Private Pension and Welfare Plans, the American Institute of Certified Public Accountants, the Retirement Savings Network, and other organizations with which I am and have been affiliated have made a number of recommendations relating to these concerns. Most are designed to raise contribution, benefit,

- Establish a set of retirement policy principles to guide and evaluate related legislative proposals
- Encourage individuals to plan, save, and invest for their retirement through employer-sponsored pension and savings plans and other vehicles.
- Require most employers to provide a means for employees to save on a payroll deduction and tax favored basis (e.g., Section 401(k) plans or Section 403(b) arrangements).
- Provide reasonable contribution and benefit limits including additional flexibility for employers and individuals to make contributions to pension and savings plans based on accumulated lifetime versus annual limits.
- Repeal the current arbitrary 150 percent full-funding limit imposed on defined-benefit plans.
- Assure that defined-benefit pension plans are funded adequately to meet their benefit promises.
- Insist that pension and savings plan assets are managed in accordance with a strict set of fiduciary standards and that violators are held accountable (this would include disallowing firms from using money in 401(k)s as a source of checking funds and being sure of some independent trustee supervision).
- Streamline and simplify the nondiscrimination and other applicable rules.
- Restore the minimum vesting periods applicable to multi-employer (union sponsored) plans to parallel these applicable to other plans.
- Enhance the portability of defined-benefit plan assets by increasing individuals' ability to take their accrued pension benefits with them when they change jobs and enable them to contribute the value of any related benefit to a defined-contribution plan maintained by their new employer.
- Require individuals to preserve their employer contributions for retirement income purposes and limit individuals' ability to obtain lump-sum distributions prior to retirement except in situations of real, significant, and unexpected hardship.
- Ensure the long-range financial integrity and equity of the PBGC insurance program, including revising the current risk-related premium structure to make it more equitable and in line with real versus perceived risk.
- Assure that all employer-sponsored pension and savings plans, including governmental and multiemployer plans, are required to disclose important information on a timely basis and in a useful manner.
- Eliminate the current restrictions on the ability of independent auditors to review activity relating to employee benefit plan assets held by banks, insurance companies, and trust companies.

and funding limits to more reasonable levels and reduce related administrative burdens. Fortunately the Small Business Job Protection Act of 1996 (see Appendix B), which was passed by the Congress in August 1996, contains a number of positive first steps, including pension simplification and excellerated multi-employer plan vesting. However, more can and should be done.

Employer-sponsored pension and savings plans will have an increasingly important role to play in the twenty-first century as the Social Security retirement program faces greater financial strains, particularly if people continue to save inadequately.

Questions remain: Will employers be able to maintain and adequately fund these plans based on existing tax laws? Furthermore, will employers be willing and able to continue these plans given increasing competitive pressures, existing regulatory burdens, and possible major changes in the tax system? Solutions must be found and soon. I have my own views which I share frequently with the Congress and the Administration. However, this is not a public policy book so let's move on.

CHAPTER FIVE

Employer-Provided Retiree Health Benefits

MYTH 7   Employer retiree health programs won't change.
False by a long shot. Three things are certain in life: death, taxes, and change. Most employers that offer retiree paid or subsidized health care are moving to curb their costs and, in some cases, cancel plans outright. These plans are not afforded the same federal law protections as pension and savings plans. Employers are likely to continue to take steps to curb costs associated with the plans as long as they are not legally bound to maintain them.

The 1960s was the decade of the Beatles, flower children, the Vietnam War and former President Lyndon B. Johnson's Great Society. Fueled by the Vietnam War, the economy boomed. As businesses thrived, many employers started sharing some of their spoils with employees in the form of health-care benefits for retirees.

BACKGROUND/HISTORY

Employer-provided retiree health benefits were virtually unheard of before the 1960s. Some enlightened employers, mostly those with a paternalistic culture, had begun to provide them, though they did so as the smart business step to take and in a vastly different economic landscape than exists today. Health benefits were affordable and could be better controlled. The percentage of individuals over 55 who worked was higher (Exhibit 5-1), and the ratio of retirees per active employee was lower (Exhibit 1-4).

Many employers eased into the retiree health business slowly. A number tested the waters by providing health insurance coverage to

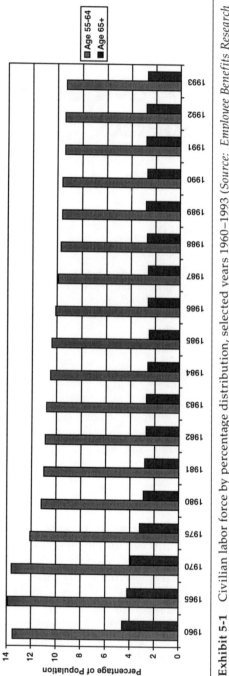

Exhibit 5-1 Civilian labor force by percentage distribution, selected years 1960–1993 (*Source: Employee Benefits Research Institute Databook on Employee Benefits*, 1995.)

workers who retired before they were 65 and eligible for Medicare. When the climate seemed right, employers added a smattering of supplemental policies to address specific health-care expenses not covered by Medicare, such as deductibles, co-pays, and amounts in excess of applicable benefit caps.

In these cases, most employers initiated and expanded programs as an incidental benefit to health-care coverage for then-active employees, though many acted before calculating the true long-term cost of providing these benefits. Ditto for employers who provided generous coverage to those who took early retirement before age 65 as part of an employer-sponsored voluntary workforce reduction program. In many cases, employees jumped at the opportunity to retire early. Those who didn't take the sweetened offers were sometimes later pushed into retirement without additional compensation.

The retiree health option proved to be shortsighted and pricey and bit a big hole in many corporate bottom lines. While some employers may have achieved the desired headcount reduction, they did so at great expense and, in most cases, at much greater costs than they expected. For example, General Motors and other large employers would experience such surprises in connection with their "downsizings" in the late 1970s and early 1980s, although in a number of cases the surprise was delayed.

The result was an employer expectation gap. It became apparent that it was much more expensive for employers to provide a stated level of retiree health insurance coverage for 55- to 65-year-olds than for those a decade older, because, although health insurance costs increase with the age of the insured, at 65, Medicare became the primary payer of these costs.

Because of the expectation gaps and the sky-high and escalating costs of retiree health-care coverage today, many employers who offered these programs have now reduced or eliminated them. There has been a significant drop in employer-paid or subsidized retiree health coverage over the last few years, a trend that is expected to continue.

Pittston Coal attempted to terminate its retiree health contributions outright in 1988 when it realized the magnitude of the related costs, which ran in the hundreds of millions of dollars. The United Mine Workers (UMW) struck in 1989 after negotiations failed on these issues. In the end, Pittston partially restarted retiree health benefits and resumed contributions to the 1950 UMW Benefit Trust and a new 1974 UMW Benefit Trust.

The employer-oriented expectation gap is just one point of view. The other is that employees and retirees who expect to receive these benefits during their retirement years may be shortchanged. The gaps here are wider. Many think that these benefits are sacrosanct, protected by the federal laws that guard pension programs. The reality is quite different.

I predicted this scenario in 1987 when I gave my first speech as U.S. Assistant Secretary of Labor and referred to retiree health programs as a "ticking time bomb." A number of publications and people adopted my analogy. It has turned out to be a truism based on employer reductions and eliminations of these programs in the 1990s.

Why? Because the expectation gap associated with employer-provided retiree health programs was, and remains, the most prevalently misunderstood of any retirement security element—more so than Social Security, employer-sponsored pension and savings programs, and Medicare programs. To put things into perspective, less than 15 percent of current retirees have employer-paid retiree health insurance, which is far less than private pension, Social Security, and Medicare coverage rates.

TYPES OF RETIREE HEALTH PLANS

Benfit Types

To convey the full scope of the quandary, three different employer-provided retiree health plan arrangements need to be explained. The simplest and fastest-growing plan is designed to give retirees the ability to purchase health insurance at group rates. These rates may or may not be subsidized directly or indirectly by an employer.

By subsidized, I mean that the retiree may not have to shoulder the full cost of his health insurance coverage as if it were priced for retiree-only groups. The premium is calculated on the basis of whether the retiree has a separate premium rating to avoid any subsidization of retiree health benefits by active employees and the employer. This is predicated on the fact that certain classes of retirees (e.g., under 65) usually incur higher employer paid health care costs than active employees (Exhibit 5-2). The employer may decide to directly subsidize the retiree's premiums by paying a portion of the retiree's cost. Alternatively, the employer may decide to indirectly subsidize a portion of the cost by not charging retirees the full cost of a separately calculated retiree-only premium. In this case, active employees may also serve to effectively subsidize retiree health coverage, if they pay all or part of the cost for their own health insurance coverage.

In the second type of plan, the employer provides retirees with access to health care at group rates and makes a stated fixed contribution to help the retiree pay. These so-called defined-dollar benefit plans

	1992	1993	1994	1995
Retiree:				
Total	$2,548	$2,751	$2,859	$3,131
Under 65	4,858	5,219	a	5,252
65 and over	1,650	1,793	a	1,803
Active	3,301	3,578	3,443	3,476

a = N/A.

Exhibit 5-2   Average employer medical plan costs active employee versus retiree, 1992–1995 (*Source:* A. Foster Higgins & Co., Inc., *National Survey of Employer-Sponsored Health Plans, 1994 and 1995* (Princeton, NJ: A. Foster Higgins & Co., Inc., 1995 and 1996) and EBRI tabulations.)

usually stipulate that the employer pays a stated dollar amount per year of service toward a retiree's health insurance cost, perhaps $10 per month times the retiree's number of work years. In this arrangement, since the employer's contribution is fixed, the retiree bears the risk and costs associated with future health-care inflation.

A third type is one in which the employer provides a stated level of health-care coverage to retirees and the employer pays or subsidizes the retiree's cost, which may fluctuate. Under this arrangement, the employer is exposed to additional costs due to health-care inflation and other factors such as an increase in use of services, level of treatment, and longer life spans.

Many employers who offer this type arrangement impose a ceiling on overall cost. Some might cap total annual retiree health costs at a specified amount such as $3,000 times the number of retirees. Others index the active and retiree premiums associated with the plans to the plan's actual health-care inflation rate to assure that their employees and retirees pay a stated percentage of the overall cost of the plan, perhaps 50 percent. Additional active and retiree costs come in the form of higher premiums, deductibles and copays or lower benefit levels or dollar limits. In some instances, employers may take multiple steps to control these costs, thereby employing a "belt and suspenders" approach (double insurance).

Relatively new to emerge on the benefits scene is the aggressive use of managed-care approaches to control costs. This includes the use of health maintenance organizations (HMOs), preferred-provider organizations (PPOs) and point-of-service arrangements (PSOs). Employers also control benefit costs for active employees and retirees by demanding second surgical opinions or requiring referrals by primary care physicians before a person can be reimbursed for a specialist or for going outside of the managed-care network.

The aggressive exploration and implementation of managed care by employers has dramatically reduced the rate of growth in their annual health-care costs within the past several years. This sparked Congress's interest in expanding the use of managed-care arrangements under Medicare and other government-sponsored health programs.

Funding Arrangements

In addition to the type of plan, the type of funding arrangement is crucial to completing the total health-care benefits picture. Two primary funding strategies exist. The plan can be self-funded with the employer paying for benefits out of its general assets or by establishing a separate trust fund. In these type of arrangements, the employer's financial condition can have a direct impact on the security of the promised benefits. Since most retiree health programs are unfunded (no seperate trust fund), they represent a "naked promise to pay."

The second major funding arrangement is an insured plan. This is similar to any insurance policy. The employer transfers all risk associated with providing the promised benefits for a stated period of time to an insurance company in exchange for paying a specified premium. The insurance company promises to pay the guaranteed benefits and administers the claims process. Premiums, of course, can rise annually depending on claims history. Many employers faced double-digit increases in annual health insurance costs until they began to pursue aggressively new and enhanced managed-care initiatives coupled with plan design changes in the 1990s. Many of the plan design changes resulted in the shifting of certain costs and risks to employees.

Some employers outsource the claims administration process to an insurance company or third-party administrator. If an insurance company only administers claims, it is referred to as an *administrative services-only arrangement (ASO)*. If another entity administers claims, it is called a *third-party administrator (TPA)*. Under either, the arrangement may be self-funded or partially insured.

If self-funded, the employer retains a primary responsibility for meeting the promised benefit obligations. Under a partially insured arrangement, an employer is obligated to foot the bill for a portion promised and may deflect the risk associated with certain benefits such as individual or accumulated claims in excess of a stated amount(s).

For example, some employers will purchase insurance from a third-party insurance company to pay individual catastrophic claims in excess of a stated annual limit, such as $10,000, or total claims amounts in excess of a specified limits such as $10 million. Most retiree health benefits are self-funded or partially insured because few insurance companies will fully insure retirees. In the last few years, most employers have embraced self-funded arrangements with ASO or TPA features. Many of these have stop-loss insurance policies, and virtually all call for some retiree premiums, deductibles, copays and benefit caps.

FEDERAL LAW PROTECTIONS (ERISA)

More often than not, employer-sponsored retiree health arrangements are a part of an active employer's health care plan. Most of these plans are subject to ERISA guidelines, but they are not subject to a number of the same important protections that apply to employer-sponsored pension and savings plans. Specifically, employers are not required to fund these plans in advance or hold most of any related plan assets in trust. The primary exception are plans that require employee after-tax contributions. Because retiree health plans are so exposed, they're commonly referred to as naked promises to pay on behalf of the employer. The security of the benefit depends directly on the sponsor's financial well-being or, in cases of insured plans, the insurance company's viability.

Unlike pension and savings plans, retiree health plans are not subject to ERISA's minimum coverage, participation, funding, and vesting provisions. In addition, they are not subject to the anticutback provisions applicable to employer-sponsored pension and savings plans.

Retiree health plans that do hold plan assets in trust are subject to the same fiduciary responsibility, reporting and disclosure, and independent audit requirements as employer-sponsored pension and savings plans.

Unlike 401(k) salary reduction contributions, which must be placed in trust on a timely basis and which are normally held for longer-term investment, Section 125 contributions, which are named after the related IRC section, salary reduction contributions by employees under employer-sponsored health and welfare benefit plans are not currently required to be placed in trust. These Section 125 contributions relate to employee contributions and typically employee-health insurance premiums made in connection with an employer-sponsored cafeteria or flexible-benefit plan. Typically, these plans provide employees with the opportunity to pick certain benefits such as health or disability from a menu of choices subject to certain predetermined employer contribution limits.

Adding to the precariousness of this scenario is that many employers have the unilateral right to walk away from related promises without notifying employees or retirees in advance. The only major exceptions are employers who are in bankruptcy and must comply with certain notification requirements and those employers who are held to have entered into binding contracts by a court, including collective bargaining agreements, contractual promises to nonunion employees based on the nature of the promise and related communications to employees and retirees.

Because several important ERISA protections do not apply to retiree health plans, these benefits essentially are usually in the same position as pension promises made before ERISA's enactment in 1974. While many ERISA protections accorded to employer-provided pension and savings plans do not apply to retiree health plans, one additional provision does: that retirees are entitled to continue their coverage at their own expense, but at employee group rates, for a period of up to 18 months if they choose this right under COBRA. This ensures that retirees can get coverage, though it does not help pay for it.

THE DECLINE AND FALL OF RETIREE HEALTH PROGRAMS

Since the late 1980s, retiree health programs have been in a state of free fall for several reasons. Economic and demographic factors have affected these programs, but most employers did not realize the financial impact until the accounting treatment for these benefits changed from a cash basis to an accrual one. This evolution occurred after the Financial Accounting Standards Board (FASB) undertook a project to review and reconsider the accounting treatment for postretirement benefits such as health and life insurance. This project was long and controversial. It culminated in the promulgation of Statement of Financial Accounting Standards No. 106 (SFAS No. 106), Employer Accounting for Health and Other Post-Retirement Benefits, in December 1990.

Under the prior cash basis accounting rules, employers didn't recognize the costs associated with retiree health benefits in their financial statements until the benefits were paid. Under the current accrual basis, the employer is required to recognize the present value of all direct and indirect current and future costs and the related obligations associated with benefits during the employee's active service period.

Moreover, the change from the cash to the accrual basis was only one of two shoes that the FASB dropped in employers' laps in connection with retiree health accounting. The other required employers to project the future cost of providing retiree health insurance and to record amounts based on the discounted present value of these future payments in their current financial statements. At the time, average health insurance costs were climbing at double-digit rates and at rates significantly above the general inflation rate.

These changes may not seem significant, but they had serious adverse implications for the income statements and balance sheets of companies that sponsored these retiree plans. In fact, in 1988, the change in accounting was estimated to have an effect of over $300 billion on the combined equity of the employers who provided these benefits.

For many employers, running the numbers in connection with the implementation of SFAS No. 106 was the first time they attempted to calculate the current and projected costs of these benefits. The calculations were both a revelation and a shock. Employers saw in black and white that, given the projected rise in their retiree population, the cost of these programs and related financial statement results was stratospheric. These revelations came on the heels of Medicare's cutbacks in its cost reimbursement rates to providers beginning in 1983, which meant that health-care providers had shifted certain costs to employer-sponsored health plans. Additional cost transfers began to take place in 1986 after Medicare was changed to give employers primary responsibility for health insurance coverage for individuals who worked past age 65. The switch meant that employer-sponsored health programs, not Medicare, became first in line to pay the health costs of active employees 65 and over. The result: an increase of billions in additional annual health costs to employers.

Retiree costs ultimately rose as well, resulting from the reductions and caps imposed on the amounts that the HCFA would pay for Medicare services measures that Congress occasionally dredges up again to reduce Medicare-related costs. In many cases, providers—hospitals and physicians—began to charge more to employees covered by employer-sponsored programs to make up for the reductions in Medicare reimbursements. This went on until employers woke up and took steps to control their health-care costs through aggressive implementation of various managed-care approaches.

The expansion of managed-care approaches in the private sector in turn reversed the flow of costs, with the annual increase in health-care costs ricocheting back to Medicare and the individual and away from the employer for the first time in three decades. From 1965 to 1992, the percentage of total health-care costs shouldered by employees declined from 63 percent to 34 percent, while the portion of total health-care costs borne by employers and government during the same period increased from 16 percent to 27 percent and from 20 percent to 35 percent respectively (Exhibit 5-3).

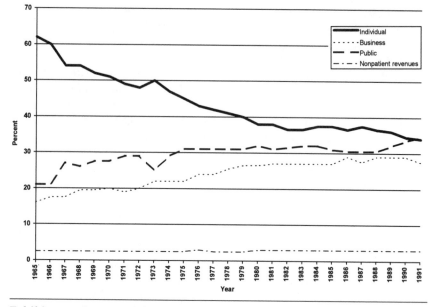

Exhibit 5-3   Percent of expenditures for health services and supplies, by payer 1965–1991 (*Source:* U.S. Healthcare Financing Administration.)

Now, however, competitive and shareholder pressures on employers, and budgetary and taxpayer pressures on the federal government are prompting more costs to be shifted to the employee in the form of increased premiums, increased deductibles, increased cost sharing, lower benefit caps, and lower benefit levels.

These changes have had a ripple effect. They have increased the pressure on employers and government to aggressively address escalating health-care costs in the years ahead, both in the United States and around the world. While the number of union work stoppages has declined significantly in the past decade, those that occur are increasingly attributable to proposed changes in active and retiree health-care programs. For example, several Caterpillar unions went out on strike in 1995 for an extended period of time due largely to disputes over health-plan coverage and cost allocation. In addition, France experienced a nationwide work stoppage in certain sectors as a result of its attempt to curb rising health-care costs associated with its national health insurance program.

Many employers continue to restructure (downsize or rightsize) because of escalating benefit costs, hemorrhaging bottom lines, and increasing shareholders pressures. What this means to the retirement security picture is that there will be fewer active employees available to support a growing retiree population. In addition, employers are more acutely aware of the additional costs associated with retiree versus active health insurance coverage, especially pre-Medicare-eligible retiree health coverage (Exhibit 5-2).

Does this sound hauntingly familiar? Basically, employers realized, albeit too late, that they had created, in many cases voluntarily, mini-Medicare programs because of positive, competitive, and economic conditions that existed in the 1960s. The climate was ripe. They were making money. The world was less competitive. Health-care costs were lower and more controllable. There were fewer retirees, more active employees to support the retirees, and the accounting profession allowed them to defer recognition of related expenses and obligations. Also, ERISA didn't prohibit them from unilaterally terminating or amending these plans, even if it meant taking away or reducing benefits attributable to service that had already been rendered.

While politicians may not want to address the challenges that face the Medicare programs, CEOs in corporate America have been quick to take a second look at their mini-Medicare programs, particularly because of more vocal shareholder activism and the fact that a significant part of their compensation may be tied to the net income or stock price of their companies.

Given these factors, corporate America as a whole began a concerted effort to restructure the design, delivery, and funding of these benefits to reduce related costs and better sensitize retirees to the costs they will face in connection with these benefits beginning in the late 1980s and early 1990s.

In some cases, action was drastic. Employers terminated the health-care programs outright. Most, however, met employees partway. They raised the eligibility criteria, changed the cost sharing arrangements, set in place managed care arrangements, and imposed certain benefit limits.

AT&T restructured its retiree health program to place an overall limit of the annual per-person cost of retiree health coverage. AT&T also pursued various managed-care strategies to limit future cost escalation. The combined purpose of these changes was to reduce the rate of increase in retiree health costs and to shift more costs from AT&T to retirees.

Some employers changed from providing and paying for a defined level of benefit coverage to furnishing retirees with the ability to purchase retiree health care at group rates and making a contribution to assist retirees to pay for coverage (the defined-dollar-benefit plans). For example, TRW revised its plan in 1988 to move to a defined-dollar-benefit/type approach.

Because of this and the fact the SFAS 106 requires employers to calculate and recognize both direct and indirect costs associated with retiree health coverage, many employers calculate separate or higher premiums that apply to retiree health coverage. This results in elevated costs for retirees and lower costs for employers and active employees. The lower employer costs also translate to lower SFAS 106 amounts. These actions serve to reduce the pressure on employers to terminate these plans.

Virtually all major employers have modified their retiree health program to impose separate and higher premium rates on retirees versus active employees for their annual health insurance coverage. This action serves to significantly reduce the effective subsidy of retiree health coverage by active employees and the company.

Other employers provided access and didn't directly or indirectly subsidize the benefit. Specifically, employers allowed retirees to purchase retiree health coverage at a separately calculated (and higher) retiree-only rate. While these rates were higher than a blended group insurance rate, they were usually much lower than the rate the retiree would have to pay for an individual health insurance policy purchased independently.

As costs soar, employer-sponsored retiree health plans are becoming dinosaurs. While they should be of increasing importance in the next century due to reforms and related benefit reductions that will ultimately be required in connection with the Medicare programs, they are not likely to step in with more help in the employer-paid benefits arena.

Even if we see an increase in the willingness of employers to offer extended retiree health coverage at more affordable group rates, any real employer subsidies are likely to decline. Employees should not count on them during their golden years.

CHAPTER SIX

Other Income and Assets

MYTH
8

Saving a little and early on in life won't make a meaningful difference.
    That's simply not true, particularly if you begin early on and literally save your spare change. The reason? The magic of compounding, especially tax-free compounding.

It's time to retire. Based on a recent study by Merrill Lynch, most people will fall short of their expectations unless they save at least 10 percent of their income once they turn 30 assuming they retire at age 65 (Exhibit 6-1). If they didn't sock away enough to maintain the same standard of living once they retire, they may find they have to work longer than age 65, continue on a part-time basis, or reenter the workforce after retirement—all not part of the scenario imagined.

What went wrong? Unfortunately, Medicare and Social Security, once the safety nets of retirement security, have become a double-edged sword, as we've learned.

Where will the extra needed monies come from? Several elements will play a more important role in funding retirement: personal savings, investments and inheritances, and earnings from continued employment. In both cases, money needs to be saved as early as possible and invested as wisely as possible for the long term. If the assets don't grow by at least the inflation rate, they actually decline in real terms.

Those who haven't yet started a personal savings plan shouldn't panic. It's never too late to begin, and this chapter discusses various investment vehicles and which offer the best results.

First, people should know that they'll ultimately need to answer these questions: How much money will I need to afford the retirement I've dreamed about? To what extent will Social Security and pensions replace my preretirement income? What percentage of my preretirement income should go into personal savings? What's the smartest

Desired Retiree Income as a	Years to Retirement					
Percent of Annual Salary	10	15	20	25	30	35
30%	36%	21%	13%	9%	6%	4%
40	48	27	18	12	8	6
50	60	34	22	15	10	7
60	72	41	26	18	12	9
70	84	48	31	21	14	10

Exhibit 6-1   Required saving as a percent of income (*Source:* T. Rowe Price Associates. The underlying assumptions are as follows: [1] A 9 percent annual investment return prior to retirement and 8 percent after retirement, [2] an inflation rate of 3 percent, [3] retirement income lasts 30 years.)

asset allocation mix in terms of stocks, bonds, real estate, and government securities for my personal savings to ensure growth, income investment, and tax breaks in retirement? What are safe, good options if I'm risk-averse? What are the best savings vehicles for a young versus older saver? Is it okay to redo a portfolio as I get older, and how do I do so?

There are many choice investment possibilities, in fact too many to address in one chapter. So, I'll touch briefly on several, in addition to the employer-sponsored pensions and savings plans such as 401(k)s already discussed and delved into in greater detail in Chapter Twelve. This chapter is a good place to begin gathering answers to those crucial questions.

TYPES OF PERSONAL SAVINGS

When it comes to personal savings, there are four major categories, each with its own pros and cons: tax-deferred, tax-exempt, taxable, and nontaxable:

- Taxable savings methods include directly held bank accounts/CDs, money market funds, mutual funds, stocks, corporate bonds, Treasury securities, and collectibles.

- Tax-deferred savings vehicles encompass employer-sponsored pension and savings plans, SEP-IRAs/Keoghs, annuities, and home equity.

- Tax-exempt savings plans include state and municipal bonds, municipal bond funds, tax-free money market funds, and state and municipal notes.

- Nontaxable savings vehicles, which don't accrue interest, include hiding your money under the mattress and possibly, though not preferably, inside a piggybank or cookie jar.

One of the best overall ways to save for retirement is by maximizing the use of employer-sponsored savings vehicles such as a Section 401(k) plan, though employees will need other forms of personal savings as well if they are to enjoy a comfortable retirement.

Taxable Savings

Everybody should try to have some form of taxable savings. One of the most popular is a bank account—a checking or savings account or a CD. These vehicles are appealing because of their liquidity and perceived security, even though they usually offer lower interest rates. Generally, CD rates range from 200 basis points (a basis point is $\frac{1}{100}$th of 1 percent) to 400 basis points above inflation for larger investments. Savings and checking account rates are lower. Many checking and savings account rates do not keep pace with inflation. As a result, you shouldn't use these vehicles for midrange or long-term savings.

Taxable money market funds typically pay approximately 200 basis points above the current inflation rate. Tax-exempt money market funds are also available at lower rates of return. These rates may, however, be higher net of tax depending on your tax bracket. We all need money that we can get our hands on quickly. Many of us have several major preretirement savings pools such as a home and money for our children's education, which can be tapped into without a penalty. On the other hand, to withdraw funds early from a tax-deferred savings account subjects that money to a 10 percent additional tax in addition to normal income taxes, thereby wiping out some funds.

It's also comforting to have some liquid funds available for emergencies or important unexpected purchases. The cost of borrowing to meet normal preretirement needs may not make economic sense if you do it with a credit card. Typically, you have to pay between 15 and 18 percent interest plus an annual credit card fee for the privilege. And beware. Using plastic makes it tempting to run up those total charges unwittingly and put yourself in debt.

Tax-Deferred Vehicles

Another form of individual savings, one that is tax-deferred, is the individual retirement account (IRA). While IRAs are considered qualified retirement plans under the IRC, in substance, they are essentially tax-favored individual retirement savings arrangements. With the exception of SEP and SIMPLE-IRAs (Appendix B), they do not require employer involvement.

IRAs are available to both employees and self-employed individuals. All individuals with adjusted gross income of $25,000 or less and couples who file jointly with adjusted gross income of $40,000 or less a year may make fully tax-deductible contributions of up to $2,000 per person a year to an IRA provided they each have at least $2,000 each in earned income. Partial deductions are allowed when an individual's or couple's (filing jointly) adjusted gross income ranges between $25,000–$34,999 and $40,000–$49,999 if they are covered under an employer-sponsored plan. Importantly, individuals not covered under an employer-sponsored plan, including certain non-working spouses who file joint tax returns, can make deductible IRA contributions up to $2,000 per year.

Even people with income in excess of the limit can make nondeductible contributions to IRAs. In all cases, the earnings on the IRA contributions are tax-deferred until withdrawn. However, money cannot be withdrawn serendipitously. Any distributions taken prior to age 59½ or because of death, disability, or retirement are subject to a 10 percent additional tax.

Self-employed workers may want to investigate establishing a Keogh plan to defer a portion of their earnings—currently up to 15 percent of self-employment earnings with a cap of $30,000 per year. Unfortunately, based on the reduction in the maximum amount of compensation ($150,000) that a person may consider for contributions to qualified retirement plans, many self-employed will be able to make Keogh contributions of only up to $22,500 (15 percent of $150,000).

All Keogh and IRA contributions must be set aside within two and one-half months and three and one-half months, respectively, the following tax year to which they apply, or by March 15 and April 15, respectively, for calendar-year taxpayers. These amounts grow tax-free and are subject to an income tax when withdrawn from the plan. Withdrawals prior to age 59½ are also subject to a 10 percent additional tax. IRA's are also subject to the same age 70½ minimum distribution rule as qualified pension and savings plans.

Another tax-deferred vehicle is annuities or other insurance products such as whole, variable, or split-dollar life insurance. Annuities represent investments that yield fixed payments for the entire retirement period or for fixed periods of time. Whole, variable, and split-dollar life insurance policies provide a combination of life insurance protection and an opportunity for tax free build-up. While you won't get a deductions for any related premiums, you will get tax free build-up on your investment account balance.

These types of arrangements are available to anyone, typically through an insurance agent, and do not require that savings be made in

	Average Charge
Investment management fee (provides for the expense of managing your money)	0.49%
Mortality and expense fee	1.12
Annual contract fee (on average, this fee equals .19% of assets)	Flat fee of $25 to $40 per year
Total	1.80%

Exhibit 6-2 Significant costs of insurance products (*Source: Manager's Magazine,* Vol. 69, Iss. 7, July 1995, pp. 14–15.)

the downsides are there is no deduction for related contributions and significant management or custodial fees (Exhibit 6-2).

Home Equity

The largest form of personal savings most people have is home equity. Many current retirees, especially parents of baby boomers, enjoyed significant appreciation by owning a home. Home ownership also offered a significant amount of forced savings. The monthly mortgage payments served to reduce the related mortgage obligation and thereby increased the person's net worth (and savings) at a progressively greater rate.

Home ownership was a particularly important factor in the accumulation of wealth in the 1970s and part of the 1980s, when housing prices soared. In 1990, housing wealth accounted for more than 50 percent of total wealth for people aged 55 to 74.

Even for those who manage to accumulate significant savings through home ownership, questions remain regarding the owner's willingness and ability to tap into this asset for retirement. While many homeowners have made a conscious decision to preserve this asset for inheritance purposes, others have decided to sell or borrow from this asset for retirement income, particularly during the last few years of their lifetime if they need funds for health care, long-term care, and other purposes.

This trend is likely to continue because of evolving new ways to access the economic value of home equity through reverse mortgages or similar arrangements, which have been a major source of retirement income in countries such as France. Under reverse mortgages, a person borrows against the equity in their home in exchange for a lump sum, or a fixed monthly payment for a stated period of time (e.g., lifetime or 10 years). The loan is not repaid until the home is sold or the borrower moves away or dies. This serves to convert home equity into retirement income while allowing the person to remain in his home. The tax consequences of these arrangements vary.

But I must play devil's advocate for a moment. Some experts warn that today it is no longer savvy to count on the equity in your home to bail you out in retirement. This vehicle probably will not offer the same appreciation opportunities over coming decades. Although few real estate observers expect a significant decline in home prices, other than in selected markets, most don't expect home prices to rise by an amount much in excess of the rate of inflation over the longer term. There will, however, be significant variances based on local market conditions.

Some sellers already have found that if they bought their homes at the peak of the market—in the late '80s and early '90s, they are getting less when they go to sell. Many Houston homeowners lost money after the oil boom bubble burst in the early 1980s, and many California homeowners face similar conditions today.

The primary reason for the likely cooling of appreciation in home prices is the changing demographics noted earlier. The aging baby boomers followed by the baby bust generation has begun and will continue to have a significant impact on the total amount of real estate demand as well as specific demand—single-family versus attached housing or town homes. Furthermore, if Congress reforms the nation's individual tax laws and moves to a flat income tax or consumption tax approach, the current home mortgage interest deduction could be slashed. If so, many believe that the result would be lower current and prospective housing prices.

Collectibles

Collectibles are another way to save for investment purposes. They are also a tax-deferred investment that can offer personal gratification. However, many investments in collectibles offer no guarantee in a particular year, and the swings in value, depending on the overall economy and personal tastes, can be volatile. The price of silver went up dramatically and fell just as quickly when the Hunt brothers, Lamar and Bunker, attempted to corner the world silver market but failed in 1979.

On the other hand, many of the most popular collectibles now enjoy a resurgence—precious metals such as gold and silver, art (the high end of the market is now returning after a disastrous downswing), antiques, baseball memorabilia, automobiles, and wine.

Collections also are something tangible to pass down to another generation. However, if you invest in them, don't count on significant appreciation, and be willing to sell them if you must.

Gifts/Inheritance

Inheritance is another source of savings income for some retirees. Some baby boomers will gain substantial sums from their parents and other relatives. It has been reported that the current generation under age 50 will inherit more money than any other generation. Under current tax laws, up to $10,000 each year may be gifted tax-free to certain family members, or $20,000, if gifts are made jointly by a husband and wife. This form of wealth transfer, however, is not without its glitches.

Most of us will not be able count on this pot of gold for several reasons. First, parents are living longer—into their 80s and 90s—and they are hanging on to their money knowing that extended-care costs can be staggering. Nursing homes can be expensive and vary in price depending on the quality of the facility along with its amenities and geographic location. The average cost of a nursing home was approximately $40,000 per year in 1994. Care for debilitating diseases such as Alzheimer's can increase monthly costs.

Also, estate taxes can eat up an inheritance if proper planning has not been done. Under current federal tax laws, estates of up to $600,000 can be left on a tax-free basis. Amounts in excess are subject to 55 percent estate taxes. My best advice is not to get complacent in your retirement planning contingent on inheriting funds. You may never see a dime.

Earnings from Employment after Retirement

A final source of retirement income, the antithesis of what we expect during retirement, is earnings from employment. For a variety of reasons, more of us may have to rely on this if we fail to take adequate steps to save and invest properly early on.

WHERE TO PLACE YOUR MONEY WHEN YOU INVEST

Where you put your money when you invest is also crucial. Care must be taken in choosing any financial institutions and financial instruments. While most financial institutions now pay interest on a broad range of deposits, including checking accounts, the amount of interest paid is paltry, and in many cases, less than the current inflation rate.

Shop around for the best offer and review the bank's financial statements if your savings are not fully insured amounts in excess of $100,000 per individual. A better alternative in many cases is to invest in money market funds, which typically pay higher rates than CDs and definitely higher than savings and checking accounts.

It is important to research the creditworthiness of any companies with whom you invest tax-deferred annuity contracts. This can been done by reviewing the company's financial statements and its ratings from various rating agencies such as Moody's, Duff & Phelps, and Best. Several major insurance companies have reorganized recently, such as First Executive Life and Mutual Benefit Life. An annuity contract is only as good as the company that issues it. We'll address this in Chapter Twelve.

A caveat about any form of savings. Some traditional ways of squirreling away money aren't what they used to be. Don't discount new options. The future holds some ominous and changing signs that must be considered, such as current and pending changes in the federal tax laws that will affect income and estate taxes. Congress is debating the possibility of creating new tax-favored savings vehicles such as family savings accounts and medical savings accounts, which will allow individuals to save additional funds on a tax-favored basis for medical expenses, for example.

There is little question that we must assume more responsibility for individual retirement security. No longer can we count on government, employers, or families to provide windfalls. Most of us will need to save more and invest more wisely. Saving today, the only way to compound your money, may be worth far more tomorrow.

Now let's examine ways to develop your personal retirement security plan.

PART TWO

Developing and Implementing a Personal Retirement Security Plan

CHAPTER SEVEN

A Retirement Planning Framework

MYTH 9

Saving (assuming 8 percent return) on a tax-favored (e.g., employer-sponsored plans, IRAs, Keoghs) versus nontax-favored basis doesn't matter much.

Not true. Tax-free versus taxable-compounding can make big differences in your retirement nest egg over time. For example, $100,000 invested for 25 years with a tax-free buildup will amount to $458,848 (after a 33 percent tax in year 25) while a 33 percent combined federal and state income tax rate imposed on each year's investment income would reduce this amount to $368,888.

Part One presented a sizable amount of information to digest and probably proved a hard landing for those who haven't thought about such issues. I hope it made you uncomfortable enough to take action today regarding retirement planning rather than at some distant date.

I'm also certain that by this point in the book you're probably thinking, the information in Part One was revealing, but I need more concrete ideas about how I can plan my retirement security. That's what Part Two is about. It provides more practical tips and details to develop a personal retirement security plan. It will also address selected key retirement savings and investment principles for you; it uses as examples our hypothetical family of James and Carol from St. Charles, Illinois, their two children (James has one child from a former marriage), their parents, including one stepparent. While they may not represent all American families today, their retirement issues will raise a number of important questions that all of us need to consider.

A final comment before we proceed. This book is not intended to be a tax or estate planning guide, even though some related points will be covered.

KEY RETIREMENT PLANNING PRINCIPLES

Before I present my suggested retirement planning framework, let's reiterate some key principles. The most important are:

- Be responsible and realistic.
- Start now.
- Save early and smart.
- Invest wisely.
- Be disciplined.
- Don't eat your retirement nest egg.

Let's go over each.

Be responsible and realistic. To be responsible for your retirement security means that you must accept the fact that the Social Security program as it exists today won't provide the same level of benefits tomorrow. The Medicare program, too, will have to be fundamentally reengineered and reduced in the twenty-first century. Like it or not, some sweeping changes already are on the horizon. Employers are moving toward defined-contribution plans that give you more choice but also more responsibility and risk. At the same time, most employers are moving rapidly to cut back rather than to add to their retiree health programs.

To add to this sense of unease, home equity, once an investment staple, is not likely to generate nearly as much in appreciation and personal savings as it has in the past. Furthermore, we're kidding ourselves if we count on receiving an inheritance or winning the lottery to underwrite our retirement.

Start now. You should begin today to review your current plan in light of the trends discussed in Part One and the planning approach outlined in the following pages. While I keep stressing that it's never too late to make a difference, the longer you wait, the tougher it will be to make a *meaningful* difference.

I can't say it enough: save early and smart. Do so even if it's not much. Why? Because of the magic of compounding, which is especially helpful if your earnings are growing on a tax-deferred basis such as in a 401(k) savings plan. Over time, especially if you successfully adopt a plan and have better-than-expected investment results, you may need to adjust your taxable versus tax-deferred savings patterns such as in qualified 401(k)s and Keoghs to avoid excise taxes on your retirement distributions.

Invest wisely. While your personal savings efforts are essential, savings represent only one side of the retirement security coin. The other is how you invest the funds. It is crucial to invest wisely to assure that your hard-earned savings multiply at a reasonable rate. Many individuals tend to be overly conservative in investing their retirement dollars.

It is possible—and wise—to divvy up how you invest. Some funds should be invested conservatively, others for high growth. Don't fall into the trap of targeting your investment horizons at the time of retirement rather than looking at the bigger picture of your full-life expectancy. You also need to give appropriate consideration to diversification, historical rates of return over time, inflation protection, portfolio volatility, tax considerations, and other important matters in determining your overall asset allocation. We'll address this in greater depth in Chapter Twelve.

Be disciplined. Once you develop your retirement security plan, don't be a Teflon saver. Stick to it, which can be tough. There are various ways to do so. Many people use mechanisms like annual budgets, payroll deductions, automatic savings programs, and annual retirement plan checkups as ways to keep themselves on track. Some people feel that if they don't touch their money, they are less likely to spend it. Others get help from professional personal financial planners and money managers, which I recommend.

Don't spend your retirement savings prematurely. If you take the necessary steps to save and invest for retirement, it's important that you don't undermine your efforts by withdrawing your hard-earned savings prior to retirement. Not only does this serve to mortgage your retirement security, but in many cases it will cause you to spend your own money too early. You'll also have to pay income and excise taxes on the withdrawn amounts. There are much better alternatives to pre-retirement withdrawals, such as borrowing from employee benefit plans and home equity loans.

RETIREMENT PLANNING FRAMEWORK

To develop your personal retirement security plan, you need a framework. I believe there are seven basic chronological steps necessary to achieve your personal retirement security plan:

1. Define your retirement goals.
2. Determine your retirement needs.

3. Review your retirement resources.
4. Define and fill your retirement gap.
5. Develop a savings and investment strategy.
6. Implement your savings and investment strategy.
7. Monitor the results and make necessary adjustments.

Before you can develop your retirement plan, define your goals: when you plan to retire, what you want to do during your retirement years, where you will retire.

After you have specified your basic retirement goals, you must ascertain your retirement needs. As discussed in Part One, every person has two basic retirement security needs. The first is to have an adequate stream of income throughout your retirement years. The second is to have access to affordable health coverage.

In determining your basic needs, review and assess your current and projected spending. Do so by major categories of expenditures: housing, food, clothing, transportation, insurance, travel. The total annual amounts will need to be translated into the amount of investments and convertible assets that you need at retirement time in order to meet your objectives.

Once you have pinpointed your retirement needs, you need to review your retirement resources, probably from existing savings, investments, and convertible assets, projected Social Security, Medicare, employer-sponsored pension, and retiree health benefits. Certain adjustments (such as increased health-care costs and lower commuting expenses) will have to be made to these amounts to develop your personal retirement security plan.

Now it's time to calculate your retirement gap: the difference between the total amount of savings, investments, and convertible assets that you are projected to have at retirement and the real amount that you will need to meet objectives. I say *retirement gap* because a vast majority of Americans currently face a shortfall (or deficit) in calculating their projected needs versus resources based on their savings and investment patterns. In most cases, gaps are significant.

How will you fill the gap? There are several ways. You could change your retirement goals by delaying your planned retirement date. You could cut back on your standard of living in retirement or your children's inheritance. You could plan to work part-time during some or all of your retirement years. These, however, are not very attractive options. Alternatively, you could save more before you retire and invest what you save better, a double benefit that can pay off long term. Most people will need to adopt a combination of options.

Once you modify your retirement plan and determine your savings and investment strategy, it's time to set it into motion. This will involve a variety of factors: What type of savings vehicles should you use (taxable versus tax-deferred)? What type of asset allocation makes sense—stocks, bonds, real estate, collectibles; international versus domestic? What type of investment approaches should you consider—mutual funds, individual stocks and bonds? Who, if anyone, should assist you in addressing these issues? How should these factors change as you age?

After you have decided on or modified your initial plan, monitor your progress. Compare your actual savings rates, asset allocations, and investment results against your plan. You also need to review your projected retirement needs and other resources.

To avoid unpleasant retirement-related bombshells, get busy designing your personal retirement security investment plan without delay.

CHAPTER EIGHT

Setting Your Retirement Goals

MYTH 10   Individuals need 70 percent to 80 percent of their preretirement income to achieve retirement objectives.

False. Despite the fact that many so-called retirement experts say that you need to have income equal to those percentages of your final pay prior to retirement to maintain your standard of living in retirement, life and retirement planning for later in life aren't that simplistic. Actual income needs vary from 40 percent to 80 percent of preretirement levels, depending on various factors such as income level, retirement dates, and other retirement goals.

Throughout our lives, most of us set goals for ourselves—grades in school, low golf scores, job promotions, car or house purchases, weight losses. Many of us set and reset our goals annually, often at the start of a new year. Such New Year's resolutions unfortunately are often broken or otherwise go unachieved, as do many of our other goals.

Retirement planning should be added to the list of goals in order to reach your desired destination. But unlike a New Year's resolution, these goals should not be broken. The game of retirement security is too important for you not to plan for, work for, and ultimately win at it.

Any goals set for retirement are likely to be more vague if you are just beginning your career, but more specific the closer you are to your intended retirement age.

RETIREMENT GOAL SETTING

My advice will be structured accordingly. There are several basic elements to retirement goal setting:

- When do you want to retire?
- What standard of living do you want to enjoy in your retirement years?
- What do you want to do in your retirement years?
- Where do you want to retire?
- Who, other than yourself, will you be responsible for during your retirement years?
- What type of inheritance do you want to leave for your children or others?

Setting your preferred retirement date(s) is a logical and concrete place to begin your retirement planning process. By *retirement date*, I mean the date(s) or age(s) at which you and your spouse, if applicable, want to stop working full-time for wages. You may technically retire from more than one employer if you have the requisite number of years of service. Many government workers retire after 20 years of employment and begin a new full-time career in the private sector. Conversely, you may decide to retire from full-time employment and devote your time to community service work or other charitable activities or decide to continue to work part-time as you head into your retirement years.

I say your *preferred retirement date(s)* because in some cases this date may be set for you by your employer in situations where it is legal because of corporate downsizing or failing health. In other cases, your preferred date may have to be delayed because you haven't taken the necessary steps or achieved the expected investment results. Here again there can be significant expectation gaps relating to your actual retirement date. In some cases, it may involve multiple dates—if you are married (one date for you and one for your spouse), or if you have to reenter the workforce after initially retiring because your retirement nest egg cracks due to insufficient funds.

Most people set their initial retirement dates in accordance with the retirement dates for their current employer's pension and retiree health programs. Others refer to the date for eligibility for OASI benefits, which currently is 62 for reduced early retirement benefits and from 65 to 67 years of age depending on your birth year for normal retirement benefits, and 65 for Medicare benefits. This is understandable, but these represent only a portion of the elements that anyone needs to retire securely. The other major element is personal savings, including convertible assets.

In the final analysis, your targeted retirement date(s) should be based on when you can afford to retire, rather than when you want to retire, and should be a by-product of an informed and disciplined retirement planning process.

Many people view retirement as a date; others view it as a point in time. Both are relevant to your planning efforts. Even though it sounds macabre, it is important to estimate the number of years that you expect to live.

Estimating your life expectancy and those of loved ones should take into account several factors. Are you a male or a female? Females typically live longer. Do you smoke? According to the latest statistics, nonsmokers can live up to 15 years longer than regular smokers. How long did your parents and grandparents live? Life spans are a function of heredity, lifestyle, and other external factors such as accidents. Longevity may run in your family. If so, you may want to take that into consideration in developing your own retirement security plan. Finally, it may be helpful to refer to the latest available data on average life expectancies published by the government. (See Appendix C for ordering such charts.)

Overlaying all these considerations is a realistic determination of your desired retirement standard of living compared to your prior standard of living. Most people want to maintain that standard, but don't know what it takes.

The exact percentage of preretirement monies needed will vary depending on a person's preretirement income level, employment status—self-employed versus employee, form of retirement savings—taxable versus tax-deferred, and expected expenditures during the retirement years.

AVOID OVER-SIMPLIFIED APPROACHES

In my opinion, you should not resort to simplified percentage-oriented guidelines to estimate the amount of income that you will need. Doing so may result in a significant over- or underestimation of your retirement targets. Instead, the best way is to estimate what your annual expenses are likely to be, based on today's dollars. These amounts will need to be converted to future dollars to account for future inflation.

In addition to determining your desired standard of living, you need to decide what you want to do during your retirement years. This will have a direct bearing on estimating expenses. Your choices will depend partly on your health. You may want to travel more than you did during your working years or stay home and play golf, a pricey game.

Where you want to retire also should be factored in. You may want to join the millions of retirees who migrate to Florida and other Sunbelt states. Or you may want to spend the winter in a warmer climate and the summer in the mountains. Such desires will affect the amount of retirement expenses, particularly if you have to cover the cost of maintaining dual residences.

Even if you don't have two residences, it's expensive to relocate. You need to consider the differential cost of living between your current and future locations, including different tax rates. To help you, Appendix D summarizes the cost of living indexes for a number of U.S. cities. Appendix E also summarizes each state's current individual income tax rates. If a state does not have a personal income tax rate, it may have higher sales, personal property, and other tax rates to raise operating revenues.

Also consider whether you need to provide for anyone else during your retirement years. You may have a spouse who is younger. If so, you need to consider not only any additional expenses associated with providing for two persons but also the additional number of years that your spouse may survive you.

You may have other loved ones who will also rely on you during your retirement. You may have one or more parents or in-laws who need to be cared for. All of you may be counting on government-sponsored retirement or welfare programs to provide financial assistance. But remember, as noted earlier, cutbacks are inevitable.

As I said at the beginning of this chapter, goal setting is an integral part of any worthwhile endeavor. Retirement planning is no exception. You need to consider a plethora of elements, be realistic, and periodically review and revise your goals based on changes in your life, other family members' lives, the economy, and government and employer retirement programs. And no, this doesn't preclude hoping for or planning on the off chance that you may one day win the lottery or inherit a bundle.

CHAPTER NINE

Defining Your Retirement Needs

MYTH
11

Divorced spouses have few rights in connection with the pension benefits and retiree health of their former spouse.

False. Most divorce settlements and court-ordered property divisions address the treatment of pension and other retirement savings. These amounts can be significant, particularly in the case of a nonworking spouse. The affected spouse should obtain a Qualified Domestic Relations Order (QDRO) and present that document to the plan administrator of the ex-spouse's pension or retirement plan. The QDRO must specify certain information to be valid. If it is deemed to be valid, the plan administrator must comply with the division of property, and any payments must be in accordance with the terms of the employer's plan. Importantly, there are no federal law protections for divorced spouses in connection with retiree health benefits.

Now that you have pinpointed some of your primary retirement goals, you need to convert them into more concrete terms, namely, specific dollar amounts necessary to retire comfortably.

But how do you do that? There's the rub. Few of us have the time or patience to tackle the arcane mathematics of budgets and projections, and doing so can leave you dizzy with confusion. Fortunately, making sense of a retirement plan isn't as difficult as it looks or sounds, though it requires time.

Start by reviewing the major preliminary retirement goals that you set for yourself. *Preliminary* implies flexibility—after you initiate a more thorough and objective retirement planning review, you may find it necessary to revise some of your initial goals. You may not be able to afford to retire at your initial targeted age, based on your desired standard of living, anticipated life expectancy, and projected retirement resources. You may have to work several years longer, assuming you remain healthy. Alternatively, you may need to save more or invest more

119

wisely if you don't want to alter your targeted retirement age or proposed standard of living.

Whether you need to revise your initial goals or modify your retirement savings and investment actions, all will become more intelligible after you complete the personal security model in Chapter Eleven. Let's return to estimating your retirement needs.

SETTING RETIREMENT OBJECTIVES

Decide on your primary retirement objective. Is it to have enough money to support yourself during your expected lifetime? If so, and you're married, you will need to take appropriate steps to provide for your spouse as well. Take into account the fact that women are expected to live several years longer than men, according to actuarial tables.

What about other relatives you may need to support after you retire, such as parents or in-laws who didn't do their own adequate retirement planning or who lived longer than they expected. Their housing, possibly a nursing home or some assisted-living or continuing-care facility, and medical costs may prove staggering. Additionally, you may find yourself supporting your grown children long after you expected to; or, heaven forbid, they may return home to roost if their entry-level jobs don't provide a large enough salary to cover their rent and basic expenses.

Even if you were willing to allow your relatives to live alone or, alternatively, if you plan to take advantage of certain existing loopholes in federal and state poverty programs, (many poverty programs don't consider the assets of the children in determining whether a parent is eligible for assistance even if the parent transfers considerable sums to their children in their retirement years), you may not be able to. Greater pressures on both federal and state budgets, which will increase exponentially with the decrease in the ratio of workers to retirees, probably will result in a crackdown on any related asset transfer efforts.

Even if you don't have expenses connected with your parents, you may want to leave an inheritance for your children. If so, you need to include any related targeted amounts in your retirement planning. Under current federal estate tax laws, you may leave an unlimited dollar amount to your spouse tax-free. However, you may leave only $600,000 to others without incurring estate taxes. Transfers above that amount are subject to a 55 percent tax rate. Six hundred thousand dollars may sound like a lot of money—and yes, it is—but don't forget that it includes the value of your home and the proceeds from any insurance that may be a part of your estate.

In addition, the $600,000 exemption is not currently indexed for inflation. Therefore, the relative value of the current estate tax exclusion will erode over time in real terms. While some on Capitol Hill are currently discussing the need to lessen the current estate tax burdens after the significant increase a few years ago, you shouldn't count your chickens before they hatch. After all, a little conservatism in your planning is advisable so that you will have only pleasant surprises.

These supplemental retirement needs should be evaluated and the resulting amounts included in the appropriate section of the worksheet shown in Exhibit 9-1.

Major Recurring Expense Categories	Current Recurring Annual Expenses	Adjustments (+ or - a Given Amount for Retirement)	Detailed Budget for First Year of Retirement
Housing:			
Mortgage	___	___	___
Homeowners Insurance	___	___	___
Utilities	___	___	___
Maintenance	___	___	___
Property Tax	___	___	___
Total	___	___	___
Food	___	___	___
Clothing	___	___	___
Transportation			
Car Payments	___	___	___
Gas	___	___	___
Maintenance	___	___	___
Parking	___	___	___
Total	___	___	___
Education	___	___	___
Insurance			
Life	___	___	___
Disability	___	___	___
Total	___	___	___
Health Care	___	___	___
Travel/Vacations	___	___	___
Recreation/Entertainment	___	___	___
Taxes			
State and Local	___	___	___
Payroll	___	___	___
Total	___	___	___
Savings	___	___	___
Other	___	___	___
TOTAL	___	___	___

Supplemental Retirement Expenses			Current Value
Retirement Condo			___
Country Club			___
Dream Trip			___
Family Assistance			___
Children's Inheritance			___
TOTAL			___

Exhibit 9-1 Total estimated retirement expenses worksheet (current dollars)

BASIC RETIREMENT NEEDS

Let's turn to your basic retirement needs. As noted in the last chapter, I do not subscribe to the generalization that everyone should estimate his retirement income needs at 70 to 80 percent of preretirement income. Life isn't that clear-cut. Needs vary, and retirement planning should reflect this by employing a more serious, thorough approach. Namely, you should estimate in a detailed budget (Exhibit 9-1) what your estimated retirement expenses, including income taxes, will be in your first year of retirement. These include expenses such as housing, food, transportation, insurance, travel, entertainment, health care, and taxes.

Even if you don't currently follow an annual budget, this approach is helpful as a means to apply some discipline to your current financial affairs and spending patterns. It is not difficult, and employing it may encourage you to use an annual budgeting approach to your spending, savings, and other recurring financial affairs prior to retirement.

What expenses should you budget for and how will they differ from your current spending patterns? We'll review and estimate those in the balance of this chapter.

Current Expenses

When estimating your projected retirement expenses, the best place to start is with your current outlays. This will enable you to deal with numbers that are current and verifiable. Exhibit 9-1 includes a list of major recurring expense categories.

Appropriate Adjustments

After estimating your current recurring annual expenses, make appropriate adjustments based on the differences between expenses during your working and retirement years. Most people understand the seesaw effect of spending before and after retirement—certain expenses will go down while others will go up.

Current Expenses That May Decline

Many will have paid off their mortgage by the time they retire, eliminating the related principal and interest payments (and the related interest deductions) on their primary residence. At the same time, there are annual property taxes, homeowner's insurance, and maintenance expenses. You may also have expenses associated with a second home.

Similarly, most people can expect that certain recurring expenses incurred during working years may decline in retirement. For example:

- Annual commuting expenses, unless you expect to have the equivalent of a second full-time profit- or nonprofit job.

- Clothing expenses, since you won't have to maintain a full range of business attire, though you'll probably have some different clothing needs—more warm-up suits and sweaters.

- Education expenses for you and your family, especially if your children are out of college.

- Life insurance since it is typically designed as a means to replace your income if you die prior to retirement or as a retirement savings vehicle.

- Additional savings. While planned savings may not be an expense, it should be an annual line item on your budget prior to retirement.

Following this approach will help you treat savings as a required expenditure rather than a by-product of not spending all that you earn in a given year so that you have something to sock away. Some may consider that form over substance, but form counts and can make a difference in your mind-set as well.

Current Expenses That May Increase

On the flip side of the coin, certain recurring annual expenses can be expected to increase during retirement years. For example:

- Most people's annual health-care expenses will rise, in some cases significantly. Most employers do not provide employer-paid or subsidized retiree health insurance, and those that do, are, at a minimum, not likely to subsidize it at current levels in the next century.

  Check with your employer regarding any benefits that you may be eligible for and estimate your additional expenses in retirement such as higher premiums, deductibles, and co-pays. For those who are, or expect to be, eligible for an employer subsidy, the amount of subsidy your employer provides at retirement is likely to be less than for active employees. It also will decline.

  You will also have to assess the likelihood of whether you will continue to receive any employer-paid or subsidized health benefits when you retire based on possible changes. In most cases, you'll want to assume a reduction in current benefit levels if your employer currently offers subsidized retiree health-care coverage, because that clearly has been a trend in recent years and one that is likely to continue.

- The most significant increase in health-care costs is likely to be attributable to changes in the Medicare programs (HI and SMI programs). Both the HI and SMI programs are in need of dramatic and fundamental reform. This translates to significant benefit reductions and tax increases over time.

While more aggressive pursuits of managed-care approaches and tougher enforcement can reduce the rate of increase in program costs, they can't change the demographic trends and won't come close to solving the financial imbalance in the Medicare programs. Remember that according to the 1995 Annual Trustees' Report, the HI program is projected to have a $758 billion operating deficit in 2025 alone.

While you are likely to have more choices regarding the level of benefit coverage that you can purchase under the Medicare program, you may not be willing to accept the additional risk in exchange for lower premiums.

- In addition to increasing Medicare costs, most people will want to purchase a Medigap policy to cover certain expenses not paid for by Medicare.

- Miscellaneous health-care expenses can also be expected to increase, including prescription drugs that aren't covered under Medicare. The average retiree currently can spend hundreds of dollars per year on prescription drugs even if they're fairly healthy. Add a chronic illness, such as high-blood pressure or diabetes, and the costs zoom.

- Most people can also expect their average annual travel and recreational expenses to increase in retirement. After all, what is retirement all about? It may be the first time that you really have the time to travel, play golf, and take advantage of any other recreational opportunities that you have always wanted to.

Exhibit 9-1 includes a column to make adjustments to your current annual expenses based on changes in your spending patterns that are likely to occur in your retirement years. You should consider these changes and insert the appropriate adjustments (higher or lower incremental expenses) in your individual worksheet.

Nonrecurring Retirement Expenses

Now that you have determined your estimated recurring expenses in retirement, what about selected nonrecurring retirement expenses or capital needs?

- You may decide to purchase the second home that you have been talking about for years, allowing you to spend winters in a warmer climate and summers close to family at your current home.

- You may decide to swallow hard, pony up the ante, and join some type of club since you and your spouse now have time for tennis, swimming, and golf.

- In addition to increasing your recurring travel, you may want to take the dream trip you couldn't while you were working. This can be expensive.

- You may be required to provide financial assistance to one or more of your parents or in-laws for a period of time after you retire. Alternatively, you may need to provide assistance to one or more of your children, whether or not they return home.

- If you are a widow or single woman, you will need to plan even better because odds are you will live longer than men, and you may not have accumulated as much in retirement resources, depending on your employment history.

- If you are married for a second time, you also have other considerations, possibly stepchildren who add to the complicated process of figuring out who provides for whom. High rates of divorce and remarriage have made a patchwork of the American family.

- Finally, don't forget about your plans to leave something for the children, any stepchildren, and other loved ones.

You need to consider the preceding line items as an add-on to your recurring retirement expenses. Exhibit 9-1 contains a column to insert these nonrecurring retirement expenses and capital requirements.

Geographic Adjustments

Some or all of the expenses just cited need to be adjusted based on your expected retirement location. You may decide not to move in your retirement years and use your current city as a base from which to travel. Alternatively, you may want to move your primary residence to a warmer climate. If so, you may need to adjust certain retirement expenses by a cost-of-living differential factor, especially if the cost of living is higher in your desired versus current location. For example, San Francisco is more costly than St. Charles, Illinois.

Again, consult Appendix D, which contains the current cost-of-living index for a number of cities in the country. Personally, I would not adjust your estimated expense numbers unless the adjustment factor causes your estimated expenses to increase. This more conservative approach

Major Recurring Expense Categories	Current Recurring Annual Expenses	Adjustments (+ or − a Given Amount for Retirement)	Detailed Budget for First Year of Retirement
Housing:			
Mortgage	$17,700	− $17,700	$0
Homeowners Insurance	$1,200	$0	$1,200
Utilities	$3,700	$0	$3,700
Maintenance	$2,400	$0	$2,400
Property Tax	$3,000	$500	$3,500
Total	$28,000	− $17,200	$10,800
Food	$8,000	− $1,500	$6,500
Clothing	$5,000	− $2,000	$3,000
Health Care	$1,500	$5,000	$6,500
Transportation			
Car Payments	$4,600	− $1,500	$3,100
Gas	$2,900	− $500	$2,400
Maintenance	$600	$0	$600
Parking	$1,200	− $1,000	$200
Total	$9,300	− $3,000	$6,300
Education	$10,000	− $10,000	−$0
Insurance			
Life/Disability	$1,400	− $1,400	$0
Auto	$1,600	− $1,600	$0
Total	$3,000	− $3,000	$0
Travel/Vacations	$4,500	$8,000	$12,500
Recreation/Entertainment	$3,500	$4,000	$7,500
Taxes			
State and Local	$19,500	− $9,500	$10,000
Payroll	$8,300	−$8,300	$0
Total	$27,800	− $17,800	$10,000
Savings	$6,500	− $6,500	$0
Other	$1,350	− $350	$1,000
TOTAL	$108,450	− $44,350	$64,100

Supplemental Retirement Expenses	Current Value
Retirement Condo (Sarasota)	$100,000
Country Club	$15,000
Dream Trip	$7,600
Family Assistance	$40,000
Children's Inheritance (Minimum)	$25,000
TOTAL	$187,600

Exhibit 9-2   James' and Carol's total estimated retirement expenses worksheet, Sarasota, Florida

will help assure that you don't get caught short. Exhibit 9-2 has been completed based on the assumption that our hypothetical couple, James and Carol, want to keep their home in St. Charles, a far western suburb of Chicago, but purchase a condo in Sarasota in which to spend at least six months a year when they retire.

How to Convert Current Expenses from Now to Then (Retirement)

Once you complete your total estimated retirement expenses worksheet, you will need to translate the resulting amounts that you calculated into a lump sum that you will need at retirement. Exhibit 9-3 represents a worksheet that will help you perform this translation based on the nature and timing of the expense, your expected retirement date, your

Current ages	a	
Retirement ages	b	
Years to retirement	b-a	(See Appendix C-Use the longer life expectancy of you or
Life expectancy	c	your spouse and add at least two years to this number to
		be conservative.)
Years in retirement	c-b	(Use the higher of you or your spouse)
Inflation rate	4%	

Detailed budget total for first year of retirement		(Exhibit 9-1)
Cost of living ("COL") in current city		(Appendix D)
Cost of living in retirement city		(Appendix D)

If COL in retirement city is greater than COL in current city, then complete Column 1. If COL in current city is greater than COL in retirement city, then complete Column 2.

Column 1	**Column 2**
Step 1: (COL in retirement city) - (COL in current city) = _____	Since COL in current city is greater than COL in retirement city, no adjustment is necessary. Thus, your detailed budget total for the first year
Step 2: 1 + (result from Step 1) = _____	of retirement is unchanged. Enter this result on the first line below.
Step 3: (detailed budget total for first year of retirement) x (result from Step 2) = _____	
Enter this result on the first line below.	
_____	_____
	_____ (From above)
	(Continued)

Exhibit 9-3 Translation worksheet (translate total estimated retirement expenses to sum needed at retirement)

Translation to future value using 4% inflation and number of years to retirement:

1) Determine your number of years to retirement.
   _____

2) Using the chart on the following page, determine your appropriate inflation factor under the 4% column. _____

3) Multiply this factor by the result from either Column 1 or 2. _____

Results = future value of the budget total for the first year of retirement

_____

Supplemental Retirement Expenses:

Cost of retirement condo _____ (Exhibit 9-1)

Translation to future value using 3% inflation and number of years to retirement:

1) Using the chart on the following page, determine your appropriate inflation factor under the 3% column. _____

2) Multiply this factor by the cost of your retirement condo.

_____
(Line 2)

Cost of country club + dream trip
+ family assistance _____ (Exhibit 9-1)

Translation to future value using 4% inflation and number of years to retirement

1) Using the chart on the following page, determine your appropriate inflation factor under the 4% column. _____

2) Multiply this factor by the (cost of country club + dream trip + family assistance).

_____
(Line 4)

Result = Sum of lines 2 and 4 = Future value of supplemental retirement expenses needed at retirement

_____

Exhibit 9-3 *(Continued)*

INFLATION FACTORS

Years to	Inflation			
Retirement	2%	3%	4%	6%
40	2.20804	3.26204	4.80102	10.28572
39	2.16474	3.16703	4.61637	9.70351
38	2.12230	3.07478	4.43881	9.15425
37	2.08069	2.98523	4.26809	8.63609
36	2.03989	2.89828	4.10393	8.14725
35	1.99989	2.81386	3.94609	7.68609
34	1.96068	2.73191	3.79432	7.25103
33	1.92223	2.65234	3.64838	6.84059
32	1.88454	2.57508	3.50806	6.45339
31	1.84759	2.50008	3.37313	6.08810
30	1.81136	2.42726	3.24340	5.74349
29	1.77584	2.35657	3.11865	5.41839
28	1.74102	2.28793	2.99870	5.11169
27	1.70689	2.22129	2.88337	4.82235
26	1.67342	2.15659	2.77247	4.54938
25	1.64061	2.09378	2.66584	4.29187
24	1.60844	2.03279	2.56330	4.04893
23	1.57690	1.97359	2.46472	3.81975
22	1.54598	1.91610	2.36992	3.60354
21	1.51567	1.86029	2.27877	3.39956
20	1.48595	1.80611	2.19112	3.20714
19	1.45681	1.75351	2.10685	3.02560
18	1.42825	1.70243	2.02582	2.85434
17	1.40024	1.65285	1.94790	2.69277
16	1.37279	1.60471	1.87298	2.54035
15	1.34587	1.55797	1.80094	2.39656
14	1.31948	1.51259	1.73168	2.26090
13	1.29361	1.46853	1.66507	2.13293
12	1.26824	1.42576	1.60103	2.01220
11	1.24337	1.38423	1.53945	1.89830
10	1.21899	1.34392	1.48024	1.79085
9	1.19509	1.30477	1.42331	1.68948
8	1.17166	1.26677	1.36857	1.59385
7	1.14869	1.22987	1.31593	1.50363
6	1.12616	1.19405	1.26532	1.41852
5	1.10408	1.15927	1.21665	1.33823
4	1.08243	1.12551	1.16986	1.26248
3	1.06121	1.09273	1.12486	1.19102
2	1.04040	1.06090	1.08160	1.12360
1	1.02000	1.03000	1.04000	1.06000

Exhibit 9-3 *(Continued)*

estimated life expectancy, and your assumed inflation rate between now and the date of your retirement.

With regard to inflation, it's important to remember that for every $10,000 of annual expenses that you need today, you'll need $21,911 in 20 years based on a 4 percent average annual inflation rate (which is the long-term inflation rate assumed by the Social Security and Medicare Trustees in their 1995 annual report). You may also want to assume a higher inflation rate for selected expenses such as health-care costs when you estimate how much additional health care costs you may incur in retirement.

SAMPLE RETIREMENT NEEDS MODEL FOR A HYPOTHETICAL COUPLE (JAMES AND CAROL)

Now that we have covered the basics of determining how to estimate your retirement needs, let's do so for James, 46, and Carol, 45. They both have careers. They have two children, one a freshman in a private college and one a freshman in a public high school. (James also has a grown son from a prior marriage, whom he no longer supports, but wants to provide for upon death. His ex-wife remarried and he no longer pays alimony.)

They estimate that a condo in Sarasota would cost about $100,000 today, but they know that it will probably rise in price about 3 percent per year between now and retirement. Our couple's parents are all still alive. They expect to have to help support two of them during the early years of retirement at an estimated current cost of $1,000 per month. They calculate that these expenses will increase at an annual rate of 4 percent and that they will need to provide this supplemental income until about five years after they retire. The other two parents are comfortably situated and are gifting them funds each year as part of their estate plan.

James and Carol want to retire when he reaches 63, or in 17 years. When they do, they plan to take a two-week dream trip to Hawaii, visiting all four islands. A top-of-the-line tour and related expenses today would cost them about $7,600, with airfare and all meals included. They estimate that the cost of the trip and all their current expenses, other than health care, will increase by 4 percent annually.

They expect that their total annual health-care costs in retirement will increase by $5,000, including possible changes in the Medicare program, reductions in employer health-care subsidies and payments on a Medigap policy. Finally, they would like to leave their primary residence in St. Charles in equal shares to all three children if possible. They are unsure as to whether they will have other assets to bequest.

Exhibit 9-2 shows an estimate of our hypothetical couple's current annual expenses, including taxes. This exhibit also includes the appropriate adjustment for post- versus preretirement expenses and our couple's major nonrecurring expenses. Exhibit 9-4 shows our couple's retirement needs translation worksheet.

This example is only an illustration. Your projections may vary considerably. In fact, you may want to plug in your numbers using a copy of the blank form in Exhibit 9-1. But when you do, remember to err on the side of conservatism. Specifically, if in doubt, estimate higher versus lower retirement amounts.

The amounts that you calculate using the worksheet will be inserted into the overall retirement security model that will be covered later. We must, however, estimate your projected resources at retirement and your related retirement gap to complete the model. To do so, we'll continue to follow our couple's model as a rough guide.

Current ages	46/45	
Retirement ages	63/62	
Years to retirement	17	(See Appendix C-Use the longer life expectancy of you or
Life expectancy	84	your spouse and add at least two years to this number to
Years in retirement	22	be conservative.)
Inflation rate	4%	(Use the higher of you or your spouse)

Detailed budget total for first year of retirement	$64,100	(Exhibit 9-2)
Cost of living ("COL") in current city	N/A	(Appendix D)
Cost of living in retirement city	98.9	(Appendix D)

If COL in retirement city is greater than COL in current city, then complete Column 1. If COL in current city is greater than COL in retirement city, then complete Column 2.

Column 1	**Column 2**
Step 1: (COL in retirement city) - (COL in current city) = _____	Since COL in current city is greater than COL in retirement city, no adjustment is necessary. Thus, your detailed budget total for the first year of retirement is unchanged. Enter this result on the first line below.
Step 2: 1 + (result from Step 1) = _____	
Step 3: (detailed budget total for first year of retirement) x (result from Step 2) = _____	
Enter this result on the first line below.	
	$64,100 (From above)

(Continued)

Exhibit 9-4   James' and Carol's translation worksheet (translate total estimated retirement expenses to sum needed at retirement)

Translation to future value using 4% inflation and
number of years to retirement:

1) Determine your number of years to retirement.
   _17_

2) Using the chart on the following page, determine
   your appropriate inflation factor under the 4%
   column. _1.94790_

3) Multiply this factor by the result from either
   Column 1 or 2. _124,860_

Results = future value of the budget total for the first
year of retirement $124,860

Supplemental Retirement Expenses:

Cost of retirement condo $100,000   (Exhibit 9-2)

Translation to future value using 3% inflation and
number of years to retirement:

1) Using the chart on the following page, determine
   your appropriate inflation factor under the 3%
   column. _1.65285_

2) Multiply this factor by the cost of your
   retirement condo.   165,285
                                              (Line 2)

Cost of country club + dream trip
 + family assistance   87,600   (Exhibit 9-2)

Translation to future value using 4% inflation and
number of years to retirement

1) Using the chart on the following page, determine
   your appropriate inflation factor under the 4%
   column. _1.94790_

2) Multiply this factor by the (cost of country club +
   dream trip + family assistance).   170,636
                                              (Line 4)

Result = Sum of lines 2 and 4 = Future value of
supplemental retirement expenses needed at
retirement $335,921

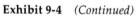

Exhibit 9-4   *(Continued)*

INFLATION FACTORS

Years to Retirement	2%	3%	4%	6%
40	2.20804	3.26204	4.80102	10.28572
39	2.16474	3.16703	4.61637	9.70351
38	2.12230	3.07478	4.43881	9.15425
37	2.08069	2.98523	4.26809	8.63609
36	2.03989	2.89828	4.10393	8.14725
35	1.99989	2.81386	3.94609	7.68609
34	1.96068	2.73191	3.79432	7.25103
33	1.92223	2.65234	3.64838	6.84059
32	1.88454	2.57508	3.50806	6.45339
31	1.84759	2.50008	3.37313	6.08810
30	1.81136	2.42726	3.24340	5.74349
29	1.77584	2.35657	3.11865	5.41839
28	1.74102	2.28793	2.99870	5.11169
27	1.70689	2.22129	2.88337	4.82235
26	1.67342	2.15659	2.77247	4.54938
25	1.64061	2.09378	2.66584	4.29187
24	1.60844	2.03279	2.56330	4.04893
23	1.57690	1.97359	2.46472	3.81975
22	1.54598	1.91610	2.36992	3.60354
21	1.51567	1.86029	2.27877	3.39956
20	1.48595	1.80611	2.19112	3.20714
19	1.45681	1.75351	2.10685	3.02560
18	1.42825	1.70243	2.02582	2.85434
17	1.40024	1.65285	1.94790	2.69277
16	1.37279	1.60471	1.87298	2.54035
15	1.34587	1.55797	1.80094	2.39656
14	1.31948	1.51259	1.73168	2.26090
13	1.29361	1.46853	1.66507	2.13293
12	1.26824	1.42576	1.60103	2.01220
11	1.24337	1.38423	1.53945	1.89830
10	1.21899	1.34392	1.48024	1.79085
9	1.19509	1.30477	1.42331	1.68948
8	1.17166	1.26677	1.36857	1.59385
7	1.14869	1.22987	1.31593	1.50363
6	1.12616	1.19405	1.26532	1.41852
5	1.10408	1.15927	1.21665	1.33823
4	1.08243	1.12551	1.16986	1.26248
3	1.06121	1.09273	1.12486	1.19102
2	1.04040	1.06090	1.08160	1.12360
1	1.02000	1.03000	1.04000	1.06000

Exhibit 9-4 *(Continued)*

CHAPTER TEN

Identifying Your Resources

MYTH 12
Your investment horizon and strategies should be based on your expected retirement age rather than your expected lifetime.
Wrong again. Doing so results in many people's failing to achieve their desired investment returns and prematurely adjusting their investment portfolios to more conservative investments as they approach retirement. The average 65-year-old male in 1996 is currently expected to live another 13.8 years. Women are expected to live about four years beyond that. You need to make sure that your investment horizon and strategies are not myopic. Consider your full life span rather than your working years in determining your investment horizon, particularly if you want to retire early.

We can use a rash of tools to peek into our retirement crystal ball. This is not voodoo or magic but is based on pragmatic planning, projections, and calculations. In the last chapter we figured out how to estimate resource needs at retirement. In this chapter, we'll review how to estimate expected retirement benefits and current resources. Until you pick apart and analyze these factors, you haven't gleaned a full picture.

We'll start by reviewing the seven major elements of retirement security that were outlined in Chapter 7, then discuss how to plug in present and future dollar amounts to arrive at your custom retirement plan.

SEVEN MAJOR RESOURCE ELEMENTS

Social Security Benefits

Appendix A contains a chart that will help you estimate the amount of benefits you'll be eligible for when you retire, based on the current Social Security program and a targeted retirement age of 65. These amounts represent a reasonable estimate of your benefits under the current program. If you plan to retire before or after age 65, you'll need to adjust your estimated benefit by the factors noted in Exhibit 2-4. You can obtain a more exact calculation by requesting a personal benefits statement from the Social Security Administration (call 1-800-772-1213 or write the nearest local office of the Social Security Administration).

Whether you estimate or go with a more exact figure, you need to decide whether to discount the projected benefit amount based on possible changes in the program between now and the time that you retire.

As noted earlier, I contend that the Social Security program can and must be saved. I also believe that it will be altered and that these changes are likely to result in lower relative benefit levels, particularly for baby boomers and busters.

While it is possible that a movement to a two-tiered Social Security program could result in the same or higher relative benefit levels for younger boomers and busters, there is a significant possibility that this will not happen, which should cause you to take a more conservative approach. Then you may be pleasantly surprised with a larger nest egg. Better safe than sorry, right?

If you concur, you may want to discount your projected Social Security benefit from 10 percent to 33 percent, depending on your age, income level, and outlook regarding the program's future. Generally, the older you are, the less likely that your benefit levels will be cut because any related reductions are likely to be phased in. Beside a possible reduction in relative annual benefits, you may want to factor in the chance that there will be an increase in the Social Security retirement age from 67 to 70 on a gradual basis. Finally, keep in mind that the earliest retirement age is likely to be raised to 65 or higher.

Medicare Benefits

As mentioned earlier, you need to adjust your estimated health-care expenses in retirement to reflect future changes in Medicare programs. Since these changes are treated as an adjustment to postretirement expenses, no adjustments to your estimated retirement resources are necessary.

Employer-Sponsored Pension and Savings Programs

There are two types of benefit amounts that you will need to obtain to complete your retirement security model. The first is the estimated amount of defined-benefit pension benefit that you will be eligible to receive from your current or prior employers. The second amount(s) will relate to the current balance in any employer-sponsored savings plans under which you may be covered. For example, your employer may have profit sharing, stock bonus, ESOP, or other types of retirement savings plans. Regarding any defined-benefit pension benefit that you may be eligible for, once a year you have the right to request an estimate of your current and projected pension benefit. This request should be directed to the plan administrator of the respective plan(s). If you aren't sure who the plan administrator is, contact the head of human resources at your current or former employer.

Once you know your projected annual pension benefit, you need to consider how secure that benefit is, in terms of both the funding status of the plan and your employer's financial strength. You can do this by reviewing your plan's latest financial statements and annual report (Form 5500 filing). These can be obtained for a modest fee from your plan administrator or the DOL's public disclosure office (call (202) 219-5000 or write the U.S. Department of Labor, Pension and Welfare Benefits Administration, Public Disclosure Office, 200 Constitution Ave. N.W., Washington, DC, 20210).

When it comes to your individual account balance in any employer-sponsored, defined-contribution plan, most employers automatically provide a statement at least quarterly. If it's unavailable or outdated, contact your plan administrator or human resources department.

Employer-Sponsored Retiree Health-Care Programs

This item should be handled in the same way as Medicare expenses. Adjust your estimated postretirement annual health-care expenses so that no additional adjustments are necessary. If you aren't sure you have any related benefits, contact your human resources department.

Personal Savings and Likely Inheritance

Study your latest bank, brokerage, mutual fund, and insurance policy statements for your account balances. If they're not available, contact the proper institutions. Also, estimate the value of your home, other real estate and any collectibles, and net related selling costs such as commissions and closing costs. You may decide that you don't plan to sell some of these assets when you retire. If so, exclude these related amounts in estimating your retirement resources. If you plan to set aside certain property such as a primary residence for your children, you shouldn't include any related amounts in your listing of retirement resources or supplemental retirement needs.

If you have purchased an individual annuity policy, you will need to review and consider the financial strength of the insurer to determine if you are likely to receive your full annuity payments. Most

Moody's	Standard & Poor's	Duff & Phelps	Explanation
Aaa	AAA	AAA	Best quality—Capacity to pay interest and repay principal is extremely strong. The risk factors are negligible, being only slightly more than the risk-free U.S. Treasury debt.
Aa	AA	AA+ AA AA−	High-quality—Very strong capacity to pay interest and repay principal. Differs from the higher-rated issues only in small degree. Risk is modest but may vary slightly from time to time because of economic conditions.
A	A	A+ A A−	Upper-medium grade—Strong capacity to pay interest and repay principal although it is somewhat more susceptible to the adverse effects of changes in circumstances and economic conditions than debt in higher-rated categories. Risk factors are more variable and greater in periods of economic stress.
Baa	BBB	BBB+ BBB BBB−	Medium-grade—Adequate capacity to pay interest and repay principal. Adverse economic conditions or changing circumstances are more likely to lead to a weakened capacity to pay interest and repay principal for debt in this category than in higher-rated categories. Considerable variability in risk during economic cycles.
Ba	BB	BB+ BB BB−	Speculative—Faces major ongoing uncertainties or exposure to adverse business, financial, or economic conditions which could lead to inadequate capacity to meet timely interest and principal payments. Overall quality may move up or down frequently within the category.
B	B	B+ B B−	Undesirable—Adverse business, financial, or economic conditions will likely impair capacity or willingness to pay interest and repay principal. Potential exists for frequent changes in the rating within this category or into a higher or lower rating grade.

Exhibit 10-1   Company ratings (*Sources: Moody's Bond Record,* Dec. 1995, p. 3; *Standard & Poor's Bond Guide,* Feb. 1996, p.12; *Duff & Phelps DCR Rating Scales,* Mar. 1996.)

Moody's	Standard & Poor's	Duff & Phelps	Explanation
Caa	CCC	CCC	Poor standing—Has a currently identifiable vulnerability to default, and is dependent upon favorable business, financial, and economic conditions to meet timely payment of interest and repayment of principal. Well below investment grade securities. Risk can be substantial with unfavorable economic/industry conditions, and/or with unfavorable company developments.
Ca			Speculative in a high degree—Such issues are often in default or have other marked shortcomings.
Ca			Lowest rating—Can be regarded as having extremely poor prospects of ever attaining any real investment standing.
	D	DD	Payment default—Used when interest payments or principal payments are not made on the date due even if the applicable grace period has not expired. Also used upon the filing of a bankruptcy petition if debt service payments are jeopardized.

Exhibit 10-1   *(Continued)*

people receive their full benefit. Some insurance companies, however, have failed in recent years, shortchanging their policyholders. If you are uncertain about your provider's financial strength, you should inquire about the funding arrangement. Some annuities and insurance policies are backed by a segregated pool of assets, while others are backed only by the general assets and financial strength of the insurance company. You should periodically monitor this situation if you have a significant sum tied up in such contracts.

You can do this by reviewing the annual reports issued by the provider and, if the contract is backed by only the provider's general assets, inquire about the current rating of the company, as reported by any one of several major rating services—Moody's, Standard & Poors, Duff & Phelps (Exhibit 10-1). Doing so will help you gauge the relative financial strength of your contract provider.

Earnings from Future Employment

Be it the same job, a new career, or part-time work, this will be an option that most people may have to resort to if they plan inadequately.

Employer-Provided Health-Care Benefits during Retirement

If you continue to work after you retire, you may be eligible for certain employer-paid or subsidized health-care benefits. If you work 1,000 or more hours in a year, you are probably eligible for certain health-care benefits that active employees receive.

If you choose to continue to work more than 1,000 hours in a year after you retire, you should consider the potential value of any related employer-provided or subsidized health-care benefits when estimating your overall health-care expenses. If you aren't sure of what the future holds, your health-care expenses should be adjusted upward.

Once you gather the preceding numbers, you need to plug these into the worksheet in Exhibit 10-2, which is designed to help you project your retirement resources at retirement. To do so thoroughly, you also need to make certain assumptions regarding future inflation and earnings rates. Exhibit 11-1 should be used to project the value of your employer-defined contribution accounts and individual savings arrangements.

As a point of reference, the Social Security and Medicare Trustees assumed a 4 percent average long-term inflation rate in their 1995 Annual

Elements	Amount
Social Security benefits for first year of retirement (Appendix A)	_____
Employer-sponsored pension—annual payment	_____
Employer-sponsored savings program—401(k)—balance	_____
Personal savings—IRA—balance	_____
Other personal savings—balance	_____
Inheritance/Gifts	_____
Earnings from continued employment—Annual salary	_____

Exhibit 10-2   Total estimated retirement resources worksheet

Report and a 5 percent increase in average wage levels. Your investment earnings rates will vary based on your individual investments.

HOW TO CONVERT CURRENT RESOURCES TO FUTURE ONES—JAMES AND CAROL

Now that we have determined how to estimate your resources at retirement, let's show how the retirement resource projection model would work for James and Carol.

James anticipates that he will earn the maximum Social Security benefit based on his career earnings record to date, and Carol estimates that her Social Security benefit will be based on an average

Elements	Annual Amount
Future Benefits:	
Social Security benefits for first year of retirement:	
James	$22,790*
Carol	$16,700*
Employer-sponsored pension—annual payment:	
James	0
Carol	$30,000**
Current Savings:	
Employer-sponsored savings program—401(k)-balance:	
James	$30,000†
Carol	$20,000†
Personal savings—IRA—balance:	
James	$20,000†
Carol	$20,000†
Other retirement savings—balance	$20,000§
Other:	
Inheritance/Gifts	$75,000‖
Earnings from continued employment:	
James	$ 0
Carol	$ 0

*James and Carol estimated their benefits using Appendix A and the early retirement reduction factors in Exhibit 2-4. They expect their Social Security benefits to be reduced by 20 percent each by the time they retire. This 20 percent reduction is shown in the estimate of their benefits in 2013.

**Estimated benefit in 2013 dollars.

†James and Carol expect these balances to grow at 8 percent annually.

§James and Carol expect their savings to grow at 4 percent annually after income taxes.

‖James and Carol expect this amount to grow at a 4 percent inflation rate.

Exhibit 10-3   James' and Carol's complete retirement resources worksheet

earnings level of $37,000 in today's wages, or about 50 percent above today's average wage.

They both estimate that their Social Security benefits will be reduced by 20 percent from the projected benefit levels by the time they retire. Both expect their Medicare benefits to be cut by 50 percent when they retire. They included the related Medicare adjustment in projecting their estimated health-care expenses in retirement. James estimates that he will not be eligible for an employer-sponsored defined-benefit pension. Based on a review of her plan and discussions with her employer, Carol estimates that she will be eligible for a defined-benefit pension of $30,000 (in 2013 dollars) beginning at age 62.

Neither expects that his or her employers will provide them with company-paid retiree health benefits when they retire, although Carol's employer has recently provided some company-paid retiree health benefits to employees who voluntarily retired early. As a result, they have made an appropriate adjustment in their projected health-care expenses in retirement.

James has a 401(k) account balance of $30,000, net of the amount that was awarded to his former wife via a QDRO, which he thinks will grow at 8 percent per year. Carol has a 401(k) balance of $20,000 that she also expects will grow at 8 percent per year.

Both have IRAs with current balances of $20,000, and both expect their IRAs to grow at 8 percent annually. They also have additional savings of $20,000 that they expect will grow 4 percent annually after income taxes. The couple expects to inherit $75,000 from her parents around their retirement, 20 years down the road. Neither, therefore, expects to have earnings or health-care benefits from continued employment.

Exhibit 10-3 represents their completed retirement resources worksheet. They estimate that they will have a dollar total of $601,397 in resources upon retirement.

After you estimate your expected resources at retirement, we'll determine whether you have a retirement gap, and its extent, then determine what you can do about it.

CHAPTER ELEVEN

Defining and Filling Your Retirement Gap

Completing Your Personal Retirement Security Model

MYTH 13
Spouses have their retirement interests fully protected by federal law.

False. Federal pension laws require certain types of pension plans (for example, defined-benefit plans) to provide joint and survivor annuities as their primary form of benefit. They also require written consent to any other form of benefit (such as, single life annuity, lump sum). These protections do not, however, apply to certain types of retirement and savings plans (including, profit sharing plans, Section 401(k) plans, ESOPs). In addition, there are currently no federal law protections for spouses in connection with retiree health-care programs.

It's time to define and fill your retirement gap. This process is much like filling your gasoline tank before you take a long road trip. In case there aren't gasoline stations along the way, you don't want to get caught short and run out of fuel.

It's the same with a retirement gap. Most people find that if they do not have sufficient resources at retirement to meet their objectives, they may be living on fumes, or even worse, running on empty. This deficiency is referred to as a *gap*.

DEFINING YOUR RETIREMENT GAP

To calculate the gap, simply subtract. Start with your estimated resources (Exhibit 10-3), subtract your estimated needs (Exhibit 9-2), and voilà, you've hit the magic number we've been waiting for, perhaps impatiently, since you began reading this book.

If you get a positive number, congratulations. You're in good shape. You have a projected retirement surplus based on your current assumptions and resources. But don't crack open the champagne—at least not yet. Your job isn't over.

A projected retirement surplus is just that—a projection based on assumptions at one specific point in time, such as your estimated retirement date, retirement needs, and projected investment returns, any of which can change in the blink of an eye, because of a single glitch or altered plans.

Also, as we all know, projections are only as good as the assumptions that underlie them. Review your assumptions and be sure that they are reasonable. If you think equity from the sale of your house, which you're planning to use as retirement income, will bring $75,000 in the current market, don't raise the amount for five years down the road because of inflation. The reality is that your home may not escalate in value.

Don't overlook the little extras. You may not have budgeted for graduate school for your children. Your daughter may decide to go to medical school. Even though she has volunteered to foot some of the bill or take out a partial loan, you're still going to help bankroll a major portion of the cost. Some medical schools are as pricey as $25,000 or more a year in tuition alone (excluding room and board and expenses), and it's a long road ahead.

What about potential long-term care needs for you, your spouse, or a parent? Consider your health and that of your relatives as well as your family histories in assessing the relative probability that you may incur these expenses.

Have I dampened your optimism? That's not the point. I'm here to make sure that you cover your bases.

If by chance you arrive at a negative number when you do your subtraction and have a projected gap, don't panic. A vast majority of Americans end up with a negative number. The more important question is: What are you going to do about it? And when? Fortunately, there are many solutions.

FILLING YOUR RETIREMENT GAP

If you have a gap in your teeth, you wear braces. If you have a gap in your checking account, you add money. It's the same principle in retirement planning. There are two primary and basic ways to close your retirement gap. You can reduce your estimated retirement needs and/or increase your estimated retirement resources.

To reduce your needs, you can delay your retirement date by a few years. This enables you to earn a salary and save longer. You can lower your standard of living before you retire so you save more money (perhaps skip the annual summer trip and go every other year; or, instead of sending your children to private colleges, choose less expensive state schools). You may choose also to reduce your objectives once you hit retirement. Perhaps you can vacation for a few weeks each winter rather than buy a second home in a warm climate. You can work part-time during all or part of your retirement years. Alternatively, you can cut your children's inheritance.

Based on the size of your gap and the number of years until you plan to retire, review your retirement assumptions and goals and decide whether and what changes you can stomach. If you want to estimate how much of a difference any changes would make, you can redo the

---

Step 1: Determine the amount needed in savings to fund the detailed budget total for the first year of retirement.

Future value of budget total for first year of retirement:	_____	(Exhibit 9-3)
Social Security annual benefit(s):	= _____	(Exhibit 10-2)
Employer-sponsored pension annual payment(s):	= _____	(Exhibit 10-2)

Future value of annual earnings from continued
 employment:
    1) Determine your number of years to retirement. _____
    2) Refer to the Inflation Factors Chart on the following
        page to determine your appropriate inflation factor
        under the 4% column. _____
    3) Multiply: (annual earnings) x (result from Step 2)   = _____
Result--Amount needed in savings to fund first year
    detailed budget: _____

Step 2: Using the result from Step 1, refer to the chart on the following page to determine the amount of savings needed to fund annual retirement budget.

Amount: _____

Step 3: Add the future value of the supplemental retirement expenses (Exhibit 9-3) to the amount in Step 2.

Amount from Step 2:	_____	
Future value of the supplemental retirement expenses:	_____	*(Exhibit 9-3)
Sum:	_____	

        *This approach assumes that all of the supplemental retirement
        expenses will be covered in the first year of retirement.

(Continued)

Exhibit 11-1   Retirement gap (difference between retirement resources and retirement needs)

Step 4: Determine the future value of current savings.

1) Using Exhibit 10-2, determine the following:
   401(K) balance _____
   IRA balance _____
   Other savings balance _____
   Inheritance _____

2) Determine your number of years to retirement _____

3) Determine your expected rates of return for the balances in Step 1:
   401(k) expected rate of return _____
   IRA expected rate of return _____
   Other savings expected rate of return _____
   Inheritance expected rate of return _____

4) Using your number of years to retirement and your expected rates of return, refer to the Return Factors Chart on the following page to determine your appropriate return factors for each of your balances:
   401(k) return factor _____
   IRA return factor _____
   Other savings return factor _____
   Inheritance return factor

5) Multiply your return factors (Step 4) by your current balances (Step 1) to determine the future value of your current savings:
   (401(k) balance) x (401(k) return factor) _____
   (IRA balance) x (IRA return factor) _____
   (Other savings) x (other saving return factor) _____
   (Inheritance) x (Inheritance return factor) _____

6) Sum the results from Step 5   _____

Step 5: Subtract the sum in Step 3 from the sum in Step 4.

Sum (Step 4)   _____
Sum (Step 3)   _____
Difference--retirement gap   _____

Exhibit 11-1   *(Continued)*

worksheet in Exhibit 11-1 based on alternative assumptions. For each year that you delay your retirement past age 62, the typical person needs 30 to 40 percent less on average in annual resources upon retirement to pay for normal recurring expenses. This does not count other retirement objectives, and needs vary considerably by individual.

Fortunately, there are other alternatives that I have addressed before. First, you can increase the amount of resources that you have at retirement by boosting your personal savings and investing better. Both require conscientious planning and personal discipline. They also probably demand the assistance of a financial planner who can advise you about what to do during peak periods and hold your hand during down cycles to keep you from panicking. (We'll address how to select an adviser in Chapter 13.)

Using Exhibit 11-2, you can determine the exact amount that you must save each month to fill your retirement gap based on variable

Number of Years in Retirement	Savings Needed to Fund Annual Retirement Budget (From Worksheet)					
	$20,000	$30,000	$40,000	$50,000	$75,000	$100,000
10	$184,000	$276,000	$368,000	$ 460,000	$ 689,000	$ 919,000
15	263,000	395,000	527,000	659,000	988,000	1,317,000
20	336,000	504,000	672,000	840,000	1,259,000	1,679,000
25	402,000	602,000	803,000	1,004,000	1,506,000	2,008,000
30	461,000	692,000	923,000	1,155,000	1,730,000	2,307,000

(Continued)

Example: James and Carol Smith determined from the worksheet that they need $40,000 in their first year in retirement. They estimate that they will live for 25 years in retirement. Thus, James and Carol determine that they need to have a total of $803,000 in savings by the time they retire.

- You can see that the earlier you decide to retire (and thus the more years you will be in retirement), the more money you will need to accumulate as a nest egg.
- The table takes into account that there will likely be regular increases in the cost of living. Therefore, you will need more money in each year of retirement to keep up with those increases. The table takes this into account by assuming an annual inflation rate of 4 percent while you are retired. If the actual rate is higher, you will need more money.
- The table reflects the assumption that your nest egg investments will earn 6 percent each year after retirement. If the actual rate is lower, you will need a larger nest egg to begin with.
- The assumption is that you will spend all of your nest egg—the amount you have on the day you retire, as well as the income earned on that money during retirement. So, if you live exactly as long as you anticipate, there will be no money left to be inherited by your family.

Exhibit 11-1 *(Continued)* (Source: Saving for a Secure Retirement, AICPA.)

earnings rates and different numbers of years until you retire. The rates of return noted are current after-tax rates. Be aware that investments in nontax-favored investment vehicles will have to earn enough to cover the current related tax costs, whereas investments in qualified pension and savings plans, IRAs, Keoghs, and other tax-advantaged savings vehicles will grow on a pretax (tax-deferred) basis.

If you have investments in stocks or taxable bonds outside tax-favored savings vehicles, the dividends, interest, and realized gains on the sale of these investments will be subject to current taxation. A 10 percent pretax rate of return on such investments for a person with a combined federal and state effective tax income rate of 30 percent translates to a 7 percent current after-tax rate of return. Importantly, if your taxable bond fund and stock investments pay $5,000 in interest and dividends in

INFLATION FACTORS

Years to Retirement	Inflation			
	2%	3%	4%	6%
40	2.20804	3.26204	4.80102	10.28572
39	2.16474	3.16703	4.61637	9.70351
38	2.12230	3.07478	4.43881	9.15425
37	2.08069	2.98523	4.26809	8.63609
36	2.03989	2.89828	4.10393	8.14725
35	1.99989	2.81386	3.94609	7.68609
34	1.96068	2.73191	3.79432	7.25103
33	1.92223	2.65234	3.64838	6.84059
32	1.88454	2.57508	3.50806	6.45339
31	1.84759	2.50008	3.37313	6.08810
30	1.81136	2.42726	3.24340	5.74349
29	1.77584	2.35657	3.11865	5.41839
28	1.74102	2.28793	2.99870	5.11169
27	1.70689	2.22129	2.88337	4.82235
26	1.67342	2.15659	2.77247	4.54938
25	1.64061	2.09378	2.66584	4.29187
24	1.60844	2.03279	2.56330	4.04893
23	1.57690	1.97359	2.46472	3.81975
22	1.54598	1.91610	2.36992	3.60354
21	1.51567	1.86029	2.27877	3.39956
20	1.48595	1.80611	2.19112	3.20714
19	1.45681	1.75351	2.10685	3.02560
18	1.42825	1.70243	2.02582	2.85434
17	1.40024	1.65285	1.94790	2.69277
16	1.37279	1.60471	1.87298	2.54035
15	1.34587	1.55797	1.80094	2.39656
14	1.31948	1.51259	1.73168	2.26090
13	1.29361	1.46853	1.66507	2.13293
12	1.26824	1.42576	1.60103	2.01220
11	1.24337	1.38423	1.53945	1.89830
10	1.21899	1.34392	1.48024	1.79085
9	1.19509	1.30477	1.42331	1.68948
8	1.17166	1.26677	1.36857	1.59385
7	1.14869	1.22987	1.31593	1.50363
6	1.12616	1.19405	1.26532	1.41852
5	1.10408	1.15927	1.21665	1.33823
4	1.08243	1.12551	1.16986	1.26248
3	1.06121	1.09273	1.12486	1.19102
2	1.04040	1.06090	1.08160	1.12360
1	1.02000	1.03000	1.04000	1.06000

Exhibit 11-1   (Continued)

a given year and their fair market value increases by $15,000, you will only have to pay current income tax on the interest and dividends.

The gain will not be taxed until you sell the respective investment(s). More important, the principal amount of taxable investments is not subject to income tax. As a basis of comparison, the same investments held in an IRA, Keogh, or qualified pension or savings plan will result in no current taxation. Rather, the interest, dividends, and capital gains, as

RETURN FACTORS

Years to	Rate of Return			
Retirement	4%	6%	8%	10%
40	4.80102	10.28572	21.72452	45.25926
39	4.61637	9.70351	20.11530	41.14478
38	4.43881	9.15425	18.62528	37.40434
37	4.26809	8.63609	17.24563	34.00395
36	4.10393	8.14725	15.96817	30.91268
35	3.94609	7.68609	14.78534	28.10244
34	3.79432	7.25103	13.69013	25.54767
33	3.64838	6.84059	12.67605	23.22515
32	3.50806	6.45339	11.73708	21.11378
31	3.37313	6.08810	10.86767	19.19434
30	3.24340	5.74349	10.06266	17.44940
29	3.11865	5.41839	9.31727	15.86309
28	2.99870	5.11169	8.62711	14.42099
27	2.88337	4.82235	7.98806	13.10999
26	2.77247	4.54938	7.39635	11.91818
25	2.66584	4.29187	6.84848	10.83471
24	2.56330	4.04893	6.34118	9.84973
23	2.46472	3.81975	5.87146	8.95430
22	2.36992	3.60354	5.43654	8.14027
21	2.27877	3.39956	5.03383	7.40025
20	2.19112	3.20714	4.66096	6.72750
19	2.10685	3.02560	4.31570	6.11591
18	2.02582	2.85434	3.99602	5.55992
17	1.94790	2.69277	3.70002	5.05447
16	1.87298	2.54035	3.42594	4.59497
15	1.80094	2.39656	3.17217	4.17725
14	1.73168	2.26090	2.93719	3.79750
13	1.66507	2.13293	2.71962	3.45227
12	1.60103	2.01220	2.51817	3.13843
11	1.53945	1.89830	2.33164	2.85312
10	1.48024	1.79085	2.15892	2.59374
9	1.42331	1.68948	1.99900	2.35795
8	1.36857	1.59385	1.85093	2.14359
7	1.31593	1.50363	1.71382	1.94872
6	1.26532	1.41852	1.58687	1.77156
5	1.21665	1.33823	1.46933	1.61051
4	1.16986	1.26248	1.36049	1.46410
3	1.12486	1.19102	1.25971	1.33100
2	1.08160	1.12360	1.16640	1.21000
1	1.04000	1.06000	1.08000	1.10000

Exhibit 11-1 *(Continued)*

well as all principal amounts other than those attributable to any after-tax employee contributions, will be subject to income tax when withdrawn from the plan or account. Exhibit 11-3 contains a summary of several major types of investment vehicles and instruments and the related income tax treatment.

Now that we've reviewed how you'll tackle the personal retirement security model, let's take a peek at how James and Carol have fared. We

Years to Retirement	Total Amount Needed at Retirement Date							
	$200,000				$300,000			
	4%	6%	8%	10%	4%	6%	8%	10%
40	$ 169	$ 100	$ 57	$ 31	$ 253	$ 150	$ 85	$ 47
35	218	140	87	52	327	210	130	78
30	287	198	133	77	431	297	200	132
25	388	287	209	149	582	4371	313	221
20	543	431	337	261	815	646	506	392
15	810	684	574	479	1,215	1,026	861	718
10	1,354	1,214	1,086	96	2,031	1,822	1,629	1,452
5	3,007	2,852	2,704	2,561	4,510	4,278	4,056	3,842

Years to Retirement	Total Amount Needed at Retirement Date							
	$400,000				$500,000			
	4%	6%	8%	10%	4%	6%	8%	10%
40	$ 337	$ 200	$ 114	$ 63	$ 422	$ 250	$ 142	$ 78
35	436	279	173	104	545	349	217	131
30	574	396	267	175	718	495	333	219
25	775	574	418	299	969	718	522	374
20	1,087	861	675	522	1,359	1,077	843	653
15	1,620	1,369	1,148	957	2,025	1,711	1,435	1,196
10	2,707	2,429	2,172	1,937	3,384	3,036	2,715	2,421
5	6,013	5,705	5,408	5,123	7,517	7,131	6,760	6,403

Exhibit 11-2   Monthly savings needed to fill retirement gap

already estimated that they would need $1,335,921 upon retirement to meet their retirement objectives. We also estimated that together they'd have projected resources of $518,052, excluding Social Security and defined benefit pension amounts. Based on these calculations, they project that they have a current retirement gap of $817,869 (see Exhibit 11-4).

Like many of us, they assumed they were saving enough. They're obviously disappointed, though not shocked. They realize in hindsight that they shouldn't have been so quick to buy a new car every few years or to take a two-week family vacation every summer. They also should

Years to Retirement	Total Amount Needed at Retirement Date							
	$600,000				$700,000			
	4%	6%	8%	10%	4%	6%	8%	10%
40	$ 506	$ 300	$ 171	$ 94	$ 590	$ 350	$ 199	$ 110
35	654	419	260	157	764	489	303	183
30	862	594	400	263	1,005	693	467	307
25	1,163	862	627	448	1,357	1,005	731	523
20	1,630	1,292	1,012	784	1,902	1,507	1,181	914
15	2,430	2,053	1,733	1,436	2,835	2,395	2,010	1,675
10	4,061	3,643	3,258	2,905	4,738	4,250	3,801	3,389
5	9,020	8,557	8,112	7,684	10,523	9,983	9,464	8,965

Years to Retirement	Total Amount Needed at Retirement Date							
	$800,000				$900,000			
	4%	6%	8%	10%	4%	6%	8%	10%
40	$ 675	$ 400	$ 228	$125	$ 759	$ 450	$ 256	$ 141
35	873	559	346	209	982	629	390	235
30	1,149	792	533	351	1,292	891	600	395
25	1,551	1,149	836	598	1,745	1,292	940	673
20	2,174	1,723	1,349	1,045	2,446	1,938	1,518	1,175
15	3,240	2,737	2,297	1,914	3,645	3,079	2,584	2,154
10	5,415	4,857	4,344	3,873	6,092	5,465	4,887	4,357
5	12,026	11,409	10,816	10,246	13,530	12,835	12,168	11,526

(Continued)

Exhibit 11-2   *(Continued)*

have insisted that their children save half of the money earned from their summer jobs, no matter how small.

They can take some comfort in the fact that they are typical. Another boon is that they aren't waiting for a crisis to shake them into changing, but are planning ahead. Because both have always worked they're prepared to dig in their heels and take decisive steps to turn their negative number into a positive one, rather than adjusting their basic retirement objectives or desired standard of living at retirement.

Years to Retirement	Total Amount Needed at Retirement Date							
	$1,000,000				$1,100,000			
	4%	6%	8%	10%	4%	6%	8%	10%
40	$ 843	$ 500	$ 285	$ 157	$ 928	$ 550	$ 313	$ 173
35	1,091	698	433	261	1,200	768	476	287
30	1,436	991	667	439	1,580	1,090	733	483
25	1,939	1,436	1,045	747	2,132	1,579	1,149	822
20	2,717	2,154	1,686	1,306	2,989	2,369	1,855	1,437
15	4,050	3,421	2,871	2,393	4,455	3,764	3,158	2,632
10	6,769	6,072	5,430	4,841	7,445	6,679	5,973	5,326
5	15,033	14,261	13,520	12,807	16,536	15,688	14,872	14,088

Years to Retirement	Total Amount Needed at Retirement Date							
	$1,200,000				$1,300,000			
	4%	6%	8%	10%	4%	6%	8%	10%
40	$ 1,012	$ 600	$ 341	$ 188	$ 1,096	$ 650	$ 370	$ 204
35	1,309	838	520	313	1,418	908	563	340
30	1,723	1,189	800	526	1,867	1,288	866	570
25	2,326	1,723	1,253	897	2,520	1,867	1,358	972
20	3,261	2,584	2,024	1,567	3,533	2,800	2,192	1,698
15	4,860	4,106	3,445	2,871	5,265	4,448	3,732	3,111
10	8,122	7,286	6,516	5,810	8,799	7,893	7,059	6,294
5	18,040	17,114	16,224	15,368	19,543	18,540	17,575	16,649

Exhibit 11-2   *(Continued)*

Because they are 17 years from their planned retirement, they feel they have time to fill their gap, and they do.

They plan to concentrate on altering their current savings and investment strategy. Using Exhibit 11-2, they note that they need to save approximately $1,960 per month ($23,520 per year) in order to fill their projected retirement gap, assuming they can achieve an overall 8 percent after-tax rate of return on their investments (using Exhibit 11-2, $817,869/800,000 \times [2297 - (2297 - 1349) \times .4]$). That represents approximately $1,230 of additional savings per month (Exhibit 13-10). They are concerned as to whether they can achieve that savings rate even by being

| Years to Retirement | Total Amount Needed at Retirement Date | | | | | | | |
| | $1,400,000 | | | | $1,500,000 | | | |
	4%	6%	8%	10%	4%	6%	8%	10%
40	$ 1,181	$ 699	$ 398	$ 220	$ 1,265	$ 749	$ 427	$ 235
35	1,527	978	606	366	1,636	1,048	650	392
30	2,010	1,387	933	614	2,154	1,486	1,000	658
25	2,714	2,010	1,462	1,046	2,908	2,154	1,567	1,121
20	3,804	3,015	2,361	1,828	5,076	3,230	2,530	1,959
15	5,670	4,790	4,019	3,350	6,075	5,132	4,306	3,589
10	9,476	8,500	7,602	6,778	10,153	9,108	8,145	7,262
5	21,046	19,966	18,927	17,930	22,550	21,392	20,279	19,210

| Years to Retirement | Total Amount Needed at Retirement Date | | | | | | | |
| | $1,600,000 | | | | $1,700,000 | | | |
	4%	6%	8%	10%	4%	6%	8%	10%
40	$ 1,349	$ 799	$ 455	$ 251	$ 1,434	$ 849	$ 484	$ 267
35	1,745	1,117	693	418	1,854	1,187	736	444
30	2,298	1,585	1,066	702	2,441	1,684	1,133	746
25	3,102	2,297	1,671	1,196	3,296	2,441	1,776	1,271
20	4,348	3,446	2,698	2,090	4,620	3,661	2,867	2,220
15	6,480	5,474	4,593	3,828	6,885	5,816	4,880	4,068
10	10,830	9,715	8,688	7,746	11,507	10,322	9,231	8,230
5	24,053	22,818	21,631	20,481	25,556	24,245	22,983	21,772

Exhibit 11-2   *(Continued)*

disciplined, and take full advantage of the 401(k) savings plans offered by their employers, whose plans offer a 50 percent match for each $1 they save, up to 6 percent of their annual pay. However, they are already saving $6,500 per year and receiving some match for their current 401(k) plan contributions for a total of $8,748 per year (Exhibit 13-10).

James and Carol call a family meeting with their three children to lay down the law regarding expenses and savings.

To save the additional amounts necessary, they will need to cut their current annual expenses by approximately $1,230 per month or $14,760 per year or otherwise adjust their plan. To do so, they agree to take a

Investment Category	Savings Deductible	Earnings (Interest and Dividends Tax Deferred	Withdrawals Taxable
IRAs	Maybe*	Yes	Yes/Maybe**
401(k)s	Yes	Yes	Yes
Insurance	No	Yes	Maybe**
Annuities	No	Yes	Maybe**
Mutual Funds	No	No	No***
Municipal Bonds	No	Yes	No***
Stocks	No	No	No***
CPS/Taxable Bonds	No	No	No***

*If neither you nor your spouse (if married) is an active participant in an employer-maintained retirement plan, you may deduct up to $2,000 in contributions to an IRA. If either you or your spouse (if married) is an active participant in an employer-maintained retirement plan, this $2,000 limit may be reduced, depending on your adjusted gross income ("AGI").

1) Single individual (including a head of household)—No deductions if AGI is $35,000 or more. If AGI is $25,000 or less, the full $2,000 deduction is available. For AGI between $25,000 and $35,000, compute the deductions as follows:

$$[(35,000 - AGI)/10,000] \times 2,000 = \text{deduction.}$$

2) Individual filing joint return with spouse—No deduction if AGI is $50,000 or more. If AGI is $40,000 or less, the full $2,000 deduction is available. For AGI between $40,000 and $50,000 compute the deductions as follows:

$$[(50,000 - AGI)/10,000] \times 2,000 = \text{deduction.}$$

3) Married individual filing separately—same procedures as previous with an AGI range of $10,000 to $20,000.

**Nondeductible contributions are not taxed on withdrawal; however, earnings on the contributions are taxed on withdrawal.

Distributions may be subject to excise taxes if taken out before age 59½ (IRAs and annuities only).

Loans against the cash value of an insurance policy are not taxed.

***Sale of these investments may result in taxable capital gains.

Exhibit 11-3   Summary of major investment categories

Step 1: Determine the amount needed in savings to fund the detailed budget total for the first year of retirement.

Future value of budget total for first year of retirement:	$124,860	(Exhibit 9-4)
Social Security annual benefit(s):	−39,490	(Exhibit 10-3)
Employer-sponsored pension annual payment:	−30,000	(Exhibit 10-3)
Future value of annual earnings from continued		
employment (Exhibit 10-3):		

    1) Determine your number of years to retirement. __17__
    2) Refer to the Inflation Factors Chart on the following
       page to determine your appropriate inflation factor
       under the 4% column. __1.94790__   __N/A__
    3) Multiply: (annual earnings) x (result from Step 2)
Result--Amount needed in savings to fund first year
    detailed budget: $55,370

Step 2: Using the result from Step 1, refer to the chart in Exhibit 11-1 to determine the amount of savings needed to fund annual retirement budget.

Amount: $1,000,000

Step 3: Add the future value of the supplemental retirement expenses (Exhibit 9-4) to the amount in Step 2.

Amount from Step 2:	$1,000,000	
Future value of the supplemental retirement expenses:	335,921	*(Exhibit 9-4)
Sum:	$1,335,921	

       *This approach assumes that all of the supplemental retirement
       expenses will be covered in the first year of retirement.

Step 4: Determine the future value of current savings.

    1) Using Exhibit 10-3, determine the following:
       401(K) balance __50,000__
       IRA balance __40,000__
       Other savings balance __20,000__
       Gifts/Inheritance __75,000__
    2) Determine your number of years to retirement __17__

    3) Determine your expected rates of return for the balances in
       Step 1:
       401(k) expected rate of return __8%__
       IRA expected rate of return __8%__
       Other savings expected rate of return __4%__
       Gifts/Inheritance expected rate of return __4%__
    4) Using your number of years to retirement and your expected
       rates of return, refer to the Return Factors Chart on the
       following page to determine your appropriate return factors
       for each of your balances:
       401(k) return factor __3.70002__
       IRA return factor __3.70002__
       Other savings return factor __1.94790__
       Gifts/Inheritance return factor __1.94790__

(Continued)

Exhibit 11-4   James' and Carol's retirement gap (difference between retirement resources and retirement needs)

5) Multiply your return factors (Step 4) by your current balances
(Step 1) to determine the future value of your current savings:

(401(k) balance) x (401(k) return factor) _185,001_
(IRA balance) × (IRA return factor) _148,000_
(Other savings) × (other saving return factor) _38,958_
(Gifts/Inheritance) × (Gifts/Inheritance return factor) _146,093_

6) Sum the results from Step 5 $ 518,052

Sum (Step 4)	$ 518,052
Sum (Step 3)	$(1,335,921)
Difference—retirement surplus (deficit)	**$ (817,869)**[1]

[1] Without considering the effect of future planned savings.

INFLATION FACTORS

Years to Retirement	Inflation			
	2%	3%	4%	6%
40	2.20804	3.26204	4.80102	10.28572
39	2.16474	3.16703	4.61637	9.70351
38	2.12230	3.07478	4.43881	9.15425
37	2.08069	2.98523	4.26809	8.63609
36	2.03989	2.89828	4.10393	8.14725
35	1.99989	2.81386	3.94609	7.68609
34	1.96068	2.73191	3.79432	7.25103
33	1.92223	2.65234	3.64838	6.84059
32	1.88454	2.57508	3.50806	6.45339
31	1.84759	2.50008	3.37313	6.08810
30	1.81136	2.42726	3.24340	5.74349
29	1.77584	2.35657	3.11865	5.41839
28	1.74102	2.28793	2.99870	5.11169
27	1.70689	2.22129	2.88337	4.82235
26	1.67342	2.15659	2.77247	4.54938
25	1.64061	2.09378	2.66584	4.29187
24	1.60844	2.03279	2.56330	4.04893
23	1.57690	1.97359	2.46472	3.81975
22	1.54598	1.91610	2.36992	3.60354
21	1.51567	1.86029	2.27877	3.39956
20	1.48595	1.80611	2.19112	3.20714
19	1.45681	1.75351	2.10685	3.02560
18	1.42825	1.70243	2.02582	2.85434
17	1.40024	1.65285	1.94790	2.69277
16	1.37279	1.60471	1.87298	2.54035
15	1.34587	1.55797	1.80094	2.39656
14	1.31948	1.51259	1.73168	2.26090
13	1.29361	1.46853	1.66507	2.13293
12	1.26824	1.42576	1.60103	2.01220
11	1.24337	1.38423	1.53945	1.89830
10	1.21899	1.34392	1.48024	1.79085
9	1.19509	1.30477	1.42331	1.68948
8	1.17166	1.26677	1.36857	1.59385
7	1.14869	1.22987	1.31593	1.50363
6	1.12616	1.19405	1.26532	1.41852
5	1.10408	1.15927	1.21665	1.33823
4	1.08243	1.12551	1.16986	1.26248
3	1.06121	1.09273	1.12486	1.19102
2	1.04040	1.06090	1.08160	1.12360
1	1.02000	1.03000	1.04000	1.06000

Exhibit 11-4   *(Continued)* (Source: Saving for a Secure Retirement, AICPA.)

RETURN FACTORS

Years to Retirement	Rate of Return			
	4%	6%	8%	10%
40	4.80102	10.28572	21.72452	45.25926
39	4.61637	9.70351	20.11530	41.14478
38	4.43881	9.15425	18.62528	37.40434
37	4.26809	8.63609	17.24563	34.00395
36	4.10393	8.14725	15.96817	30.91268
35	3.94609	7.68609	14.78534	28.10244
34	3.79432	7.25103	13.69013	25.54767
33	3.64838	6.84059	12.67605	23.22515
32	3.50806	6.45339	11.73708	21.11378
31	3.37313	6.08810	10.86767	19.19434
30	3.24340	5.74349	10.06266	17.44940
29	3.11865	5.41839	9.31727	15.86309
28	2.99870	5.11169	8.62711	14.42099
27	2.88337	4.82235	7.98806	13.10999
26	2.77247	4.54938	7.39635	11.91818
25	2.66584	4.29187	6.84848	10.83471
24	2.56330	4.04893	6.34118	9.84973
23	2.46472	3.81975	5.87146	8.95430
22	2.36992	3.60354	5.43654	8.14027
21	2.27877	3.39956	5.03383	7.40025
20	2.19112	3.20714	4.66096	6.72750
19	2.10685	3.02560	4.31570	6.11591
18	2.02582	2.85434	3.99602	5.55992
17	1.94790	2.69277	3.70002	5.05447
16	1.87298	2.54035	3.42594	4.59497
15	1.80094	2.39656	3.17217	4.17725
14	1.73168	2.26090	2.93719	3.79750
13	1.66507	2.13293	2.71962	3.45227
12	1.60103	2.01220	2.51817	3.13843
11	1.53945	1.89830	2.33164	2.85312
10	1.48024	1.79085	2.15892	2.59374
9	1.42331	1.68948	1.99900	2.35795
8	1.36857	1.59385	1.85093	2.14359
7	1.31593	1.50363	1.71382	1.94872
6	1.26532	1.41852	1.58687	1.77156
5	1.21665	1.33823	1.46933	1.61051
4	1.16986	1.26248	1.36049	1.46410
3	1.12486	1.19102	1.25971	1.33100
2	1.08160	1.12360	1.16640	1.21000
1	1.04000	1.06000	1.08000	1.10000

Exhibit 11-4   *(Continued)*

two-week summer vacation every other year and to visit family or stay close to home in the off years. This should save them $3,600 every two years (or about $150 per month).

In addition, they agree to go out to dinner only every other Friday rather than every Friday. This should save them about $100 per month. Finally, they agree to buy new cars only every five years rather than every three years. This should save them about $250 per month between reduced car payments and insurance costs. The grand total:

such cutbacks on spending will enable them to save about $500 per month or $6,000 a year, a nice tidy sum. It's a good start but it's only about one-half of the additional amount they need to save. They agree they need to speak with a qualified retirement planner to go further.

Even after they determine how to achieve the additional savings, they need to figure out how best to save and how to make their savings grow. They agree that the best thing to do is take greater advantage of their employers' 401(k) plan. This will enable them to save through payroll deduction so they won't be tempted to touch the money. It will also permit them to take advantage of the matching contributions offered under their employers' plans.

In addition to determining how to achieve their additional savings or otherwise close enhance their retirement resources, they find another major hurdle in achieving their targeted 8 percent annual after-tax rate of return, which they're not sure they'll be able to maintain given their past experience. This is a particular challenge since they have put a significant amount of their current savings in a money market fund paying 5.5 percent. Fortunately, James has a number of years left until he retires and a number of years he's expected to live thereafter. As a result, James and Carol would be smarter to invest a larger portion of their retirement savings in stocks and other investments with higher expected rates of return to achieve a higher overall rate of return.

One thing is certain: If they fall short of their targeted rate of return over time, they'll need to have a backup plan and save more per month through a further reduction in their spending. Otherwise they'll need to make other changes to their retirement plan.

Before we see how James and Carol meet with their financial planner to help them close their gap and map out their investments, we need to cover some basic savings and investment principles to give them the most bang for their bucks and lead to the most secure retirement.

CHAPTER TWELVE

Personal Savings and Investment Strategies

MYTH 14	Most investment returns are gained by market timing and stock picking. False. A 1992 study of major institutional investors such as pension funds disclosed that 91.5 percent of all investment returns relate to asset allocation decisions and not market timing or stock picking. Many people make decisions based on very recent market trends or tips, which puts them behind the curve on trying to time the market or pick individual stocks.

Taking a family through retirement security planning isn't easy, as you now know. To top it off, you probably have a retirement gap staring you in the face that's wider than the Atlantic Ocean. But at least it's not as wide as the Pacific.

If you're ready to pull out your hair, worrying how to possibly fill that gap, don't despair. The main focus of this chapter is achieving goals and attaining peace of mind.

Thanks to a variety of actions, including additional savings and smarter investing, planning for your retirement now can turn out to be a decent investment for the future if you're prepared to make some adjustments and hold on for the long term.

James and Carol are in the same boat as most of you. They, too, have a retirement gap and are grappling with how to fill it. There is a logical way that's easier said than done. It involves the basics of simply saving more and investing more wisely. Although in their mid-40s, they could start saving $500 per month now and accumulate approximately $294,500 in 20 years if they achieve an overall annual 8 percent after-tax rate of return on their investments (Exhibit 12-2). At the same time, they would have to increase their monthly savings rate to $638 per month to accumulate that desired amount if they achieve only an annual after tax rate of return of 6 percent.

BASIC RETIREMENT SAVINGS PRINCIPLES

The three basics of retirement saving principles and techniques are: save early, save wisely, and don't eat your nest egg.

First and foremost, as Sherlock Holmes said to his sidekick: "It's elementary, my dear Watson." The earlier you start, the easier it is to achieve your objective because, as I've said repeatedly, the miracle of compounding will help you.

Exhibit 12-1 demonstrates how a dollar invested today can accumulate over time, based on different annual rates of return. Exhibit 12-2 demonstrates how saving $100 per month will accumulate over time based on different compounded annual rates of return. For example, if you save $100 per month starting at age 25 or 35 or 45 or 55, you will accumulate $349,101, $149,036, $58,902, and $18,295, respectively, by age 65 based on an 8 percent annual compounded rate of return (Exhibit 12-2). Stated differently, if you assume an 8 percent rate of return, you can accumulate $100,000 by age 65 if you invest just $28.65 a month starting at age 25. If you get a later start, the amount needed to be saved each month will increase. You'd have to save $67.10 per month beginning at 35, $169.77 per month beginning at age 45, and $546.61 per month at age 55 to reach that nice round $100,000 figure by age 65.

Deferred versus Current Taxation of Savings

It's wise to save, but how you save counts too. One way is to maximize your tax-favored savings opportunities. Money will grow much faster on a tax-deferred versus a current taxation basis. Saving just $100 per month beginning at age 25 and ending at age 65 with an annual

Number of Years	Rates of Return			
	4%	6%	8%	10%
10	$1.48	$1.79	$2.16	$2.59
20	$2.19	$3.21	$4.66	$6.73
30	$3.24	$5.74	$10.06	$17.45
40	$4.80	$10.29	$21.72	$45.26

Exhibit 12-1   Future value of a dollar invested today

Number of	Rates of Return			
Years	4%	6%	8%	10%
10	$14,725	$16,388	$18,295	$20,484
20	$36,677	$46,204	$58,902	$75,937
30	$69,405	$100,452	$149,036	$226,049
40	$118,196	$199,149	$349,101	$632,408

Exhibit 12-2   Future value of saving $100 per month

compounded rate of return of 8 percent will yield $349,101. But if the annual 8 percent earnings are subject to current taxation at combined 33 percent federal and state income tax rates, the same $100 per month savings yields less, or $167,751 by age 65, a difference of $181,350.

In fairness, comparing these total accumulated savings numbers is a little like comparing apples and oranges because tax-deferred savings are subject to taxation when paid, whereas you have already paid income taxes on the principal amount associated with taxable savings. However, even if you assume that you pay a combined 33 percent federal and state income tax rate on the above tax deferred savings at retirement, you would have accumulated $66,147 more than you would have through using a taxable savings vehicle.

The reason? The miracle of compounding. In addition most individuals will be subject to lower income tax rates when they retire than while they work. The bottom line is that you will fare better on a net-of-tax basis by availing yourselves of any tax-deferred savings opportunities.

After you retire, your tax picture is likely to change significantly based on changes in your income and deductions. You will have less earned income and no payroll taxes (if you don't work and don't have self-employment earnings) and lower income taxes. Your medical expenses will go up, but the additional expenses will not be completely deductible. You probably won't have a mortgage deduction, and you may have nondeductible expenses associated with caring for your parents in nursing homes.

If you're now thinking what will happen to tax-deferred vehicles if there are future income tax rate increases, Exhibit 12-3 will flesh out how much your effective income tax rate would have to increase over a period of time to fully negate the benefits of tax-deferred versus non-tax-deferred savings. Taking a 20-year savings period, your marginal tax rates would have to go up by 22 percent to fully negate the benefits of tax deferral, assuming that you can achieve a 2 percent higher

Growth Advantage of Deferred Income (Percentage Points)

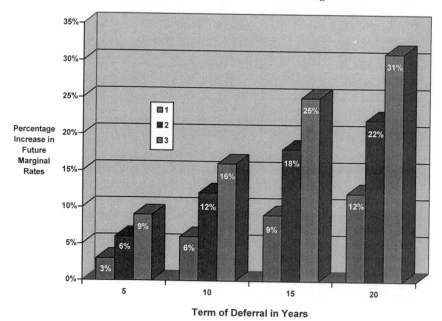

KEY POINTS

- The value of deferral depends on three considerations: How **long** the income will be deferred, **future tax rates,** and the **difference** between taxable returns and nontaxable investment returns.
- The longer the deferral period, the greater the impact of the deferral.
- For example, if you make deductible IRA contributions that remain in the account 20 years and the investment returns exceed currently taxable returns by 3 percent, marginal rates have to increase 31 points before the deferral ceases to make economic sense.
- However, if the money will be deferred only five years under the same scenario, the break-even point is nine points.
- Thus, if you put money in an IRA in 1992 and withdraw the funds in 1997, if the tax rate increases less than nine points over what it is today, it is better to defer rather than to pay the tax today and invest the funds in a currently taxable vehicle.

Exhibit 12-3   Deferred income break-even analysis (*Source:* Arthur Andersen LLP.)

compounded rate of return in a tax-deferred versus taxable savings vehicle. Such a dramatic leap in tax rates is unlikely. Also, don't forget that you can withdraw tax-favored savings gradually to spread out any related tax burden.

Beware, however; there's a catch-22 to this ingenious planning, an exception to the general rule of maximizing your tax-favored savings opportunities. Believe it or not, under current federal income tax laws, you can be penalized if you do too good a job of saving and investing. Yes, I said that correctly, although in reality this "problem" doesn't happen to many of us. But you should consider it.

Under current tax laws, most annual distributions from all employer-sponsored pension and savings plans in excess of $155,000 or lump sums in excess of $750,000 in 1996 are subject to an extra 15 percent nondeductible excise tax. This means that if you started saving early, invested wisely, and have a good pension, you may need to reallocate a portion of your additional savings later in your career to nonemployer-sponsored plans. For example, James and Carol might have to increase their nontax-favored savings and decrease their 401(k) savings if their investment results are far greater than they expect, to avoid the related 10 percent excise tax. It is likely that more people will be affected by these limits in the future as they begin to save earlier and invest more wisely, particularly if Congress fails to adjust the limits for inflation. Importantly, depending on the investment results achieved and the number of years involved, it may still make sense to save through a tax-favored savings vehicle even with a 10 percent excise tax. Whether this is the case depends on the present value of the related investment and distribution amounts. In general, the longer period of time involved the less impact the excise tax has.

SAVINGS: DON'T TOUCH THE MONEY

Another way to save wisely is to practice abstinence—don't touch the money. In order to help them save, many people elect to take advantage of automatic salary reduction and payroll deduction opportunities through employers. This might include a 401(k) plan, with its multiple benefits or other employee savings or stock purchase programs. By taking advantage of these automatic savings vehicles, you can avoid the temptation to spend the money before you save it.

Give Yourself a Raise

The last benefit is too good to pass up, as sure a thing as death and taxes. Put in financial terms, matching contributions from your employer are a way to give yourself a tax-deferred raise, or guarantee yourself an outstanding rate of return in the first year of your deferral. Furthermore, matching contributions can make a powerful difference in your ability to reach your retirement savings objectives in a shorter period of time.

If James had been able to sock away $500 a month for 20 years through his employer 401(k) savings plan, and his employer matched his contribution 50 cents for each dollar that he contributed, the resulting matching contribution could either have been viewed as a raise of $3,000 a year ($500 × 12 × $.50) or a 50 percent first-year rate of return on his savings for that year. Assuming an 8 percent annual investment return, James will have accumulated $441,765 of which $147,255 is attributable to his employer's matching contributions and the earnings on those contributions after 25 years.

To help you take full advantage of related employer matching opportunities, you might be smart to cut your current consumption or, if necessary, draw on your taxable savings and investments to fund any current year shortfall. In certain circumstances, it may make sense to consider a home equity or plan loan.

Other Automatic Savings Vehicles

Additional automatic savings opportunities and related tax advantages can be achieved through payroll deductions for IRA contributions and automatic reinvestment of dividends on nontax-favored common stock investments. With regard to an IRA contribution, even if you are unable to take a current tax deduction for an IRA because of your income level, you can benefit from the tax deferral of your compounded earnings. Exhibit 12-4 demonstrates the effect that tax-free compounding of a $2,000 IRA can have over the long haul.

Don't Spend Your Nest Egg

No matter how tempting, don't spend your nest egg once you do start saving. That brand-new four-wheel drive vehicle or kitchen remodeling probably aren't worth the consequences if you have a retirement gap.

There are, however, ways to eliminate any temptation. Specifically, explore the possibility of borrowing funds from your plan. Many

Number of Years	Rates of Return			
	4%	6%	8%	10%
5	$10,833	$11,276	$11,735	$12,212
10	$24,012	$26,363	$28,975	$31,877
20	$59,556	$73,574	$91,529	$114,557
30	$112,170	$158,122	$226,576	$329,005
40	$190,051	$309,534	$518,135	$885,230

Exhibit 12-4   Tax-free compounding of a $2,000 annual IRA contribution

defined-contribution plans, especially 401(k)s, allow employees to borrow up to 50 percent of their account balance at prevailing market rates. Here you can be your own banker, use your own funds, and avoid tax penalties. This feature allows you to get the economic benefit of your retirement savings without incurring any income taxes.

Under plan loan arrangements, you can borrow money from yourself and pay yourself tax-deferred interest income. However, it is crucial that you repay your debt within, generally, 5 years, or 15 years if the loan is related to a home purchase, so as not to undercut your retirement planning efforts and not to incur income and excise taxes on the unpaid loan amounts. In addition, don't forget that you may have to sell some of your higher returning assets (e.g., stocks) to obtain a loan. In this case, the effective cost of the loan may be higher due to the change in your asset allocation.

While some people may be able to obtain access to funds from a 401(k) plan to pay for an unexpected illness, they will pay a significant price for such access. A withdrawal of $10,000 for a person in a 33 percent effective tax bracket would yield only a net $5,200 after taxes (10 percent excise tax and 33 percent income tax).

This method of borrowing cannot be exercised with Keoghs and IRAs, however. Current income tax regulations prohibit this and result in the disqualification of these plans as well as the loss of all tax-favored treatment, including current taxation of the entire account balance.

BASIC INVESTMENT PRINCIPLES

If you want to make sound investment decisions, do good research and don't play expert. Most people aren't financial pros, much less investment experts. In fact, regardless of background and expertise, most of us have a limited amount of time to dedicate to personal affairs, no matter how important.

This section will provide you with basic investment information to enable you to make reasonably informed judgments regarding retirement savings and investing. It will also help you separate the wheat from the chaff when it comes to overly simplistic investment information that is provided by some employers and product/service providers.

Granted, there are only a few basic savings principles. But there are a plethora of basic investment precepts to keep in mind. I have compiled seven to consider when contemplating your retirement-related investment efforts:

- Focus on asset allocation and total expected returns.
- Know your investment horizon.

- Know what risk is and what your risk tolerance is.
- Know your income and liquidity needs.
- Don't forget to diversify.
- Don't try to time the market.
- Consider your tax status.

Focus on Asset Allocation and Total Long-Term Expected Returns

You've heard it before, but the most important factor in real estate investment is said to be location, location, location. The most important principle of investing is asset allocation, asset allocation, asset allocation. Asset allocation refers to dividing your investments among different investment categories or asset classes. Understanding the various classes and the differences between them is important since they define the type of individual investments that you will make (e.g., stocks versus bonds). Importantly, the expected rates and patterns of returns of different asset classes are somewhat predictable over longer periods of time.

The primary traditional asset classes are domestic stocks, domestic fixed-income instruments such as bonds, and domestic cash instruments such as money market funds or Treasury bills. There are, however, other asset classes and subclasses to consider. What about international equities and fixed-income instruments, real estate, precious metals, commodities, and collectibles? Other major asset subclasses for stocks include large cap, small cap, growth, value, and income. Major asset subclasses for fixed-income instruments include long-term, intermediate, short-term, and convertible bonds. Exhibit 12-5 includes a summary and description of the major asset classes and subclasses.

- ❐ Large Cap Equity—Those equity securities of companies with on market capitalization in excess of $5 billion.
- ❐ Small Cap Equity—Those equity securities of companies with a total market capitalization of less than $1 billion.
- ❐ Medium Capitalization—The average market capitalization ranges from $1 billion to $5 billion.
- ❐ Value Equity—Equity securities of companies believed to be undervalued or possessing lower than average price/earnings ratios, based on their potential for capital appreciation.
- ❐ Growth Equity—Equity securities of companies that are expected to have above-average prospects for long-term growth in earnings and profitability.

Exhibit 12-5   Asset classes *(Source:* Arthur Andersen LLP.)

❒ International Equity—Investments in a range of non-U.S. equity securities. A typical international fund is composed of approximately 85 percent of the Morgan Stanley Capital International EAFE index and 15 percent of the Morgan Stanley Emerging Markets Free Index. The Morgan Stanley indices include approximately 1,000 securities representing the stock exchanges of Europe, Australia, New Zealand, the Far East, Africa, Europe, and Central and South America.

❒ Broad Domestic Fixed Income—Securities in this asset class are a composite of all publicly issued, fixed-rate nonconvertible, domestic bonds. The issues are rated at least BBB, have a minimum outstanding principal of $100 million for U.S. government issues, or $50 million for other bonds, and have a maturity of at least one year. (This class includes long-term, intermediate-term, and short-term bonds, depending on the maturity.)

❒ Core Fixed Income—A fixed-income strategy that constructs portfolios to approximate the investment results of the Lehman Brothers' Government/Corporate Bond Index with a modest amount of variability in duration (a measure of interest-rate sensitivity) around the index. The objective is to achieve value added from sector or issue selection.

❒ Active Duration—Managers who employ either interest rate anticipation or business cycle timing. Portfolios are actively managed so that wide changes in duration are made in anticipation of interest rate changes and/or business cycle movements.

❒ Defensive Domestic Fixed Income—Fixed-income securities whose average maturity is two to five years are included in this asset class. The objective of allocating funds to this asset class is to minimize or reduce risk by investing in short to intermediate term securities.

❒ High Yield Fixed Income—Fixed income securities with high current income which typically are non-investment grade. Due to the increased level of default risk, security selection focuses on credit-risk analysis.

❒ Global Fixed Income—Investments in both foreign and domestic fixed-income securities which seek to take advantage of international currency and interest rate movements, differing bond yields, and/or international diversification.

❒ Real Estate—Typically consists of open- and closed-end commingled funds (including Real Estate Investment Trusts, or REIT's) managed by real estate firms.

❒ Cash Equivalents—Instruments or investments of such high liquidity and safety that they are virtually as good as cash. Examples are a money market fund and a Treasury bill. The Financial Accounting Standards Board (FASB), defined cash equivalents for financial reporting purposes as any highly liquid security with a known market value and a maturity, when acquired, of less than three months.

❒ Closely Held Asset—Represents a broadly diversified portfolio of a combination of privately placed equity and privately placed debt. The index

(Continued)

Exhibit 12-5 *(Continued)*

combines data from the venture capital, convertible security, and high-yield bond markets.

❏ Inflation—The rise in the prices of goods and services, as happens when spending increases relative to the supply of goods on the market—in other words, too much money chasing too few goods. A common measure of inflation is the Consumer Price Index (CPI). The CPI measures the average change in prices for a fixed market basket of goods and services.

Exhibit 12-5 *(Continued)*

Four factors contribute to overall investment returns: strategic asset allocation, market timing, security selection, and interaction.

- *Strategic asset allocation* refers to the targeted allocation of your investments among various asset classes based on a long-range strategy.
- *Market timing* is also known as *tactical asset allocation* or *active asset allocation*. It involves an active and conscious decision to deviate from the strategic asset allocation due to expected short-term changes in market or other conditions.
- *Security selection* means the active selection and management of individual securities within an asset class.
- *Interaction* is the interplay among the other three factors. It also includes two intangibles: sheer luck and good timing.

Which of these is most important and why? You may be surprised. It's strategic asset allocation. The rest are gravy by comparison and yet they attract the most attention from unsophisticated investors and the press. In fact, as shown in Exhibit 12-6, a 1991 study of major pension fund investors found that 91.5 percent of their annual return performance was due to strategic asset allocation. The balance of 8.5 percent was due to all the other factors combined.

In setting your asset allocation strategy you should consider your targeted rate of return target, investment horizon, tolerance for volatility of returns, income, and liquid needs and your tax status.

Targeted Rate of Return

Hand and glove with your investment strategy planning and appropriate asset allocation plan should be your targeted rate of return over time. As previously discussed, your targeted rate of return has direct bearing on how much you need to save to fill your retirement gap.

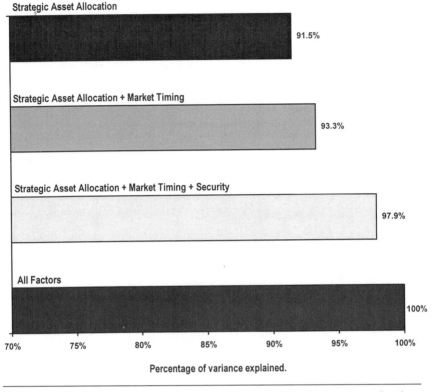

Percentage of variance explained.

Exhibit 12-6 Components most responsible for differential pension fund performance (*Source:* Graph is based on information presented in Gary P. Brinson, Brian D. Singer, and Gilbert L. Beebower, *Determinants of Portfolio Performance II: An Update, Financial Analysts Journal,* May–June 1991.)

Exhibit 12-7 shows the annual compound rates of return for a number of major asset classes and subclasses for the period between 1926 and 1995, as applicable. This exhibit also points out the average annual inflation rates during this period. As you can see, the average annual compound rates of return for the asset classes vary from a high of 12.4 percent for U.S. small cap stocks to a low of 3.7 percent for U.S. Treasury bills, the latter being only .6 percent (or 60 basis points in investment terminology) higher than annual inflation for the period. As expected, stocks outperformed bonds by a landslide.

To further extrapolate the dramatic effect of the differences in the effect of various annual compounded rates of return over time, we'll use another example. Suppose you (or your parents) had $1 to invest at the end of 1925. If you (or they) had invested in Treasury bills, your funds

Period	Asset Class	Compound Annual Return
1926-1995	U.S. Large Cap Stocks	10.4%
1926-1995	U.S. Small Cap Stocks	12.4%
1926-1995	U.S. Long-Term Corporate Bonds	5.6%
1926-1995	U.S. Long-Term Government Bonds	5.0%
1926-1995	U.S. Intermediate-Term Government Bonds	5.2%
1926-1994	U.S. Long-Term Municipal Bonds	3.9%
1926-1995	U.S. Treasury Bills	3.7%
1926-1994	U.S. Real Estate	11.1%
1970-1995	Non-U.S. Stocks	13.1%
1961-1994	Non-U.S. Government Bonds	10.1%
1976-1994	U.S. Mortgage-Backed Securities	10.2%
1971-1994	Gold	10.0%
1970-1994	Commodities	13.2%
1926-1995	U.S. Inflation	3.1%

Assumptions: No transactions costs or taxes; all cash flows are reinvested at next month-end.

Data: All data through June 1995, except municipal bonds, real estate, non-U.S. bonds, mortgage-backed securities, gold, commodities.

Exhibit 12-7   Historical asset class returns (*Source:* Ibbotson Associates.)

would have grown to $8.58 by the end of 1995. In contrast, if you (or they) had invested the $1 in the small company stocks, it would have grown to approximately $3,822 in the same period. That's a $3,814 difference—not exactly chump change, is it? (See Exhibit 12-8.) Yet since 1925 many individuals have invested in Treasury bills or similar lower risk and lower return investments. Why? Because most people haven't been afforded any meaningful investment education. In addition, some people can't tolerate the unpredictable fluctuations of short-term returns associated with stocks and other more volatile investments.

Exhibit 12-9 shows what $1,000 invested in 1925 would have grown to if it had been put in a well-diversified stock, bond, or Treasury bills portfolio. It also shows the effect inflation would have on chipping away at the same $1,000 over the same period.

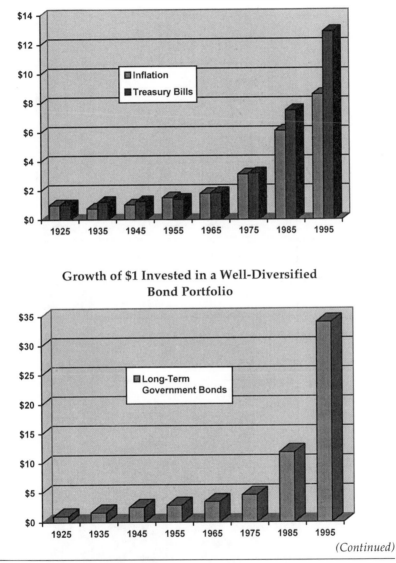

Growth of $1 Invested in a Well-Diversified Treasury Bill Portfolio versus Inflation

Growth of $1 Invested in a Well-Diversified Bond Portfolio

(Continued)

Exhibit 12-8 Growth of $1 invested in 1925 (1925–1995) (*Source:* Ibbotson Associates, *1996 Yearbook.*)

Growth of $1 Invested in a Well-Diversified
Stock Portfolio

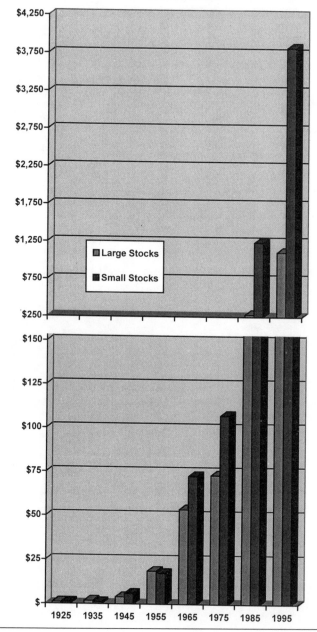

Exhibit 12-8 *(Continued)*

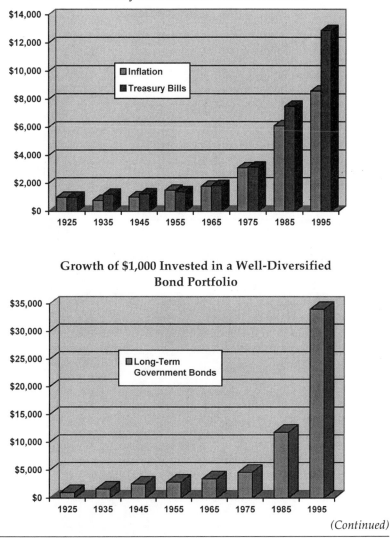

Exhibit 12-9   Growth of $1,000 invested in 1925 (1925–1995) (*Source:* Ibbotson Associates, *1996 Yearbook.*)

Growth of $1,000 Invested in a Well-Diversified
Stock Portfolio
(In Thousands of Dollars)

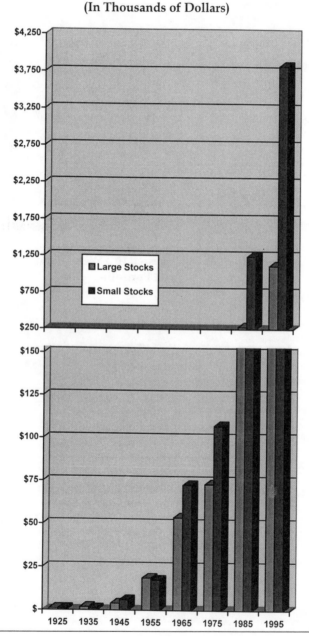

Exhibit 12-9   *(Continued)*

The gap between the inflation line and other investment lines represents the real rate of return for the respective asset class. Keep in mind that the key here is to optimize your real (inflation adjusted) versus nominal (or non-inflation adjusted) rate of return. If not, you could be losing ground based on the change in the purchasing power of a dollar over time, again because of inflation.

To eyeball the annual compounded rates of return of selected asset classes and subclasses from 1974 to 1995, glance at the summary in Exhibit 12-10. This exhibit includes several new asset classes that have evolved over the year such as international equities and fixed-income instruments such as high yield, noninvestment grade bonds (referred

Period	Asset Class	Compound Annual Return
1/74-12/95	U.S. Large Cap Stocks	13.2%
1/74-12/95	U.S. Small Cap Stocks	18.7
1/74-12/95	U.S. Long-Term Corporate Bonds	10.1
1/74-12/95	U.S. Long-Term Government bonds	10.1
1/74-12/95	U.S. Intermediate-Term Government Bonds	9.4
1/83-12/95	U.S. Long-Term Municipal Bonds (Lehman Brothers Long-Term Municipal Bond Index)	11.1
1/74-12/95	U.S. Treasury Bills	7.2
1/78-12/94	U.S. Real Estate (Russell/NCRIEF Property Index)	7.9
1/74-12/95	Foreign Stocks (Morgan Stanley/Capital International Europe, Australia, Far East Index)	13.2
1/86-12/95	Foreign Government Bonds (J.P. Morgan Non-U.S. Government Bond Index)	13.0
1/76-12/95	U.S. Mortgage-Backed Securities (Lehman Brothers Mortgaged-Backed Securities Index)	10.2
1/74-12/95	Gold (Gold Base Price)	5.8
1/74-12/95	Commodities (Dow Jones Commodity Spot Price Index)	2.2
1/74-12/95	U.S. Inflation	5.6

Exhibit 12-10   Asset class returns (*Source:* Ibbotson Associates, *1996 Yearbook;* Frontier Analytics, Inc.)

by some as "junk bonds"). It also includes the average annual inflation rate of the period, which was 5.6 percent. The highest compounded annual rate of return during this period was the U.S. Small Cap stocks class with a rate of 18.7 percent. Interestingly, the best-performing asset class in one year turned out to be a loser in the next year (small cap stocks in 1983 and 1984) and vice-versa (Treasury bills in 1993 and 1994).

While historic rates of return are interesting to chart, the past is not necessarily a predictor of the future. Therefore, when you consider an appropriate asset allocation strategy, examine both the historic as well as the projected average annual rate of return for selected asset classes over a reasonable period, perhaps five years.

No one has a crystal ball to predict the future with a high degree of certainty, but some investment consulting firms attempt to forecast future average annual rates of return in assisting their pension plan and other institutional investor clients in performing asset allocation modeling. One such firm is Callan Associates based in San Francisco. Callan is one of the largest institutional investment consulting firms. It currently provides certain information services to Arthur Andersen's individual and institutional investment consulting practices, and attempts to project the volatility of these asset classes over the same five years. The projections are good-faith estimates, and actual performance may vary significantly. The most important contribution of firms such as Arthur Andersen and Callan is that they can also provide additional information, which is useful in selecting an appropriate asset allocation mix for your accumulated retirement savings.

Asset allocation is an integral part of plotting your investment policy and strategy and should be based on your asset class preferences, your investment horizon, your risk tolerance, your liquidity and income needs, and the expected returns and related risk for various asset classes.

The last point, expected returns and related risk for various asset classes, is diagrammed in Exhibit 12-11 and presents a summary of the probability of a range of expected returns for more than a five-year period per Arthur Andersen's Institution Investment Consulting Group and based on data provided by Callan.

While these statistics represent projections and shouldn't be taken as gospel, they are based on sound statistical analysis and are a barometer for you to follow in making asset allocation decisions. In doing so, you should also consider how certain asset classes move as compared to changes in other asset classes. This is referred to as correlation and is summarized in Exhibit 12-12. Investment horizon and liquidity and income needs will be discussed in more detail later in this chapter.

Asset Class	Return	Risk*
Large Cap Equity	10.5	17.0
Small Cap Equity	12.0	23.0
International Equity	12.0	23.0
Broad Domestic Fixed Income	7.5	9.9
Real Estate	8.0	18.0
Cash Equivalents	4.5	1.8

Shown above are a typical set of assumptions about risk and return for the major asset classes used in the asset allocation analysis based upon long term market history since World War II. Expected return is the projected total rate of return (income and capital gains) for each asset class and is shown in annualized form. *"Risk" is shown as standard deviation. Standard deviation is a statistical measure of the variability of potential returns around the expected return. Approximately 68% of the returns are expected to fall within plus or minus one standard deviation of the expected return in any single year.

Exhibit 12-11 Projected risk and return for selected asset classes (*Source:* Arthur Andersen LLP.)

	Large Stocks	Small Stocks	Foreign Stocks	Bonds
Large Stocks[1]	1.00			
Small Stocks[2]	.79	1.00		
Foreign Stocks[3]	.56	.42	1.00	
Bonds[4]	.55	.30	.23	1.00

Note: Correlation's range from 1.0 (perfect correlation) to −1.0 (perfect inverse correlation).

[1] S&P 500 index.
[2] DFA small company index.
[3] Morgan Stanley Europe, Australia, Far East index.
[4] Lehman Government Corporate Bond index.

Example: Foreign stocks are a diversifying influence when mixed with large U.S. stocks, because when one of them moves, the other has demonstrated only about a 56% tendency, on a scale of 0% to 100%, to move similarly (at the same time), which is about the same correlation as U.S. stocks with U.S. bonds (.55).

Exhibit 12-12 Impact of diversification tendencies of asset classes to perform similarly (correlation's based on 22 years of market history 1973 to 1995)

DETERMINING YOUR INVESTMENT HORIZON

In financial parlance, *investment horizon* means the period of time over which an institution or individual plans to invest to meet a stated purpose, such as for retirement. Taking a look at one's investment horizon is an important piece of the total retirement picture. It should affect decisions regarding how you invest your retirement savings over time. Of primary importance is how you plan to disperse your investments among the various asset classes (stocks, bonds, real estate). I can't emphasize enough that asset allocation is your single most important decision. Setting your sights on the right horizon will affect results.

Your investment horizon does not end at the point when you retire, which is a little like running a race and stopping before the finish line You must invest now to have a stream of income for yourself, your spouse, and any other dependents, throughout, not just at the beginning of, your retirement years.

As I previously mentioned, retirement years represent a period of time, not a single point, which is key because the average 65-year-old in 1996 is projected to live 17.6 years and needs income and investments during that time.

This is even more significant if you plan to retire before 65. If you plan to retire at 55, you would be expected to live another 27.6 years. You should not ignore this long span when determining your investment horizon. This is a race that you want to finish—and win.

Understand Your Risk Tolerance

Understanding risk is crucial in determining retirement savings investment strategy. As Forest Gump says in the movie by the same name, "I know what love is!" The same applies to risk. Know what your risk tolerance is and how much you can comfortably assume.

Risk has many connotations, but there are three basic dimensions in connection with retirement investment risks: ultimate risk, volatility risk, and underlying risk.

Types of Investment Risk

Ultimate Risk　　The *ultimate risk* in retirement planning is not to meet your accumulated retirement savings goal, to have to delay your retirement date, reduce your standard of living, and/or adjust your estate objectives.

This is an unpleasant scenario at best and requires a somewhat precarious balancing act. Based on prior information, some of you may be inclined to assume a higher degree of investment risk than might be prudent, and attempt to achieve a stated total retirement savings target. Others may not assume enough risk given their needs and investment horizon. Such steps should not be taken on an automatic or uninformed basis. You need to understand and consider the relationship between risk and return. I will expound on this later.

Volatility Risk   The second dimension of retirement risk is *volatility risk*. This addresses the likelihood that your retirement investments will go up or down in value. Volatility is also the term that is most frequently used as the barometer of overall investment risk. Fortuitously, volatility in connection with most major investments can be measured,

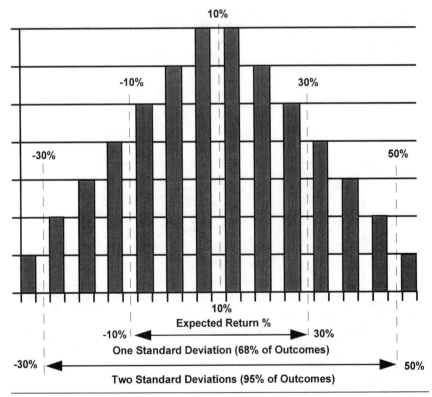

Exhibit 12-13   Expected rate-of-return graph (*Source:* Arthur Andersen LLP.)

and these measurements need to be considered when constructing your investment portfolio.

Volatility risk is typically measured in terms of the potential percentage variation from projected returns over time based on one standard deviation. For those who aren't statisticians, I'll spell it out in simpler terms. One standard deviation means that 68 percent of all expected investment returns should fall within a calculated range of investment returns. This range is calculated by applying the volatility (risk) percentage to the mean expected rate of return. For example, Exhibit 12-13 is a typical expected rate-of-return graph. Based on this exhibit, the expected rate of return is 10 percent and the annual risk (volatility) measure is 20 percent.

This means there's a 68 percent probability that actual annual return will fall within a range of negative 10 percent and positive 30 percent for any given year. In addition, there is a 95 percent probability that actual annual return will fall within a range of negative 30 percent and positive 50 percent. This 95 percent probability is based on two standard deviations from expected returns.

Exhibit 12-11 summarizes the projected five-year rate of return and the related risk (volatility measure) for several major asset classes as calculated Arthur Andersen's Institutional Investment Consulting

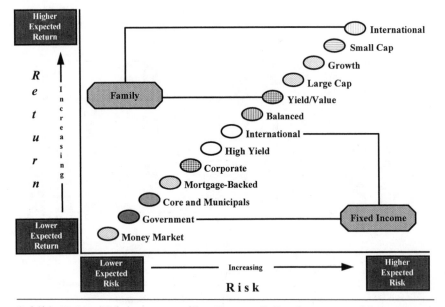

Exhibit 12-14   Risk/return profiles (*Source:* Callan Investment Management Council.)

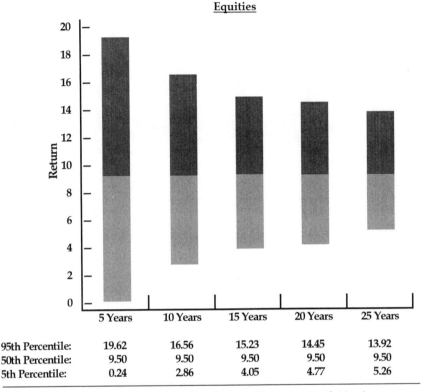

Expected Distribution of Annual Returns Based on
Expected Return and Standard Deviation

<u>Equities</u>

	5 Years	10 Years	15 Years	20 Years	25 Years
95th Percentile:	19.62	16.56	15.23	14.45	13.92
50th Percentile:	9.50	9.50	9.50	9.50	9.50
5th Percentile:	0.24	2.86	4.05	4.77	5.26

Exhibit 12-15   Stock market volatility (*Source:* Frontier Analytics.)

Group and based on data provided by Callan. Based on this schedule, you can see that equities have higher volatility rates than fixed income investments. However, they also have higher expected rates of return.

Exhibit 12-14 summarizes the risk and return profiles of a number of major asset classes, primarily equity and fixed-income subclasses. Note that the money market funds have the least risk and the international stocks have the greatest risk.

It is important to note that expected rates of return tend to moderate over longer periods of time. Exhibit 12-15 shows the volatility of the stock market and the related rates of return over 5- to 25-year time periods. In addition, Exhibit 12-16 shows the same information for intermediate bonds. Compare these graphs to the monthly volatility charts shown in Exhibits 12-17 and 12-18 for the period January 1960 through

Expected Distribution of Annual Returns Based on
Expected Return and Standard Deviation

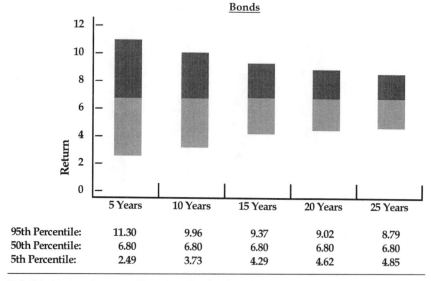

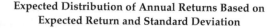

	5 Years	10 Years	15 Years	20 Years	25 Years
95th Percentile:	11.30	9.96	9.37	9.02	8.79
50th Percentile:	6.80	6.80	6.80	6.80	6.80
5th Percentile:	2.49	3.73	4.29	4.62	4.85

Exhibit 12-16   Intermediate bond volatility (*Source:* Frontier Analytics.)

Monthly U.S. Common Stock Total Returns:
January 1960—December 1995

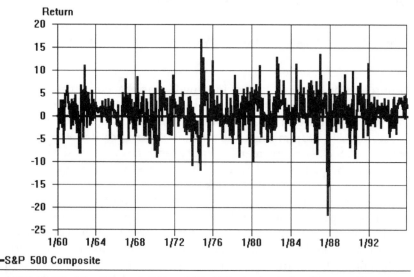

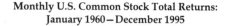

Exhibit 12-17   Monthly volatility of the U.S. stock market (*Source:* Frontier Analytics.)

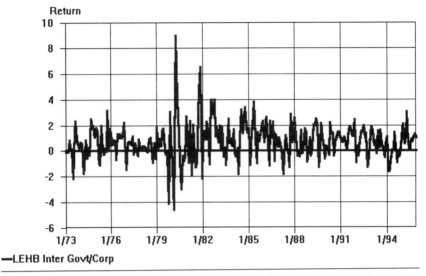

Exhibit 12-18   Monthly volatility of the U.S. bond market (*Source:* Frontier Analytics.)

December 1995. Be careful, Exhibit 12-18 is the volatility associated with intermediate-term government/corporate bonds. You can quickly see the difference. The monthly charts look more like a heart attack on an EKG, whereas the 25-year chart looks less erratic.

Given this information, your investment horizon should be a primary factor when considering the potential volatility of your accumulated retirement savings. In addition, it is crucial to consider the interrelationship between volatility and expected rates of return over your investment horizon when you are determining an appropriate asset allocation for your accumulated retirement savings.

Number of Years	Rates of Return			
	4%	6%	8%	10%
10	$14,802	$17,908	$21,589	$25,937
20	$21,911	$32,071	$46,610	$67,275
30	$32,434	$57,435	$100,627	$174,494
40	$48,010	$102,857	$217,245	$452,493

Exhibit 12-19   Accumulation of $10,000 invested today

I'll cite a tangible example. If your investment horizon is 20 years, you may want to invest a higher portion of your retirement savings in asset classes that have higher expected rates of return over time. You may experience short-term swings in the market value of your accumulated retirement savings, but in the long run you are likely to be way ahead. You can see in Exhibit 12-19 how $10,000 would accumulate over 20 years based on different expected rates of return. These expected rates of return are primarily a function of your asset allocation.

Underlying Risk   A final dimension of retirement investment risk is *underlying risk*, which includes market risk, business risk, purchasing power risk, interest rate risk, reinvestment risk, political risk, and currency risk. Underlying risk affects the volatility of a particular investment or asset class. Some of these risks are universal, and others relate only to certain types of investments.

Market Risk   *Market risk* relates to the overall volatility of the market for a particular type of asset class. As an example, Exhibit 12-17 shows the monthly volatility of U.S. stock market returns from January 1960 through December 1995. Exhibit 12-18 demonstrates the monthly volatility of long-term government bond total returns over the same period. Be careful when comparing these charts because the scales are different.

Business Risk   *Business risk* relates to the viability of a particular entity (corporations or government) and the ability of that entity to generate value for its shareholders (dividends and stock appreciation) and meet its obligations (interest and principal payments). Default risk falls into the category of a business risk since it relates to the likelihood that the entity (a corporation or government) will be able to meet its debt obligations on a timely basis. It's important to note that even governmental obligations are, at least theoretically, subject to default risk, particularly if the government involved is a city, county, or related authority. Don't forget what happened to Orange County in California in 1995.

Purchasing Power Risk   *Purchasing power risk* is a universal risk that must be considered in connection with any investment decision. In an investment context, it relates to the ability of a particular investment or asset class to outperform inflation and generate a real rate of return. When developing your overall investment and asset allocation strategy, it is extremely important to consider both the nominal rate of return on the investment and the real rate of return net of inflation. Exhibit 12-7 summarizes the rate of return for several asset classes for the period 1926 to 1994(5). You can calculate the real rates of return by subtracting the inflation rate from the compound annual rate of return.

Interest Rate Risk   *Interest rate risk* is the effect-of-interest rate fluctuations on your investment portfolio. Specifically, when interest rates go up, the value of fixed income investments such as bonds goes down. Why? Because the value of the cash flows (discounted present value of future interest and principal payments) associated with your bond has declined as compared with what you could get by investing in a new bond based on the higher rates. Conversely, when interest rates go down, the value of fixed income investments goes up. Significant swings in interest rates can have a profound impact on the payout of your accumulated retirement savings if your investment portfolio after retirement includes a preponderance of fixed-income investments. Importantly, with bonds, assuming the issuer does not default on its obligations, you should still receive the cash you expected when you invested if you hold the bonds until maturity. However, that cash amount may be insufficient to meet your needs, especially if inflation rises and causes the overall interest rates to rise.

Reinvestment Risk   *Reinvestment risk* deals with the danger of trying to attain a targeted rate of return after disposing of a particular investment. Reinvestment risk can also occur each time you collect interest on a coupon bond which you don't spend. There can be some correlation between reinvestment risk and interest rate risk, especially in situations where bonds may be recalled due to significant declines in interest rates subsequent to their issuance. In this instance, the reinvestment risk associated with reinvesting the proceeds from the recalled bonds can be considerable.

For example, you may hold a callable government bond with a coupon interest rate of 8.5 percent. The bond may be callable at a fixed conversion price. If there is a decline in prevailing interest rates to 6.5 percent, the government issuer may recall the bonds at the more favorable conversion rate. If it does, you may be left high and dry as to how you will get the prior return based on prevailing interest rates. Such recall provisions are not uncommon on certain fixed-income investments, including state and local government obligations. To avoid snags, review and consider the implications of these provisions in connection with any related investments.

Political Risk   *Political risk* relates to uncertainties about the stability of governments and political systems. This risk is associated primarily with international investments in stocks and fixed-income investments, including governmental bonds. Changes in governments and political systems can have profound effects on capital markets and the risk of governmental default. For example, Orange County, California, defaulted on its municipal bonds in 1995 after it experienced high investment losses from speculating with derivative investments.

Also, stable and long-established political systems may fail. Obviously, political risk is greater in less developed, new, and historically unstable governments than in longstanding democracies of well-developed nations. Historically, the United States has been viewed as an extremely low political risk, although this was called somewhat into question when the budget battles in Washington waged in late 1995 and early 1996, threatening to place the U.S. government in default on its obligations.

Currency Risk   The last underlying risk is *currency risk,* which relates to changes in the value of foreign investments that are denominated in foreign currency such as foreign stocks. In this case, the total risk is a combination of the volatility of the underlying investment (such as stock) and the volatility of the related currency. For example, investing in a Mexican stock on the Mexican stock exchange exposes the investor to both the risk associated with the underlying value of the stock and the Mexican peso. Many pension funds and other institutional investors will use derivatives (such as puts, calls, swaps, and other financial instruments) to moderate or mitigate the effect of foreign exchange risk such as currency risk. Exhibit 12-20 summarizes the total rates of return on selected foreign stock markets in 1995 and the real rate of return net of changes in the related foreign currency versus the U.S. dollar.

RATE YOUR LEVEL OF RISK TOLERANCE

Now that you know what risk is, it is important that you assess your risk tolerance. The questionnaire on Exhibit 12-21, which has been made available to Arthur Andersen employees, is valuable only if you are truly honest with yourself. You should complete it based on your personal opinions and in light of the information that you have been exposed to earlier in the book. You may also want to complete it again after you have finished this book because there is additional information in this chapter that could have some bearing on your opinions, including volatility of different investment classes over different periods of time. The results of this questionnaire will help you to assess your relative risk profile, but it should not be deliberated in a vacuum.

Period	Country	Compound Annual Return
1995	Australia	15.45%
1995	Austria	(11.82)
1995	Belgium	14.81
1995	Canada	11.54
1995	Denmark	4.43
1995	Finland	(7.83)
1995	France	0.53
1995	Germany	5.48
1995	Hong Kong	18.80
1995	Ireland	19.38
1995	Italy	(4.26)
1995	Japan	2.06
1995	Netherlands	16.17
1995	New Zealand	10.69
1995	Norway	1.34
1995	Spain	15.38
1995	Switzerland	25.62
1995	United Kingdom	19.24
1995	United States	37.47
1995	World	20.72

Exhibit 12-20   1995 performance of overseas equity markets (*Source: Actuaries* for all countries except the United States (S&P 500). *MSCI World Index* was used for World.)

Know Your Income and Liquidity Needs

You need to consider your current and projected income and liquidity needs when developing an appropriate retirement savings and investment strategy. These factors can have direct implications on how you save and invest.

Answer the following questions.

RISK PREFERENCE	TIME HORIZON
1. Personal Risk Assessment How do you feel about risk? • My focus is on maximizing my long-term return. I don't worry about short-term fluctuations, even if they are significantly downward. (10 points) • I'm willing to accept a reasonable amount of market risk if it means I'll have a better chance of staying ahead of inflation. (6 points) • Safety is my principal concern. Inflation is secondary. Score _____	**1. Your Retirement Goal** How many years will it be before you need your Profit Sharing Plan money for retirement income? If you're not certain, choose the earliest age you think you may need your money. • 20 or more years (10 points) • 15 years (8 points) • 10 years (6 points) • 5 years(4 points) • Less than 5 years (1 points) Score _____
2. What If . . . What if your money in the stock market dropped 15% over the next month? • I would maintain my current stock assets, because I expect peaks and valleys in my returns along the way. (10 points) • I would stay in my current stock assets, because I expect peaks and valleys in my returns along the way. (10 points) • I would sell immediately to avoid further losses. (1 point) Score _____	**2. Loan Expectations** How many years will it be before you need your 401(k) money for a loan? If you're not certain, choose the earliest time you think you may need your money. • Not at all (10 points) • 10 years (7 points) • 5 years (4 points) • Less than 5 years (1 point) Score _____ Do not choose a score that is higher than your retirement goal score, above.
Total Risk Preference Score _____	*Total Time Horizon Score* _____

Exhibit 12-21　　Risk tolerance (*Source:* Arthur Andersen LLP.)

Generally, you should use qualified plans—401(k), profit sharing, Keoghs, IRAs—as your primary vehicle for long-term savings and investing. As I said earlier, these plans will allow your investments to grow on a tax-deferred basis. But there is a negative side to them. Any early withdrawals from these vehicles will be subject to a penalty, an excise tax. If you need to access funds from these plans, use the loan and other tactics noted in the savings principles section previously. Remember, you cannot borrow funds from a Keogh or IRA.

To find your starting portfolio, use the lower of your risk preference and time horizon scores. You should use the lower score, because even if you have a high-risk tolerance but are only a short time away from when you need your money, you may not want to risk losing your principal over a short period of time.

YOUR LOWER SCORE	PEOPLE WITH THIS SCORE TEND TO
2-5	Be very conservative, and either are not comfortable accepting higher market risk, or have a relatively short time horizon until they need their money.
6-9	Be conservative, though they may be willing to accept a low degree of market risk.
10-13	Have a moderate tolerance for risk and seek a balanced investment approach.
18-20	Tolerate a high degree of risk and seek aggressive investments. For diversification, these investors may want to consider other investments that have lower inherent risk.

Exhibit 12-21   *(Continued)*

In terms of accumulated retirement savings, your investment related income and liquidity needs are likely to vary over time and probably may increase significantly during your retirement. While your ongoing monthly expenses are likely to be less than during your working years, if you cease to work, you won't have your employment earnings to use as a means to fund these and other expenses. Factor this into your planning.

If you are using qualified plans as your primary long-term investment vehicle, you are not likely to have significant need for these to be liquid or to extract income from these accumulated savings prior to retirement.

There are exceptions. The primary ones may be if you experience an unexpected hardship or if you plan to use a 401(k) or other plan as a source of periodic loans. If you decide to use your particular qualified plans as a source for perhaps a first-time home purchase, child's college education or wedding, or for periodic loans such as to buy a car, you should consider the likelihood of this beforehand and factor in the ramifications it will have on your overall related retirement investments.

Ideally, try to predict the likely amounts, the appropriate asset classes and investment vehicles to fuel these funds. For example, you may want to invest all or a portion of these funds in very liquid and less volatile investments.

Another form of long-term savings is home equity. While some liquidity can be achieved through home equity loans, this form of savings otherwise is not very liquid. After all, even if you decide to sell, doing so will take time and cost money in real estate commissions and possibly income taxes. Specifically, unless you reinvest the gains in a new home within two years after you sell it, you must pay tax on the gain at capital gains rates. Individuals over 55 get a one-time exclusion for up to $150,000 in gains on the sale of a primary residence.

In addition, some don't ever plan to sell their home. They want to will it to their children. Your views regarding any home(s) that you own are important because they can affect the nature and timing of your liquidity needs, especially after retirement. Depending on your views, you may want to exclude or include your home from your retirement savings and investment planning.

In either case, if you currently own a home, you probably have a significant amount of your net worth tied up in the real estate asset class. Keep this in mind when considering your asset allocation for the balance of your investments. We'll address this further later.

Given the preceding factors, most people will want to use their nonqualified plan savings and home equity savings as the primary means by which to meet any liquidity needs prior to retirement. As a rule, most people maintain an amount equal to one to three months of their recurring expenses in a very liquid investment vehicle such as a money market fund or a savings account for such purposes. The balance of their other savings should be invested in intermediate to longer-term investments based on the expected rate of return and volatility information noted here.

Regarding longer-term investments, you may want to consider putting a large portion of your longer-term nonqualified plan savings in investment vehicles that will allow you to defer recognition of appreciation until the investment is sold. Investing a significant portion of your long-term nonqualified plan investments in growth stocks, passive stock index funds, or certain forms of real estate can help you build your investment portfolio more quickly and benefit from lower tax rates when you retire.

As your income and liquidity needs change during your retirement years, in all probability you will want to shift your overall asset allocation approach to a less volatile and more liquid and income-oriented approach. While your portfolio is likely to change, keep your overall investment horizon (life expectancy) in mind and employ a balanced and gradual approach to changing your overall asset allocation and investment approach. You are likely to be less concerned with increasing your investment income until you retire, at least with respect to your nontax-favored investments.

However, as you approach retirement, you may want to moderate your overall investment risk on a gradual basis. Switching your asset allocation to more income-oriented investments is likely to be accomplished through your tax-favored investment vehicles so you can avoid any current taxation on the additional current income that results.

The Importance of Diversification

One of the most important principles of prudent investing is diversification. This principle is so important that one of the basic standards imposed on employee benefit plan fiduciaries is the duty to diversify to minimize the possibility of large losses.

What does diversification mean? In simplest terms, it's the "don't put all your nest eggs in one basket" mentality. The reason is simple. If your basket drops, you may end up with a bunch of broken eggs and egg all over your face. In investment terms, this means "don't put all of your investments in one mutual fund, stock, bond, real estate investment, or even one asset class."

While this description of diversification is common, it is too simplistic. Diversification has many dimensions and purposes. Savvy investors will diversify among asset classes, within asset classes, as well as across borders, time frames, industry sectors, and securities. In addition, many will diversify among mutual fund companies, investment managers, and insurance and investment contract providers when significant sums are at stake.

Most discerning investors who invest sizable sums will diversify their portfolios among stocks, bonds, and cash equivalents (money market funds and savings accounts). Some will also consider other asset classes such as real estate, insurance contracts, precious metals, and collectibles. These investors will seek to diversify within asset classes (growth, large cap, small cap, value, and income stocks; long-term, intermediate-term, and short-term bonds). Exhibit 12-22 presents how you can reduce risk in your portfolio by diversifying.

	Expected Return	Portfolio Risk*
		(Standard Deviation)

Portfolio A:
  100% Long-Term   6.2%   11.1%
  Government Bonds

Portfolio B:
  17% Common Stocks
  54% Long-Term Government   6.2%   9.4%
  Bonds
  29% Treasury Bills

Portfolio C:
  20% Common Stocks
  64% Long-Term Government   6.6%   11.1%
  Bonds
  16% Treasury Bills

▨ Common Stocks

■ Long-Term Government Bonds

▢ Treasury Bills

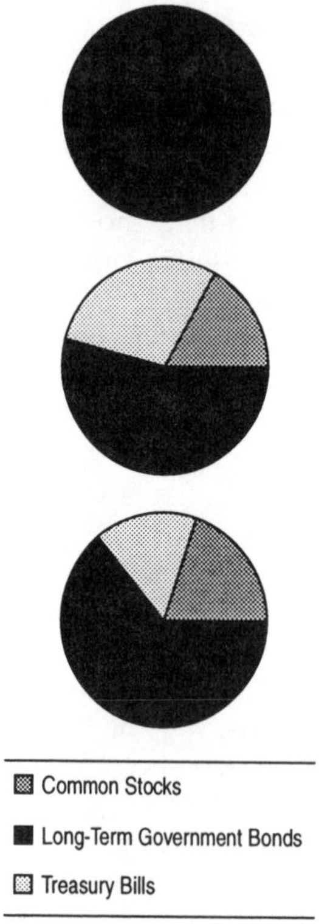

Exhibit 12-22   Diversification among asset classes (*Source:* Callan Investment Management Council.)

Since the United States represents only approximately 23 percent of global market capitalization, an ever-increasing percentage of institutional and individual investors are beginning to invest across borders in international stocks and/or global stock funds. The difference between global and international is that global funds include U.S. stocks; international ones do not. International funds can take a variety of forms, including specific country (Mexico, Japan, United Kingdom) and regional funds (Europe, Asia, Pacific, Latin America).

When considering international investments, look for opportunities to invest in countries that have not had as strong a correlation of performance with the U.S. market.

Exhibit 12-23 represents a summary of historical performance of selected overseas equity markets and the correlation of the performance of those markets to the U.S. stock market. In this exhibit, the U.S. market is considered to be 1.0. Countries with lower or negative correlations have historically resulted in better effective diversification compared to the U.S. market. While correlations are important, don't forget to take note of the expected returns and currency rate risk.

Exhibit 12-22 demonstrates how a properly diversified portfolio can enhance returns at a lower level of risk or reduce risk at certain targeted levels of return. This exhibit is based on U.S. (S&P 500) versus international (MSCI) indices using an efficient frontier software model. Efficient frontier models can be used to maximize your return at a given level of risk and to minimize your risk at a targeted level of expected return.

These software models are used by institutional investors and high net-worth individuals to help to optimize their asset allocations. You

Period	Country	Compound Annual Return	Standard Deviation
1970-1994	Australia	9.3%	30.1%
1970-1994	Austria	12.5	24.6
1970-1994	Belgium	15.2	22.8
1970-1994	Canada	9.0	21.0
1970-1994	Denmark	14.1	22.0
1970-1994	Finland	5.4	30.4
1970-1994	France	11.9	27.6
1970-1994	Germany	11.6	23.7
1970-1994	Hong Kong	21.2	54.3
1970-1994	Ireland	16.3	31.0
1970-1994	Italy	5.9	29.1
1970-1994	Japan	17.1	27.6
1970-1994	Netherlands	15.6	21.4
1970-1994	New Zealand	5.2	28.5
1970-1994	Norway	13.1	32.7
1970-1994	South Africa	9.2	40.2
1970-1994	Spain	7.8	25.3
1970-1994	Switzerland	13.0	22.1
1970-1994	United Kingdom	12.6	30.1
1970-1994	United States	11.0	17.4
1970-1994	World	11.4	16.3

(Continued)

Exhibit 12-23   Long-run performance of selected overseas equity markets. Countries other than the United States have higher volatility when returns denominated in U.S. dollars. (*Source:* MSCI for all countries except South Africa and Ireland (*Financial Times Actuaries—Actuaries Countries Index*) and United States (*S&P 500*).)

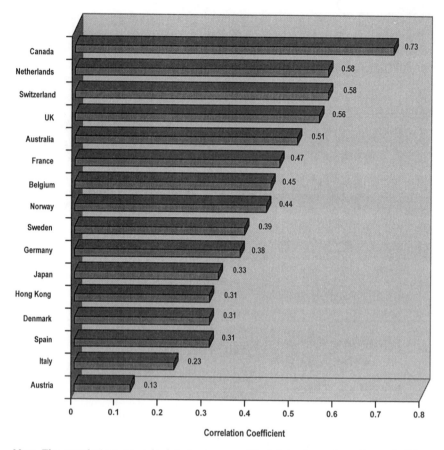

Canada 0.73
Netherlands 0.58
Switzerland 0.58
UK 0.56
Australia 0.51
France 0.47
Belgium 0.45
Norway 0.44
Sweden 0.39
Germany 0.38
Japan 0.33
Hong Kong 0.31
Denmark 0.31
Spain 0.31
Italy 0.23
Austria 0.13

Correlation Coefficient

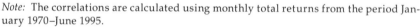

Note: The correlations are calculated using monthly total returns from the period January 1970–June 1995.

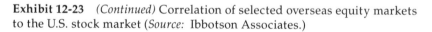

Exhibit 12-23 *(Continued)* Correlation of selected overseas equity markets to the U.S. stock market *(Source:* Ibbotson Associates.)

can purchase software programs that perform efficient number computations, but be aware that they are not cheap and must be updated periodically. For example, Frontier Analytics based in San Diego, California, has such software to which you can subscribe for between $500 and $1,000 per quarter. Most people will use a financial planner or another investment professional to run such models for them. This is important because the models are very complex and can be misused.

While efficient frontier models are not readily available or easy to use, there are a number of commercially available, more portable software tools that are simple and cost-effective. These are usually incorporated as part of a retirement or financial planning software package. Some current programs include the Quicken Financial Planner and the Vanguard Retirement Manager. Arthur Andersen provided certain assistance in the development of Vanguard's Retirement Manager Software.

Fixed-income investors will often diversify their portfolios among different time frames. Specifically, they may spread them out among a combination of short-term, intermediate-term, and long-term bonds to protect against changes in interest rates or to better match their expected liquidity needs. The weighted average discounted present value of the cash flows from a fixed-income portfolio or bond fund is referred to as its *duration*.

Portfolios or funds with longer durations are more sensitive to changes in interest rates than those with shorter durations. As a result, bond portfolios and funds with longer durations are subject to higher changes in market values due to changes in interest rates. As such, they are considered to be more volatile and, therefore, more risky.

Exhibit 12-24 demonstrates the effect of a 1 percent (or 100 basis points in the language of investment professionals) increase or decline in interest rates on three bond funds with different durations. If a bond is held to its full maturity, it will pay face (or par) value. Volatility applies only to bonds that have not yet matured. In general, the closer that a bond is to its maturity date the less volatile the market value will be.

Many investors are also concerned with diversifying among industry sectors because many industries are cyclical, and most people aren't lucky enough to time these cycles properly. In addition, some industries

Assume we have three $1,000 zero coupon bonds at an interest rate of 7%.

Interest Rate	Maturity		
	5	10	20
Base (7%)	$713	$508	$258
Increase 1%	$681	$463	$215
Percent change	4.50%	8.90%	16.70%
Decrease 1%	$747	$558	$3121
Percent change	4.80%	9.80%	20.90%

Exhibit 12-24 Effect of a 1 percent increase or decrease in interest rates on three bond funds with different durations. Assume we have three $1,000 zero coupon bonds at an interest rate of 7 percent.

do better when the economy is strong (higher-priced consumer goods, tourism) while others are less sensitive to changes in general economic conditions (health care). Some growth industries are very speculative with very high price-to-earnings multiples (biotech) while others are less volatile and more income-oriented because they pay higher dividends (utilities).

Another important way to diversify is to apportion retirement savings among a variety of securities. Clearly, investing a significant portion in one or even a few companies can lead to significant fluctuations in the value of your portfolio, possibly at the time that you can least afford it—when you may need to liquidate investments.

While diversification can be used to successfully reduce risk, it can also be used to enhance the overall risk adjusted return of an investment portfolio. Exhibit 12-22 demonstrates this.

Exhibits 12-25 through 12-29 show how a hypothetical portfolio of one-third stocks, one-third bonds, and one-third real estate would have fared during five volatile periods in U.S. investment history: the Great Depression of 1925 to 1937, the mid-1970s recession, the bond market crash of 1979 to 1981, the stock market crash of 1987, and the real estate crash of 1990 to 1993. These graphs demonstrate the benefits of diversification not only from the perspective of moderating volatility but also from the perspective of enhancing overall returns.

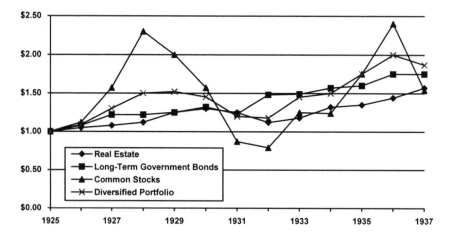

Diversified Portfolio = ⅓ stocks, ⅓ bonds, ⅓ real estate.

Exhibit 12-25   The Great Depression 1925–1937 (*Source:* Ibbotson Associates.)

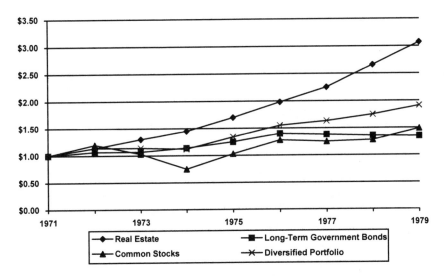

Diversified Portfolio = ⅓ stocks, ⅓ bonds, ⅓ real estate.

Exhibit 12-26   The mid-1970s recession 1971–1979 (*Source:* Ibbotson Associates.)

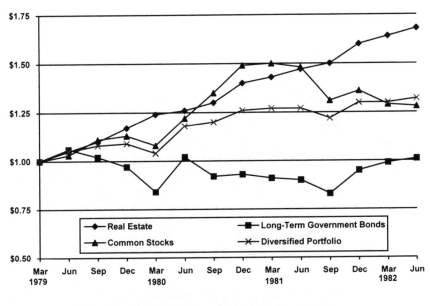

Diversified Portfolio = ⅓ stocks, ⅓ bonds, ⅓ real estate.

Exhibit 12-27   The bond crash of 1979–1981 (*Source:* Ibbotson Associates.)

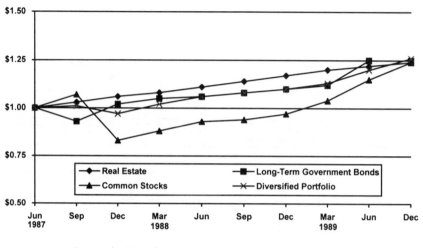

Diversified Portfolio = ⅓ stocks, ⅓ bonds, ⅓ real estate.

Exhibit 12-28   The crash of 1987 (1987–1989) (*Source:* Ibbotson Associates.)

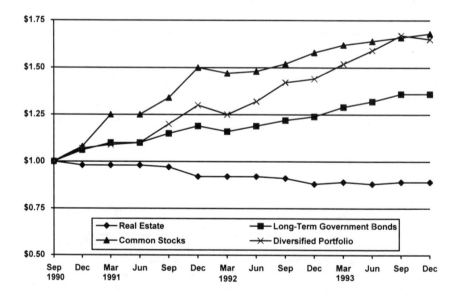

Diversified Portfolio = ⅓ stocks, ⅓ bonds, ⅓ real estate.

Exhibit 12-29   The real estate crash of 1990–1993 (*Source:* Ibbotson Associates.)

Don't Even Attempt to Time the Market with Your Long-Term Retirement Savings

One of the biggest mistakes you can make as an investor is to try to time the market with your long-term retirement savings. While the temptation is great to increase your returns, the risks that you be wrong in timing the market are usually much greater. Many investors are lag indicators. By that I mean that they get in after the market has run up considerably, and get out after it has fallen precipitously. This can have disastrous results. It also runs counter to the adage "buy low, sell high."

While the thrill of victory when you happen to be right is sweet, the agony of defeat when you're wrong can be more painful than arthritis on a damp day. To illustrate this, Exhibit 12-30 shows a best-case scenario—how well you would have done had you the foresight to successfully forecast all bull and bear markets from 1901 to 1988. It also shows how you would have done had you experienced various predictive rates versus a buy and hold strategy. Interestingly, you would have

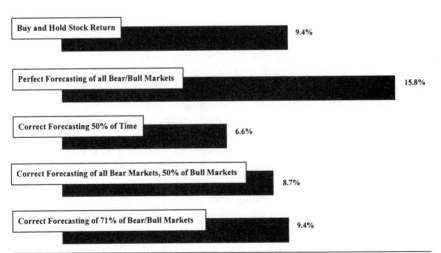

It is very difficult to improve investment performance by attempting to forecast market peaks and troughs. Forecasting accuracy of at least 71 percent is required to outperform a buy and hold strategy.

For the 88-Year Period (1901–1988)

Buy and Hold Stock Return — 9.4%

Perfect Forecasting of all Bear/Bull Markets — 15.8%

Correct Forecasting 50% of Time — 6.6%

Correct Forecasting of all Bear Markets, 50% of Bull Markets — 8.7%

Correct Forecasting of 71% of Bear/Bull Markets — 9.4%

Exhibit 12-30   Market timing (*Source:* Callan Investment Management Council, 1993.)

had to be right more than 71 percent of the time to beat a buy and hold strategy—and that's without transaction costs. Pretty long odds. The figures in the exhibit are based on total annual returns.

Most investors don't realize that the markets aren't casinos for the gambler who wants a quick buck. They generally reward patient investors over time, and they can be brutal to market timers. Most investors also forget that a vast majority of stock market returns, since 1925, have been concentrated in a block of a few months. Exhibit 12-31 demonstrates that a vast majority of stock market returns from 1926 through June 1995 came in just 30 months. This means that 99 percent of all such returns since 1926 occurred in less than 4 percent of the total months for those years.

Given these facts, how would you know for sure when to be in and out of the market? How can you know in advance which month will be a winner and which one won't? The fact is, if you did know the answers to these questions, you wouldn't be working, you'd be clipping coupons. So the moral is, develop a well-conceived plan and be patient.

Consider Your Tax Status

When reviewing and considering your savings and investment strategy, you need to keep your tax status in mind and include the tax status requirements of qualified savings vehicles, which you may be using to accumulate your retirement nest egg. We have already discussed some tax considerations, which may have an effect on your investment strategy.

First, certain types of investments, such as loans to yourself, commodities and collectibles, are prohibited by law from being done through IRAs and Keoghs. Your investment strategy must comply.

Your current and projected income tax rate can also affect how you decide to invest and which vehicles you select. If you are in a high marginal income tax bracket, you may choose to invest a portion of your nontax-favored savings in tax-exempt bonds (state and local governments and certain of their instrumentalities). Exhibit 12-32 illustrates the difference in effective rates of return between taxable and tax-exempt bonds based on various effective income tax rates.

Keep in mind when considering your effective income tax rate you need to include federal, state, and local income taxes. Alternatively, if you don't need the current interest income from the bonds to live on, you may decide to use qualified retirement and savings plans as a means to defer related taxes on nontax-exempt bonds until they are withdrawn after retirement.

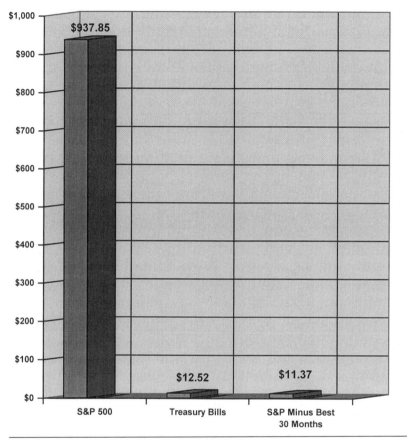

Growth of $1 Invested at
Year-End 1925 by June 1995

Exhibit 12-31   Stock market returns are concentrated in a few months
(*Source:* Ibbotson Associates.)

With regard to stocks, theoretically, if you invest in a passive investment vehicle such as an S&P 500 index fund over the long term, you
may decide to allocate a larger portion of this type of investment to
your taxable versus tax-favored savings vehicles. Fortunately, the appreciation of this investment is not taxed until realized.

Obviously there will be some dividend income and realized gains to
deal with prior to your retirement, which need to be considered. In addition, some gains and losses will result from the index fund disposing

Rates of Return	Income Tax Rates		
Taxable vs. Tax-Exempt	15% Taxable vs. Tax-Exempt	28% Taxable vs. Tax-Exempt	31% Taxable vs. Tax-Exempt
8% vs. 4%	6.8% vs. 4%	5.76% vs. 4%	5.52% vs. 4%
8% vs. 5%	6.8% vs. 5%	5.76% vs. 5%	5.52% vs. 5%
8% vs. 6%	6.8% vs. 6%	5.76% vs. 6%	5.52% vs. 6%
8% vs. 7%	6.8% vs. 7%	5.76% vs. 7%	5.52% vs. 7%

Rates of Return	Income Tax Rates	
Taxable vs. Tax-Exempt	36% Taxable vs. Tax-Exempt	39.6% Taxable vs. Tax-Exempt
8% vs. 4%	5.12% vs. 4%	4.83% vs. 4%
8% vs. 5%	5.12% vs. 5%	4.83% vs. 5%
8% vs. 6%	5.12% vs. 6%	4.83% vs. 6%
8% vs. 7%	5.12% vs. 7%	4.83% vs. 7%

Exhibit 12-32 Effective rates of return between taxable and tax-exempt bonds based on various effective income tax rates

of some of the underlying stocks to track the index. While this principle in theory would also hold true for any stock(s) that you plan to hold until retirement or beyond, how do you know you will hold them that long? Many people can't resist trading stocks within a particular asset class prior to their retirement. In addition, if you use the services of professional money managers, they will make the decisions. Keep in mind that brokers get paid based on their trades. They have a built-in incentive to buy and sell.

Obviously these tax matters are complex. In addition, they are subject to change based on variances in income tax rates, your tax status, and our overall tax structure (income versus consumption taxes). When dealing with significant sums of money, consider seeking the assistance of a qualified financial planner, CPA, attorney, banker, or investment manager.

Now that we have reviewed some of the more important investment principles, it's time to act and monitor your personal retirement security plan, your related savings and investment strategy, and zero in on which course James and Carol take on the final leg of their retirement security planning journey.

CHAPTER THIRTEEN

Putting Your Retirement Plan and Investment Strategy into Action

MYTH 15

Preparing a sound retirement plan is the toughest part of your retirement security efforts.

False. While preparing a retirement plan takes time and discipline, it's not that difficult, especially if you follow the simple seven-step method outlined in this book. The toughest part of your retirement security efforts is putting your plan into action and sticking with it. Given the importance of this effort to your future economic security, you'll probably want to get some professional help to be sure that your plan is realistic and to help you monitor it.

The moment of truth has arrived. It's time to see whether you're holding the aces you've hinted at. If you haven't picked the right cards, or in the case of retirement planning, done your homework and planned adequately, you won't be able to bluff any longer.

Many find this stage the most difficult in the game because it's easier to plan something than actually do it, particularly when it involves saving and investing. Here, actions and results speak louder than words.

Three steps are necessary to gather the best hand: First, you must document your plan by committing it to writing. Second, you must apply what you've decided on by putting it into action. Third, you must monitor your decisions, discard some cards, and add new ones if necessary and make appropriate adjustments.

DOCUMENTING YOUR PLAN

As the adage goes, without a plan, any road could lead to your destination. In the case of retirement planning, that destination could, however, be a cliff, from which you could fall to a premature end.

While a plan is a good beginning, documentation is also important. What this entails is a list of how much you will save, how you are going to save those funds—both monthly and yearly—and how you are going to invest the monies. You must deal in specifics rather than generalities. Simply saying that you plan to save "more" by cutting back on monthly expenses and that you will invest those savings "better" no longer cuts it. Or, as my Texas cronies say, "That dog don't hunt!"

Exhibit 13-1 will help you document your plan. It can also serve as a contract for you and your family regarding your agreed-on plan. For example, it lists how much you will save, what expenses you will cut, what savings vehicle that you use, and other important matters. We'll see how James and Carol went about documenting their plan later.

How much to save:
  Retirement (Exhibit 11-1)
  Monthly savings gap (Exhibit 11-2)   x

Sources of additional savings:
  Big vacation every other year, instead of every year
  Cut eating out in half
  Buy new car every five years, instead of every three years
  Other
      Total   x

Where to save:
  401(k)   /month
  IRAs
  Insurance annuities
  Personal investment account (stocks, bonds, mutual funds)
      Total   x

How to Invest:
  Stocks (mutual funds or direct investments)
  Bonds (mutual funds or direct investments)
  Cash (money market funds, CDs)
      Total   x

Exhibit 13-1   Tool to document plan

APPLYING YOUR PLAN

Next, you need to apply your plan. As discussed previously, you generally want to make maximum use of any tax-favored savings vehicles that you may be eligible for. This might include employer-sponsored retirement and savings plans, especially those that offer an employer match or automatic contributions for those who save, and individual savings arrangements such as IRAs, Keoghs, and certain insurance products (e.g., variable or whole life insurance, annuities). You should contact your employer—typically someone in the human resources or benefits administration department or, if you work at a small firm, the corporate comptroller—for information regarding plans that they sponsor. Remember, you have the right to secure information regarding these plans under ERISA, and companies should be reporting the plan's financial results at least annually.

You may also be eligible for additional non-ERISA savings arrangements such as employee stock purchase plans. Generally, some larger publicly traded companies offer these programs. The advantage of these is that you may be able to buy the stocks at a discount of 15 percent off prevailing market prices. Obviously, stock purchase programs further tie your investment portfolio to the prospects of your employer.

You can amass any detailed information you need on the cost and performance of individual tax-favored savings vehicles such as IRAs, Keoghs or annuities, and various nontax-favored savings vehicles such as savings accounts and taxable money market funds by contacting a variety of investment product providers such as banks, mutual fund companies, and insurance firms. Any brochures they publish should contain a general description of the nature of their services and applicable limits and conditions.

One caveat: Let the buyer beware. While these brochures are designed to help you, they also are meant to entice you to invest in the vehicles they sponsor, whether mutual funds, annuities, or CDs. So, do your own due diligence before jumping in.

Always comparison shop (or get a second opinion) for the best investment opportunity rather than go with the first one you hear about. You also would be wise to seek the assistance of a professional, a topic I'll discuss later in greater detail.

Asset Allocation Issues

Once you decide what type(s) of savings vehicles to invest in, you need to determine how to spread your assets among them. Your overall asset allocation should be a function of your targeted rate of return, your investment horizon, your tolerance for volatility, and your income and liquidity needs. Exhibit 12-20 will help you assess your overall risk tolerance, but it is not meant to be an automatic asset allocator. Rather, you should use it as a guide in making your own asset allocation decisions.

Investment Vehicle Options

You have a variety of options to reach your desired asset allocation. You may want to make direct investments in individual stocks, bonds, Treasury instruments, CDs, real estate, collectibles, collectively known as direct investments. A variety of research materials is available to educate you regarding various possibilities. For example, there are prospectuses for stock and bond offerings, SEC annual reports (10Ks), quarterly reports (10Qs), other filings for public companies, and research services offered by a variety of companies such as Valueline.

If your head is spinning at this point, contact a broker. He or she can explain and execute any options you decide on based on your research. Alternatively, a full-service broker can conduct this research for you, but you will pay higher brokerage fees. Before consulting a broker, however, cover your tracks. Exhibit 13-2 summarizes the factors that you should consider in selecting a financial adviser such as a Certified Public Accountant (CPA), Certified Financial Planner (CFP), Chartered Financial Consultant (ChFC), tax or a trusts and estates attorney, or a broker consultant.

The second major option available is mutual funds. These represent collective investment vehicles that can help you achieve a high degree of diversification and liquidity. Mutual funds will allow you to benefit from professional money management, more cost-effective trading and, in most instances, lower administrative expenses due to economies of scale.

Mutual funds are considered registered investment companies under the federal securities laws. As a result, they are required to file a prospectus and certain periodic reporting information with the Securities and Exchange Commission (SEC). This information is also available to current and potential investors and can be obtained from the respective mutual fund company. Check it out and see how the funds have performed over time (one, three, and five years).

Thousands of mutual funds are available to investors through mutual fund companies such as Fidelity, Vanguard, Invesco, banks, such as, NationsBank, Sun Trust, First Chicago, Northern Trust, and insurance companies such as Mass Mutual. Some are no-load, and some impose initial investment charges, known as *loads*. The cost of the funds and their relative performance can vary significantly. Exhibit 13-3

- Level of service and advice required to make investment decisions.

- Numbers and types of investment vehicles offered—do they match your plan?

- History and reputation of the firm.

- Account insurance (in excess of SIPC)

- For full-service broker, the experience and qualifications of individual handling your account.

- Performance

- Fees

- Service

- Continuity

- Experience

- Consistency

- Style

Exhibit 13-2   Factors to consider when selecting a broker (*Source:* Arthur Andersen LLP.)

summarizes the advantages and costs of mutual funds and the factors that you should consider in selecting one such as the funds investment style, expense ratios, and historical investment performance.

A number of major publications detail annual mutual fund performance summaries, but these can be misleading. Typically, they address only net (of fees and expenses) returns rather than net *risk-adjusted returns,* by which I mean the return that was achieved with the risk that was taken to achieve it factored in. For example, all small cap (generally companies with a total market capitalization of less than $1 billion) and all large cap (companies with a total market capitalization of $5 billion or more) stock funds are not alike. One may employ a greater degree of risk to reach a particular return. This needs to be taken into consideration in analyzing investment results. In addition, in most cases, the asset class or investment style attributed to the fund in these summaries is based on the fund's own assertion (self-designation) or the publisher's opinion rather than a specific and independent analysis. For example, it is not uncommon to find a bond fund that invests a significant portion of its assets in common stocks.

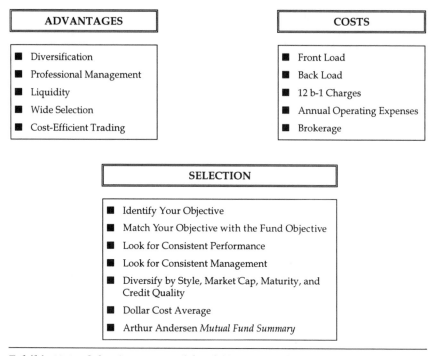

Exhibit 13-3   Selecting a mutual fund (*Source:* Arthur Andersen LLP.)

Sometimes, mutual fund or investment manager performance will vary because the fund or investment manager does not follow their professed style (small cap, large cap, growth, value) or because the fund or manager is not fully invested in its professed asset class. Also, sometimes mutual fund companies or investment managers do not stick to their published style, which can cause a positive or negative variance in their performance. For example, a large cap stock fund may buy a few small cap stocks in an attempt to achieve higher returns.

In addition, sometimes funds and investment managers do not invest all their available assets in the particular type of investment for which the fund or manager is noted such as fixed-income investments or growth stocks. The manager may maintain a large cash position (as opposed to stocks) in an attempt to time the market when it expects the market will go down in the near term. Such tactical asset allocation decisions usually involve changes in cash positions (such as short-term Treasury securities) by the manager or fund. Alternatively, a venture capital manager may not have found enough qualified entities to invest in and therefore parks (temporarily invests) certain funds in a cash or in other asset classes until a suitable investment is found and closed.

Federal law requires that mutual fund companies disclose their investment style and related criteria and restrictions in a prospectus. As a result, mutual fund companies must decide what type of disclosures and related restrictions they will place on themselves via that prospectus. Some mutual funds are very clever regarding how they handle that disclosure. Specifically, they may note a planned investment style yet provide themselves with significant, and in some cases virtually unlimited, ability to vary their investment style and asset allocation.

For example, Fidelity Magellan is the largest and most aggressive growth fund. Yet, Fidelity Magellan's prospectus provides it with considerable flexibility regarding how its fund's assets can be invested. In late 1995, the fund's investment manager decided to invest 30 to 35 percent of Magellan's assets in cash equivalents to try to time a market correction. Many people consider all of their investments in Magellan to be in aggressive growth when in fact, due to the manager's decision, they are effectively investing in a balanced fund. Investors would be in better shape if they read these documents and monitored the actual investments of the fund.

Significant net movements in inflows or withdrawals in connection with mutual funds can have an effect on the investment markets and underlying securities prices. Some believe that one of the reasons the stock market has been on a general upward trend during the past several years is the significant increase in contributions to equity-oriented mutual funds during that period. A question for the future: What will the impact be when baby boomers withdraw these funds when they retire? Only time will tell.

If you are interested in doing additional research on a particular mutual fund company, there are information services available. A well-known one is Principia from Morningstar Mutual Fund Service in Chicago, Illinois. While the Morningstar on-line service is commercially available as of 1996, it costs $195 per year with quarterly updates and $395 per year with monthly updates. Morningstar also has a mutual fund newsletter, which is available for under $100 per year. Another one is Valueline's Fund Analyzer from Valueline of New York City, New York. If you work with an investment adviser, he or she may have access to and share this service.

A third option for investing your money is to use a professional money manager. Often, professional portfolio (money) managers will invest funds on a separate or individual account basis only if the investor has a considerable amount of funds to invest—such as $250,000 or more. This is changing, however, with the advent of collective investment opportunities offered by many brokerage firms and other entities. For example, Smith Barney and other brokerage firms have formed collective investment programs that give individuals access to certain investment managers for a minimum investment of as little as $5,000 to $10,000, depending on the manager.

Separate account investment managers are not subject to the same minimum investment rules as mutual funds under federal law. They have a greater ability to attempt to time the market if they believe it is appropriate and are willing to face the music from their clients if they are wrong. The only major restriction on their investment actions other than general fiduciary principles is an investment contract, which may apply to them and their investment activities. As with Morningstar and mutual funds, there are on-line services available to conduct research and analysis on professional money managers. Three such services are Nelson's, Mobius, and Plan Sponsor Network. While these are commercially available, they are much more expensive than the mutual fund services. Nelson's, in 1996, ran $9,500 per year. As a result, most people who use professional money managers will access this information from their financial planning or investment consultant rather than on their own. Fortunately, public libraries have hard-copy versions of Morningstar, Valueline, and other research services available at little to no cost. A question remains: Are you in the best position to analyze such data?

Banks, trust companies, and insurance companies also offer professional money management investment opportunities through separate account or pooled options. Specifically, they may offer their own mutual funds. Banks may offer additional common and collective trust fund vehicles, and insurance companies may offer certain pooled separate account investments. Insurance companies also offer a range of annuity and other insurance and investment contracts. For example, they offer fixed-annuity contracts that guarantee a stated rate of return and variable-annuity contracts.

Fixed annuities offer certain additional benefits over bank CDs. First, they pay a guaranteed minimum rate, typically 3 to 4 percent forever, while paying higher specified rates for a 1–3 year period. They are typically insured by the state insurance funds and also offer tax-free build-up.

The variable-annuity option has become increasingly popular during the past 10 years. With this, investors have the option to invest their annuity contributions in one of several pooled separate accounts or mutual fund options offered by their insurance company. They have the contractual right to convert the value of their account into an annuity contract based on a predetermined conversion formula. This means that the person's annuity payment will vary based on the investment results of the options selected. In general, the insurance company will provide little or no investment guaranty in connection with these contracts. Importantly, these annuities may not be subject to state insurance fund guarantees.

There are not many readily available sources to secure information on the relative performance of these funds. Morningstar, A-M-Best Company, and Lipper Associates maintain certain information on these product providers. Otherwise, investors must rely primarily on the information provided by the insurance company and compare the performance of the respective pooled separate accounts to that of similar mutual funds, those with similar investment objectives and styles—growth, value, large cap, small cap.

MONITORING YOUR RESULTS AND MAKING NECESSARY ADJUSTMENTS

Once you document and adopt your plan, you need to monitor periodically your efforts and the inevitable variances that will occur between planned and actual numbers, which is akin to checking your deck of cards and making sure these are the cards you want to keep in your hand. This means monitoring your absolute and relative performance as well as your bottom-line progress toward achieving your stated retirement objectives. You also need to monitor the relative performance of your investments as compared to appropriate benchmarks and comparable funds or investment managers. We'll address this later in this chapter.

Based on the results you compile, you need to make appropriate adjustments in your retirement plan and actions. If you don't save as much as you expected, you need to take steps to make up the difference. You may need to save more through a 401(k) plan. Alternatively, you may need to cut your discretionary spending on travel or entertainment to have more to save.

But bear in mind, too, that your actual performance will vary in the short term in both positive and negative directions. Don't start spending more or saving less just because your investment performance has been better or worse than you expected over the short term. For example, if your investment return has averaged 12 percent during the past two years, don't cut your savings rate. Your investment returns may go down in other years and you'll be behind the eight ball.

Remember, your investment assumption is based on an average compounded rate of return. By definition, *average* means there will be interim ups and downs. If you cut back on your savings when you have favorable investment variances, you will have to increase your savings when your investment experience is below par. Chances are, you may not be able to. Set a savings plan and stick with it.

One good habit to get into is to review your plan at least once a year, kind of like an annual checkup at the doctor. Review variances between plan and actual savings rates and investment returns. Also, you should recalculate your retirement gap using Exhibit 11-1 and determine whether your current savings plan and investment strategy are still appropriate. Check whether your overall asset allocation is still in line with your target range. Your asset allocation will change based on differences in investment performance between the classes. You will need to rebalance your portfolio periodically to take these differences into account. Part of any rebalancing can and should be achieved by allocating additional savings to underweighted asset classes (less than the targeted percentage investment). This will minimize related transaction costs and related realized short-term gains and losses.

For instance, if your targeted asset allocation is 70 percent equities, 25 percent fixed income, and 5 percent cash, and the equity market rises significantly, your equity percentage will increase as compared to the other asset classes. In this case, the equity class would be deemed to be overweighted, and the other classes would be underweighted.

Typically, your asset allocation targets will provide a percentage range versus an absolute number so as not to require frequent rebalancing. The ranges for this portfolio could be 65 percent and 75 percent equities, 20 percent to 30 percent fixed income, and 2.5 percent to 7.5 percent cash equivalents.

In addition to assessing whether you need to retool your portfolio, you should determine whether there have been significant changes in the expected rates of return for various asset classes. If so, it may be appropriate to reconsider your overall target ranges. Information concerning expected rates of return by asset class will generally only be available through qualified investment professionals and their firms. You may want to have one of them assist you in your annual review.

In addition to reviewing and assessing your absolute performance of actual savings rates, investment returns, and progress toward filling your retirement gap, you need to assess the relative performance of your investments. By *relative* performance, I mean how your investments did as compared to appropriate indices (benchmarks) and similar investment managers or vehicles. After all, if your equity portfolio rose by 10 percent, but the related benchmark was up 15 percent, your absolute performance may be acceptable, but your relative performance is not.

Similarly, if an investment manager of mutual funds returns 12 percent, but the average performance for managers or vehicles with similar styles is 16 percent, then you haven't done as well as you thought. Obviously, the opposite situation could also occur, which you need to consider as well. For example, your stock mutual fund could go up by 12 percent, whereas the average performance for your type of fund was 9 percent. In this situation, you have done better than average. This could even be the case in a situation where you incur a loss. In such a circumstance, while your relative return may be better, that won't console many.

In addition to a formal annual review, you should perform a quick quarterly review of both your savings patterns and investment results. The purpose is to look for major variances, which although less likely in the short term, should be addressed if they do occur. The most likely variance is that you aren't saving at the rate you projected. Hopefully, by taking a quarterly look, you will be spurred to take quicker corrective actions.

GET ADDITIONAL HELP IF YOU NEED IT

Because many professionals are too busy to keep abreast of all the latest investment developments and their own changing portfolio, it's helpful to invest in a good retirement planning software program to crunch the numbers and run "what-if" analyses on a quick, reliable, and more detailed basis. All current software programs have individual strengths and weaknesses. Some are too simplistic, while others require too much data. Some allow you to select your own key assumptions—inflation—while others use standard assumptions. I don't feel it would be appropriate to recommend any particular software program(s), nevertheless I do feel that the Vanguard Retirement Manager and the Quicken Financial Planner software programs are useful tools. I have used both of them as supplemental tools in my retirement planning efforts. Just one note of caution, I recommend that you do all of your retirement planning on these programs in current rather than future inflated dollars. Looking at dollar amounts that have been inflated over time can give you a false sense of security, particularly in the case of your accumulated savings and investments. Software programs can help you crunch numbers, but they can't do your thinking for you.

You also would be wise to tap into some specialized and professional assistance for a variety of issues. Also consider attending related seminars and workshops conducted by firms such as Arthur Andersen. These are growing in both prevalence and importance. You may also need help putting together a retirement plan or a broader financial plan. Or you may need tax advice in connection with your plan investments or distributions, or legal advice regarding your estate plan.

You may be among those who have both the interest and the ability to be their own counsel about these matters. But even if you are, do you have the time? Most people don't, which raises an important question. Why should you potentially put your retirement security at risk by not being totally sure? If in doubt, consult a professional. There are three considerations other than price.

The Right Credentials—Choosing Professionals

The first is credentials. Does the person have any professional designation that is relevant to the task at hand? If the issue is retirement or broader-based personal financial planning, the individual should be a certified public accountant (CPA) or a certified financial planner (CFP). In addition, the American Institute of Certified Public Accountants has authorized the new designation of PFS for CPAs who have completed a standard personal financial planning training program and passed a related exam. If it's tax advice that you want, the person should again be a CPA or tax attorney. If it's investment advice that you need, you should look for a registered investment adviser, a chartered financial analyst, or a qualified broker.

The second key factor is the person's experience and how it relates to your needs. There are currently more than 400,000 CPAs in the United States, but only a small percentage have significant experience in retirement planning and investment education/assistance matters. Likewise, there are approximately 900,000 attorneys in the United States, but only a small portion have significant estate planning experience.

The key question to ask these professionals is not whether they can do what you want, but what experience they have had in doing what you want. Get references and check their track records. After all, most professionals have a difficult time saying, "No I can't do that," if there is the slightest chance that they or someone in their organization can.

The third factor to consider is objectivity. When you are seeking professional advice, it is important that the person you hire be focused solely on recommending actions that are in your best interests and yours alone rather than what lines his or her pockets. He or she should ask you the right questions such as:

1. What are your retirement objectives?
2. What is your investment horizon?
3. How do you define risk?

4. What are your opinions regarding changes in value of your investments, especially declines?

5. What are your income and liquidity needs?

You want to be sure that their compensation is not based on what they recommend or whom they recommend. As a result, you will want to assure yourself that their compensation structure does not undercut their objectivity. Be sure that their compensation does not tie into how much of certain vehicles you buy.

Also, ask some other key questions: Do they have a policy or practice of recommending only certain service providers or investment funds? Are they affiliated with certain investment funds or broker/dealers that might influence their recommendations? What size and type of clients do they typically work with?

While you must have trust in the person you are working with, you should also have confidence in the firm he or she is affiliated with because it may offer additional and worthwhile resources and services that could benefit you now or in the future or benefit other family members. For example, firms such as Arthur Andersen have extensive financial, retirement, tax and estate planning capabilities. Arthur Andersen also has 800 numbers and Internet sites. As a result, you may want to avoid "one man bands" or firms with limited resources or capabilities.

JAMES' AND CAROL'S PLAN

James and Carol previously determined that they needed to fill a projected retirement gap of $817,869. They understand that their options essentially boil down to changing their retirement objectives or modifying their savings rates and investment patterns.

Based on that fact and the information contained in the previous chapters, the couple prefers to try to enhance their current savings rates and historical investment returns rather than modify their retirement objectives, at least for now. They feel that they have enough time to make the necessary adjustments.

Referring to Exhibit 11-2, James and Carol decide that to fill their retirement gap, they can increase their expected long rate of investment return to 8 percent and save another $1,960 per month, including any employer matching contributions or achieve a 6 percent average rate of return and save an additional $2,380 per month including any employer matching contributions. Because they're concerned how they can save the lower amount much less the higher one, they decide first to focus on enhancing their expected investment return, which would justify a lower savings rate increase.

Exhibit 13-4 summarizes their current savings patterns and investments, while Exhibit 9-2 summarizes their current expenditures. These exhibits provide the basic data the couple need to implement their plan.

Based on the expected returns of Exhibit 12–11, their current investments are likely to result in an overall expected rate of return of approximately 6.5 percent. Based on their understanding of the information

	Current
Current asset allocation:	
401(k):	
Stocks	15%
Bonds	70
Short-term	15
IRAs:	
Stocks	5
Bonds	70
Short-term	25
Other personal savings	
Stocks	25
Bonds	0
Short-term	0
Savings account	75
Specific asset allocation:	
Growth stocks	
S&P 500 Index Fund	
Value stocks	
International stocks	
Small cap stocks	
Intermediate bonds	
Short-term bonds	
Money market funds	

Current savings:			
401(k)*			
James	$3,000	+	$1,500*
Carol	$1,500	+	$750
IRAs			
James	0		
Carol	0		
Other	$2,000		
Total	$6,500	=	($729/mo.)[1]

* 401(k) match of 50% up to 6% of pay.

[1] Indicating employer match.

Exhibit 13-4   James' and Carol's savings patterns and investment

contained in the prior chapter, they believe that they should be able to improve this to at least 8 percent by adopting a more optimal asset allocation consistent with their overall risk profile. To assess the feasibility of this idea, they complete the sample risk profile questionnaire in Exhibit 13-5, which shows that they have a moderate tolerance for risk. Based on their respective ages (46 and 45) and projected life expectancies (78 and 82), they decide that their investment horizon is a maximum of 32 to 37 years, while their expected retirement date puts their targeted retirement horizon at 17 years. They decide that 30 years is an appropriate estimate of their current investment horizon.

Using Exhibit 13-6 as a guide, they determine that an appropriate asset allocation for their retirement portfolio is 65 percent stocks, 30 percent fixed income, and 5 percent cash equivalents investments. These percentages are between those noted for categories D and E on Exhibit 13-5 which they feel is appropriate for them. They tentatively decide on the following specific asset allocations: (1) growth stocks, 30

Answering the following questions.

RISK PREFERENCE	TIME HORIZON
1. Personal Risk Assessment	**1. Your Retirement Goal**
How do you feel about risk?	*How many years will it be before you need your Profit Sharing Plan money for retirement income? If you're not certain, choose the earliest age you think you may need your money.*
▲ *My focus is on maximizing my long-term return. I don't worry about short-term fluctuations, even if they are significantly downward. (10 points)*	▲ *20 or more years (10 points)*
▲ *I'm willing to accept a reasonable amount of market risk if it means I'll have a better chance of staying ahead of inflation. (6 points)*	▲ *15 years (8 points)*
	▲ *10 years (6 points)*
▲ *Safety is my principal concern. Inflation is secondary. (1 point).*	▲ *5 years (4 points)*
	▲ *Less than 5 years (1 point)*
▲ *Score* _____6_____	▲ *Score* _____10_____
2. What If...	**2. Loan Expectations**
What if your money in the stock market dropped 15% over the next month?	*How many years will it be before you need your 401(k) money for a loan? If you're not certain, choose the earliest time you think you may need your money.*
▲ *I would maintain my current stock assets, because I expect peaks and valleys in my returns along the way. (10 points)*	▲ *Not at all (10 points)*
▲ *I would stay in my current stock funds until the market rebounds, then consider selling. (6 points)*	▲ *10 years (7 points)*
	▲ *5 years (4 points)*
▲ *I would sell immediately to avoid further losses. (1 point).*	▲ *Less than 5 years (1 point)*
▲ *Score* _____10_____	▲ *Score* _____10_____ *Do not choose a score that is higher than Your Retirement Goal score above.*
Total Risk Preference Score _____16_____	*Total Time Horizon Score* _____20_____

(Continued)

Exhibit 13-5 James' and Carol's profile questionnaire (*Source:* Arthur Andersen LLP.)

To find your starting portfolio, use the lower of your risk preference and time horizon scores. You should use the lower score because even if you have a high risk tolerance but you are only a short time away from when you need your money, you may not want to risk losing your principal over a short period of time.

YOUR LOWER SCORE	PEOPLE WITH THIS SCORE TEND TO	START IN ROW
2-5	Be very conservative and either are not comfortable accepting higher market risk or have a relatively short time horizon until they need their money.	A
6-9	Be conservative, though they may be willing to accept a low degree of market risk.	B
10-13	Have a moderate tolerance for risk and seek a balanced investment approach.	C
14-17	Be somewhat more aggressive and will accept risk because they expect to earn a higher return.	D
18-20	Tolerate a high degree of risk and seek aggressive investments. For diversification, these investors may want to consider other investments that have lower inherent risk.	E

Exhibit 13-5   *(Continued)*

percent; (2) S&P 500 index fund, 20 percent; (3) international stocks, 15 percent; (4) intermediate bonds, 30 percent; and, (5) money market funds, 5 percent.

Based on the expected rates of return of Exhibit 12-11, James' and Carol's new asset allocation translates to an 8.9 percent expected rate of return, which is 2.4 percent higher than their current asset allocation and comfortably in excess of their new minimum 8 percent targeted rate of return for planning purposes.

Taking into account tax and other considerations, James and Carol want to maximize their tax-deferred savings. They've decided to maximize their section 401(k) plan opportunities and reinitiate contributions to their IRAs even though they won't get a current deduction for them. Based on their new targeted rate of return and their retirement

		SAMPLE PORTFOLIO MIX*		PORTFOLIO CHARACTERISTICS
A	Most Conservative ↑	Money Market Stable Value Bond Stock Aggressive Stock	50% 25% 15% 10% 0%	This range covers the most conservative portfolios, with both the lowest risk of short-term loss and the lowest expected long-term return. As a result, portfolios in this range are expected to provide the least protection against inflation.
B		Money Market Stable Value Bond Stock Aggressive Stock	35% 25% 20% 15% 5%	This range covers somewhat less conservative portfolios, with a low to moderate risk of short-term loss and a somewhat higher long-term expected return. As a result, portfolios in this range are expected to provide somewhat better protection against inflation.
C		Money Market Stable Value Bond Stock Aggressive Stock	20% 20% 15% 25% 20%	While portfolios in this range are spread among all asset classes, they do have a somewhat higher percentage of stocks and bonds. As a result, they are expected to be more volatile in the short term but provide better long-term protection against inflation.
D		Money Market Stable Value Bond Stock Aggressive Stock	10% 10% 20% 30% 30%	This range is invested more heavily in stocks and bonds, which makes for fairly aggressive portfolios. These portfolios are expected to provide a higher long-term return, but they can be quite volatile in the short term.
E	↓ Most Aggressive	Money Market Stable Value Bond Stock Aggressive Stock	5% 5% 20% 25% 45%	This range covers the most aggressive portfolios, which have the highest risk of loss and the greatest potential for long-term return. They are expected to provide the best protection against inflation, but they can be highly volatile.

*These graphs illustrate general concepts for creating portfolio mixes and do not represent recommendations for specific percentages.

(Continued)

Exhibit 13-6   Sample portfolio characteristics

gap, they need to save an additional $1,400 per month to achieve their retirement objectives. They can achieve their additional savings objective in part by increasing their combined Section 401(k) contributions by $6,500 per year. Their contributions will be matched 50 cents per dollar up to 6 percent of their compensation.

The couple also plans to have Carol reinstigate her past IRA contributions of $2,000 per year and for James to do so in the future when they have the extra funds.

Now that they have prepared their preliminary plan, James and Carol decided that it would be prudent to seek the assistance of a qualified

PORTFOLIO COMPOSITION	DEGREE OF SHORT-TERM MARKET RISK	EXPECTED LONG-TERM PROTECTION AGAINST INFLATION	APPROXIMATE TIME FRAME	WHO MIGHT INVEST IN THESE PORTFOLIOS
Portfolios in this range tend to be concentrated among stable value investments, such as a money market fund or a stable return fund. They may include some bonds and possibly stocks.	Very low	Very low	Two years or less	People who prefer to take as little market risk as possible or who expect to withdraw their account balances soon.
Portfolios in this range tend to be spread among more asset classes. They tend to have higher concentrations of stable value investments, with some allocation to bonds and possibly stocks.	Low	Low	Three to four years	People who are comfortable with low to moderate market risk.
Portfolios in this range tend to be among all asset classes. They tend to be evenly balanced among the investment funds.	Moderate	Moderate	Four to six years	People who seek a balanced approach.
Portfolios in this range tend to be spread among stocks and bonds, with increasing concentration in more aggressive stocks, such as international stocks and small company stocks.	High	Good	Six to ten years	People who are comfortable with higher market risk.
Portfolios in this range tend to be concentrated among more aggressive stocks and small company stocks, with smaller allocations to less aggressive investments.	Very high	Very good	Ten years or more	People who aggressively assume market risk to enhance expected returns.

Please keep in mind that these portfolios are intended only to give you an idea of how you may choose to invest. You may come up with a portfolio mix that is quite different from one of these samples. Because you are responsible for the investment decisions in your account, only you can decide the portfolio mix that fits your individual objectives.

Exhibit 13-6 *(Continued)* *(Source:* Arthur Andersen LLP.)

professional to help review the reasonableness of their plan, assist them in putting it into action, and monitoring their annual performance.

They considered a number of possibilities and ultimately chose to hire Susan Kelly, a CPA and financial planning professional, whom they met through a friend. Susan has significant retirement planning and investment experience and is also knowledgeable in tax and estate planning matters. This, the couple decided, was an additional benefit, particularly in helping their parents. One set needs a nursing home; the other is trying to gift yearly amounts to the couple. In addition, Susan is one of many financial planners at her firm.

Susan reviews James' and Carol's retirement objectives and their preliminary planning efforts with them. She compliments both on their decision to get serious. While she believes they have done a good job of preliminary planning, she advises them that they still have some work and rethinking to do if they're going to achieve their goals.

James and Carol advise Susan that their first concern is their remaining retirement gap and how to fill it. Sally advises them that it is not surprising that they have such a gap since they didn't really begin their retirement planning process until their mid 40's. However, she also noted that they have several options to reduce that projected retirement gap, if they don't feel they can save any more than the additional $6,000 annually, excluding employer matching contributions, at the present time. These options include:

1. Selling their home and buying a new condo in Sarasota to live in all year around when they retire. Their St. Charles home is currently worth about $275,000 and they will have fully paid off the mortgage by the time they retire. If they sold their home and bought a nicer condo in Sarasota they could free up a considerable amount at retirement. Sally's rough estimate is that this would produce an additional $322,306 in resources at retirement net of 10% disposition costs and assuming that the home and condo increase in value by 3% between now and their retirement date (($300,000 × 1.65285) − ($175,000 − $100,000) × 1.65285) = $322,306). Taking this step would close about 70% of their retirement gap (i.e., $322,306 of $462,274). However, James and Sally may not want to take this step for personal reasons.

2. As an alternative selling their St. Charles home, they could plan on obtaining a reverse mortgage or home equity loan to free up a substantial part of the equity in their home when they retire. This would allow them to keep the home but would release its value for inheritance purposes.

3. James and Carol can save all they can now and increase their savings rate in later years, especially after their children graduate from college. Specifically, they can plan to save all or substantially all of the $10,000 per year they are currently paying for education expenses. In addition, hopefully as their wages rise they will be able to save more in the future. Unfortunately, if they take this step, they won't be able to benefit as much from the "magic" of compounding.

Based on these options, James and Sally decide to adopt option 3 because they want to try and keep their St. Charles home, planned retirement date and standard of living. They recognize, however, that life is full of trade-offs and that they will have to be much more disciplined about their retirement planning and savings in the future.

After discussing their retirement gap, James and Carol turn the discussion to their current savings and investment strategy. Sally makes the following additional observations for their consideration.

1. They can actually save more than the additional $6,000 they calculated without further cutting their discretionary spending. Specifically, by using their 401(k) plans to a greater extent they will save about $1,000 in current income taxes. As a result, they can and should save this additional $1,000.

2. They assumed an 8 percent compounded rate of return for their entire life span. While this amount is reasonable and achievable on a preretirement basis with proper asset allocation, they may want to consider assuming a lower rate of return postretirement to be a bit more conservative. This will also recognize that their asset allocation is likely to change as they approach and enter retirement and want to move toward an income versus asset accumulation strategy.

3. They want to purchase a condo in Sarasota, Florida, for cash when they retire. While they won't have a mortgage payment, they will have additional homeowners insurance, property taxes, and maintenance charges that they need to consider.

4. They need to make maximum use of their tax-favored savings opportunities. Specifically, they should attempt to max out on their 401(k) savings opportunities, particularly in light of their employers' matching policies. They should also make contributions to individual IRAs when they can even though they won't get a current deduction for their IRA contributions. They will, however, benefit from the related tax-free build-up. Based on 1996 contribution limits to James' 401(k) plan, while Carol contributes up to $4,500 (15 percent × $30,000), he can contribute up to the current limit of $9,500. This will increase in $500 increments based on future inflation.

5. They need to consider using money market funds as a liquid and short-term savings vehicle rather than maintaining a large savings account balance. Doing so will enhance their overall return while providing them the liquidity they need for short-term needs or desires.

Major Recurring Expense Categories	Current Recurring Annual Expenses	Adjustments (+ or − a Given Amount for Retirement)	Detailed Budget for First Year of Retirement
Housing:			
Mortgage	$17,700	− $17,700	$0
Homeowners Insurance	$1,200	$500	$1,700
Utilities	$3,700	$0	$3,700
Maintenance	$2,400	$600	$3,000
Property Tax	$3,000	$1,500	$4,500
Total	$28,000	− $15,100	$12,900
Food	$8,000	− $1,500	$6,500
Clothing	$5,000	− $2,000	$3,000
Health Care	$1,500	$5,000	$6,500
Transportation			
Car Payments	$2,200	$0	$2,200
Gas	$2,900	− $500	$2,400
Maintenance	$600	$0	$600
Parking	$1,200	− $1,000	$200
Total	$6,900	− $1,500	$5,400
Education	$10,000	− $10,000	$0
Insurance			
Life\Disability	$1,400	− $1,400	$0
Auto	$1,000	$0	$1,000
Total	$2,400	− $1,400	$1,000
Travel/Vacations	$2,700	$10,000	$12,700
Recreation/Entertainment	$2,300	$5,200	$7,500
Taxes			
State and Local	$18,500	− $8,500	$10,000
Payroll	$8,300	− $8,300	$0
Total	$26,800	− $16,800	$10,000
Savings	$13,500	− $13,500	$0
Other	$1,350	− $350	$1,000
TOTAL	$108,450	− $41,950	$66,500

Supplemental Retirement Expense	Current Value
Retirement Condo	$100,000
Country Club	$15,000
Dream Trip	$7,600
Family Assistance	$40,000
Children's Inheritance (Minimum)	$25,000
TOTAL	$187,600

Exhibit 13-7 James' and Carol's total estimated retirement expenses worksheet, Sarasota, Florida

Current ages	46/45	
Retirement ages	63/62	
Years to retirement	17	
Life expectancy	84	(See Appendix C—Use the longer life expectancy and add at least two years to this number to be conservative.)
Years in retirement	22	(Use the higher of you or your spouse)
Inflation rate	4%	

Detailed budget total for first year of retirement $66,500   (Exhibit 13-7)

Cost of living ("COL") in current city   N/A   (Appendix D)

Cost of living in retirement city   98.9   (Appendix D)

If COL in retirement city is greater than COL in current city, then complete Column 1. If COL in current city is greater than COL in retirement city, then complete Column 2.

Column 1	Column 2
Step 1: (COL in retirement city) - (COL in current city) = _____	Since COL in current city is greater than COL in retirement city, no adjustment is necessary. Thus, your detailed budget total for the first year of retirement is unchanged. Enter this result on the first line below.
Step 2: 1 + (result from Step 1) = _____	
Step 3: (detailed budget total for first year of retirement) x (result from Step 2) = _____	
Enter this result on the first line below.	
	_____ $66,500 _____ (From above)

Translation to future value using 4% inflation and number of years to retirement:

1) Determine your number of years to retirement. _17_

2) Using the chart on the following page, determine your appropriate inflation factor under the 4% column. _1.94790_

3) Multiply this factor by the result from either Column 1 or 2. _134,210_

Results = future value of the budget total for the first year of retirement $129,535

Exhibit 13-8   James' and Carol's translation worksheet (translate total estimated retirement expenses to sum needed at retirement)

Supplemental Retirement Expenses:

Cost of second home	$100,000	(Exhibit 13-7)

Translation to future value using 3% inflation and
number of years to retirement:

1) Using the chart on the following page, determine
your appropriate inflation factor under the 3%
column. 1.65285

2) Multiply this factor by the cost of your second
home.

	165,285	
	(Line 2)	

Cost of country club + dream trip + family assistance	87,600	(Exhibit 13-7)

Translation to future value using 4% inflation and
number of years to retirement

1) Using the chart on the following page, determine
your appropriate inflation factor under the 4%
column. 1.94790

2) Multiply this factor by the (cost of country club +
dream trip + family assistance).

	170,636	
	(Line 4)	

Result = Sum of lines 2 and 4 = Future value of
supplemental retirement expenses needed at
retirement

	$335,921

(Continued)

Exhibit 13-8   *(Continued)*

INFLATION FACTORS

Years to Retirement	Inflation			
	2%	3%	4%	6%
40	2.20804	3.26204	4.80102	10.28572
39	2.16474	3.16703	4.61637	9.70351
38	2.12230	3.07478	4.43881	9.15425
37	2.08069	2.98523	4.26809	8.63609
36	2.03989	2.89828	4.10393	8.14725
35	1.99989	2.81386	3.94609	7.68609
34	1.96068	2.73191	3.79432	7.25103
33	1.92223	2.65234	3.64838	6.84059
32	1.88454	2.57508	3.50806	6.45339
31	1.84759	2.50008	3.37313	6.08810
30	1.81136	2.42726	3.24340	5.74349
29	1.77584	2.35657	3.11865	5.41839
28	1.74102	2.28793	2.99870	5.11169
27	1.70689	2.22129	2.88337	4.82235
26	1.67342	2.15659	2.77247	4.54938
25	1.64061	2.09378	2.66584	4.29187
24	1.60844	2.03279	2.56330	4.04893
23	1.57690	1.97359	2.46472	3.81975
22	1.54598	1.91610	2.36992	3.60354
21	1.51567	1.86029	2.27877	3.39956
20	1.48595	1.80611	2.19112	3.20714
19	1.45681	1.75351	2.10685	3.02560
18	1.42825	1.70243	2.02582	2.85434
17	1.40024	1.65285	1.94790	2.69277
16	1.37279	1.60471	1.87298	2.54035
15	1.34587	1.55797	1.80094	2.39656
14	1.31948	1.51259	1.73168	2.26090
13	1.29361	1.46853	1.66507	2.13293
12	1.26824	1.42576	1.60103	2.01220
11	1.24337	1.38423	1.53945	1.89830
10	1.21899	1.34392	1.48024	1.79085
9	1.19509	1.30477	1.42331	1.68948
8	1.17166	1.26677	1.36857	1.59385
7	1.14869	1.22987	1.31593	1.50363
6	1.12616	1.19405	1.26532	1.41852
5	1.10408	1.15927	1.21665	1.33823
4	1.08243	1.12551	1.16986	1.26248
3	1.06121	1.09273	1.12486	1.19102
2	1.04040	1.06090	1.08160	1.12360
1	1.02000	1.03000	1.04000	1.06000

Exhibit 13-8   *(Continued)*

Step 1: Determine the amount needed in savings to fund the detailed budget total for the first year of retirement.

Future value of budget total for first year of retirement:	$129,535	(Exhibit 13-8)
Social Security annual benefit:	– 39,490	(Exhibit 10-3)
Employer-sponsored pension annual payment:	– 30,000	(Exhibit 10-3)
Future value of annual earnings from continued employment (Exhibit 10-3):		

    1) Determine your number of years to retirement. __17__
    2) Refer to the Inflation Factors Chart on the following page to
        determine your appropriate inflation factor under the 4%
        column. __1.94790__   N/A
    3) Multiply: (annual earnings) x (result from Step 2)

Result—Amount needed in savings to fund first year detailed
  budget: $60,045

Step 2: Using the result from Step 1, refer to the chart in Exhibit 11-1 to determine the amount of savings needed to fund annual retirement budget.

Amount: $1,100,000

Step 3: Add the future value of the supplemental retirement expenses (Exhibit 9-4) to the amount in Step 2.

Amount from Step 2:	$1,100,000	
Future value of the supplemental retirement expenses:	335,921	*(Exhibit 13-8)
Sum:	$1,435,921	

        *This approach assumes that all of the supplemental retirement
        expenses will be covered in the first year of retirement.

Step 4: Determine the future value of current savings.

    1) Using Exhibit 10-3, determine the following:
        401(k) balance __50,000__
        IRA balance __40,000__
        Other savings balance __20,000__
        Gifts/Inheritance __75,000__
    2) Determine your number of years to retirement __17__
    3) Determine your expected rates of return for the balances in Step 1:
        401(k) expected rate of return __8%__
        IRA expected rate of return __8%__
        Other savings expected rate of return __4%__
        Gifts/Inheritance expected rate of return __4%__
    4) Using your number of years to retirement and your expected
        rates of return, refer to the Return Factors Chart on the following
        page to determine your appropriate return factors for each of your
        balances:
        401(k) return factor __3.70002__
        IRA return factor __3.70002__
        Other savings return factor __1.94790__
        Gifts/Inheritance return factor __1.94790__

(Continued)

Exhibit 13-9   James' and Carol's retirement gap (difference between retirement resources and retirement needs)

5) Multiply your return factors (Step 4) by your current balances
(Step 1) to determine the future value of your current savings:

(401(k) balance) x (401(k) return factor) <u>185,001</u>

(IRA balance) x (IRA return factor) <u>148,000</u>

(Other savings) x (other saving return factor) <u>38,958</u>

(Gifts/Inheritance) x (Gifts/Inheritance return factor) <u>146,093</u>

6) Sum the results from Step 5　　　　　　　　　　　$518,052

Step 5: Subtract the sum in Step 3 from the sum in Step 4.

Sum (Step 4)	$518,052
Sum (Step 3)	($1,435,921)
Difference—retirement surplus (deficit)	($917,869)[1]

[1] Without considering the effect of future planned savings.

Exhibit 13-9　　*(Continued) (Source: Saving for a Secure Retirement, AICPA.)*

INFLATION FACTORS

Years to		Inflation		
Retirement	2%	3%	4%	6%
40	2.20804	3.26204	4.80102	10.28572
39	2.16474	3.16703	4.61637	9.70351
38	2.12230	3.07478	4.43881	9.15425
37	2.08069	2.98523	4.26809	8.63609
36	2.03989	2.89828	4.10393	8.14725
35	1.99989	2.81386	3.94609	7.68609
34	1.96068	2.73191	3.79432	7.25103
33	1.92223	2.65234	3.64838	6.84059
32	1.88454	2.57508	3.50806	6.45339
31	1.84759	2.50008	3.37313	6.08810
30	1.81136	2.42726	3.24340	5.74349
29	1.77584	2.35657	3.11865	5.41839
28	1.74102	2.28793	2.99870	5.11169
27	1.70689	2.22129	2.88337	4.82235
26	1.67342	2.15659	2.77247	4.54938
25	1.64061	2.09378	2.66584	4.29187
24	1.60844	2.03279	2.56330	4.04893
23	1.57690	1.97359	2.46472	3.81975
22	1.54598	1.91610	2.36992	3.60354
21	1.51567	1.86029	2.27877	3.39956
20	1.48595	1.80611	2.19112	3.20714
19	1.45681	1.75351	2.10685	3.02560
18	1.42825	1.70243	2.02582	2.85434
17	1.40024	1.65285	1.94790	2.69277
16	1.37279	1.60471	1.87298	2.54035
15	1.34587	1.55797	1.80094	2.39656
14	1.31948	1.51259	1.73168	2.26090
13	1.29361	1.46853	1.66507	2.13293
12	1.26824	1.42576	1.60103	2.01220
11	1.24337	1.38423	1.53945	1.89830
10	1.21899	1.34392	1.48024	1.79085
9	1.19509	1.30477	1.42331	1.68948
8	1.17166	1.26677	1.36857	1.59385
7	1.14869	1.22987	1.31593	1.50363
6	1.12616	1.19405	1.26532	1.41852
5	1.10408	1.15927	1.21665	1.33823
4	1.08243	1.12551	1.16986	1.26248
3	1.06121	1.09273	1.12486	1.19102
2	1.04040	1.06090	1.08160	1.12360
1	1.02000	1.03000	1.04000	1.06000

(Continued)

Exhibit 13-9 *(Continued)*

RETURN FACTORS

Years to Retirement	Rate of Return 4%	6%	8%	10%
40	4.80102	10.28572	21.72452	45.25926
39	4.61637	9.70351	20.11530	41.14478
38	4.43881	9.15425	18.62528	37.40434
37	4.26809	8.63609	17.24563	34.00395
36	4.10393	8.14725	15.96817	30.91268
35	3.94609	7.68609	14.78534	28.10244
34	3.79432	7.25103	13.69013	25.54767
33	3.64838	6.84059	12.67605	23.22515
32	3.50806	6.45339	11.73708	21.11378
31	3.37313	6.08810	10.86767	19.19434
30	3.24340	5.74349	10.06266	17.44940
29	3.11865	5.41839	9.31727	15.86309
28	2.99870	5.11169	8.62711	14.42099
27	2.88337	4.82235	7.98806	13.10999
26	2.77247	4.54938	7.39635	11.91818
25	2.66584	4.29187	6.84848	10.83471
24	2.56330	4.04893	6.34118	9.84973
23	2.46472	3.81975	5.87146	8.95430
22	2.36992	3.60354	5.43654	8.14027
21	2.27877	3.39956	5.03383	7.40025
20	2.19112	3.20714	4.66096	6.72750
19	2.10685	3.02560	4.31570	6.11591
18	2.02582	2.85434	3.99602	5.55992
17	1.94790	2.69277	3.70002	5.05447
16	1.87298	2.54035	3.42594	4.59497
15	1.80094	2.39656	3.17217	4.17725
14	1.73168	2.26090	2.93719	3.79750
13	1.66507	2.13293	2.71962	3.45227
12	1.60103	2.01220	2.51817	3.13843
11	1.53945	1.89830	2.33164	2.85312
10	1.48024	1.79085	2.15892	2.59374
9	1.42331	1.68948	1.99900	2.35795
8	1.36857	1.59385	1.85093	2.14359
7	1.31593	1.50363	1.71382	1.94872
6	1.26532	1.41852	1.58687	1.77156
5	1.21665	1.33823	1.46933	1.61051
4	1.16986	1.26248	1.36049	1.46410
3	1.12486	1.19102	1.25971	1.33100
2	1.08160	1.12360	1.16640	1.21000
1	1.04000	1.06000	1.08000	1.10000

Exhibit 13-9   *(Continued)*

	Current	Target
Current asset allocation:		
401(k):		
Stocks	15%	70%
Bonds	70	30
Short-term	15	0
IRAs:		
Stocks	5	70
Bonds	70	30
Short-term	25	0
Other personal savings		
Stocks	25	50
Bonds	0	0
Short-term	0	50
Savings account	75	0
Specific asset allocation:		
Growth stocks		25
S&P 500 Index Fund		15
Value stocks		15
International stocks		15
Small cap stocks		0
Intermediate bonds		30
Short-term bonds		0
Money market funds		5
		100%

Current savings: Planned savings:

401(k)*

James	$3,000	+	$1,500*	$8,280	+	$2,142*
Carol	$1,500	+	$750*	$3,220	+	$1,110*

IRAs

James	$0		$0	
Carol	$0		$2,000	
Other	$2,000		$0	
Total	$6,500	($729/mo.)[1]	$13,500	($1,396/mo.)[1]

*401(k)match of 50% on up to 6% of pay.

[1] Including employer match.

Exhibit 13-10 James' and Carol's savings patterns and investment

6. They should also consider investing in selected pooled investment vehicles, such as no-load mutual funds, to provide them
   with diversification both between and within various asset
   classes. This approach will also provide them with liquidity if
   they need it.

   Furthermore, if they are careful in their funds selection,
   they can minimize their administrative fees and achieve a
   more reasonable rate of return given their investment horizon
   and objectives.

7. They should consider investing a portion of their savings in an
   appropriate international fund to enhance their diversification
   and take advantage of the potentially higher returns. After all,
   while the United States still is the largest single capital market
   in the world, in 1995, it only had about 23 percent of total global
   market capitalization.

8. They need to be sure that they have adequate life and disability
   insurance prior to their retirement. They also need to have a
   will, and should begin to think about preparing an estate plan
   within the next five to seven years.

Based on Susan's input, the couple plan to increase their 401(k) savings and cut their transportation, travel/vacations, recreation/enter-
tainment, and auto insurance budgets to be prepared to fill in their
projected retirement gap. After they have calculated their revised annual expense budget (Exhibit 13-7), completed their revised translation
worksheet (Exhibit 13-8), and recalculated their projected retirement
gap, their new retirement gap is estimated to be $917,869 (Exhibit 13-9).
To help close this gap, they plan to increase their annual savings to
$13,500 per year and $16,752 with employer matching contributions
(Exhibit 13-10).

The couple also revised their targeted asset allocation based on their
discussion with Susan as follows: (1) growth stocks, 25 percent; (2) value
stocks, 15 percent; (3) S&P 500 index fund, 15 percent; (4) international
stocks, 15 percent; (5) intermediate bonds, 30 percent. Their revised target asset allocation serves to increase their long-term rate of return to
9.2 percent.

Now that they have finalized their plan, they decide to have Susan
help them review their plan, put it into action, and monitor their progress annually. The couple are clearly on their way. Only 17 years until
they retire comfortably, or at least that's what they hope will happen.
Time will tell.

Epilogue

It's now June of the year 2013, and James and Carol, as well as millions of other baby boomers, are preparing for their long-awaited retirement. It has been a long and winding road with a number of ups and downs to this point, but they're finally on the brink of retirement. The question is, can they retire as they initially planned 17 years ago?

Much has changed in the country and in James' and Carol's lives since they began this process. For example, the Social Security and Medicare systems were fundamentally reformed early in the twenty-first century with some phase-ins but not as long as the 1983 Social Security amendments transition. The politicians finally recognized that the existing programs could not be sustained, and the massive public education process that began in the late 1990s and the bipartisan commission that recommended specific reforms gave the Congress "political cover" and the ability to act.

The above reforms resulted in the adoption of the two-tiered benefit structure that was hotly debated. It also resulted in the full taxation of Social Security benefits for individuals with higher relative income levels, a further delay in James' and Carol's normal retirement age (until 67) and a delay in their early retirement eligibility age (until 63½).

The above changes, exclusive of the delay in retirement dates, resulted in James' and Carol's projected Social Security benefits being cut by 15 percent as compared to the 20 percent they assumed in 1996. However, more of their benefits will now be subject to income tax, and their early retirement age has increased. Their effective Medicare benefits were cut significantly, but not quite as much as they originally estimated (33 percent versus 50 percent); however, based on the reforms which were enacted, 85 percent of their Medicare benefits will be subject to income tax. In addition, they won't be eligible for Medicare benefits until they are 66½.

Employers continued their movement to defined-contribution plans as retirement income vehicles and began to employ a similar approach to health care. Specifically, after the turn of the century, they began to offer employees access to health care at group rates, and some offered a specific amount of dollars per year for employees. This approach was accelerated when the federal tax rules changed to include the value of employer-provided health-care assistance into the taxable wages of employees, both for payroll and income tax purposes.

Carol's employer followed suit in connection with the just-mentioned trend by freezing their defined-benefit plan early in the twenty-first century. The result was that Carol's projected defined-benefit pension at retirement was reduced from $30,000 to $25,000 in 2013 dollars.

While both James' and Carol's employers offer them the ability to purchase some retiree health care at group rates, they don't provide them with any funds to pay for it. The result is, they estimated that their average annual health-care costs for Medigap insurance and other aspects in retirement will run $125 higher per month than they expected.

Nationally, home prices have generally not kept pace with inflation. There have, however, been significant variances in certain markets, and first-class condos have grown faster than average home prices, especially condos in attractive retirement and vacation locations like Sarasota, Florida. As a result, James' and Carol's St. Charles, Illinois, home has not grown in value as much as they would have liked. However, they plan to will their home to their children rather than sell it or borrow on it for their retirement. As a result, it doesn't really affect their retirement plan unless they need to tap their equity as a last resort.

The faster increase in Sarasota condo prices will have an effect on their retirement plan. They now estimate that their Sarasota condo will cost them $215,000 rather than the $165,000 (in 2013) which they estimated in 1996 (see Exhibit E-1).

While the federal government has generally kept the lid on income tax rates, the effective income tax rates for states have gone up. Certain states, like Florida, finally had to adopt an income tax after years of resisting. In addition, the federal government has adopted a consumption tax approach to raising additional revenues. The combined tax changes will serve to increase James' and Carol's estimated annual tax burden in retirement by about $5,800 in 2013 dollars over what they originally estimated in 1996 (Exhibit E-1).

On the positive side, the inflation rate has been slightly less than the 4 percent which they estimated in 1996. In addition, while their annual savings rates and investment results varied during the last 17 years, they have accumulated $1,298,246 in retirement savings in addition to their Social Security benefits and Carol's defined-benefit pension. This was possible through increasing their annual savings rate, especially after their children graduated from college, and through following a disciplined investment strategy. In addition, they expected to receive gifts and other inheritance worth approximately $146,025 in 2013 dollars (Exhibit E-1).

Major Recurring Expense Categories	Detailed Budget for First Year of Retirement (1996)		Detailed Budget for First Year of Retirement (2013)**	
Housing:				
Mortgage	$0		$ 0	
Homeowners Insurance	$1,700		$3,101	
Utilities	$3,700		$6,750	
Maintenance	$3,000		$5,473	
Property Tax	$4,500		$8,210	
Total		$12,900		$23,525
Food		$6,500		$11,858
Clothing		$3,000		$5,473
Health Care		$6,500		$13,261
Transportation				
Car Payments	$2,200		$4,013	
Gas	$2,400		$4,379	
Maintenance	$600		$1,095	
Parking	$200		$365	
Total		$5,400		$9,852
Education		$0		$0
Insurance				
Life/Disability	$0		$0	
Auto	$1,000		$0	
Total		$1,000		$1,824
Travel/Vacations		$12,700		$23,170
Recreation/Entertainment		$7,500		$13,683
Taxes				
State and Local	$10,000		$26,258*	
Payroll	$0		$0	
Total		$10,000		$26,258*
Savings		$0		$0
Other		$1,000		$1,824
TOTAL		$66,500		$130,728*

Supplemental Retirement Expenses	Value 1996	Value 2013
Retirement Condo	$100,000	$215,000*
Country Club	$15,000	$30,000
Dream Trip	$7,600	$15,000
Family Assistance	$40,000	$90,000*
Children's Inheritance (Minimum)	$25,000	$25,000
TOTAL	$187,600	$375,000*

*Adjusted for 2013 actual versus 1996 estimated expenses (per the Epilogue).
** Assuming 3.6% in inflation instead of 4%.

(Continued)

Exhibit E-1   James' and Carol's total estimated retirement expenses worksheet year 2013

On the family front, Carol's mother and father were divorced about 10 years ago and Carol's father passed away about six months ago. Unfortunately, Carol's dad had a long and expensive bout with heart disease before he passed. This served to deplete his assets. Carol's mother is still living but needs financial support to the tune of about

Current ages	63/62	
Retirement ages	63/62	
Years to retirement	0	
Life expectancy	84	(See Appendix C—Use the longer life expectancy for you or your spouse and add at least two to five years to this number to be conservative.)
Years in retirement	22	(Use the larger of you or your spouse)
Detailed budget total for first year of retirement	$130,728	(Exhibit E-1 Expenses)
Adjustment for higher cost of living ("COL") in retirement city, if greater than current city	N/A	(Appendix D)
Supplemental retirement expenses total	$375,000	(Exhibit E-1 Expenses)

Exhibit E-1 *(Continued)* (Retirement) James' and Carol's translation worksheet

$1,700 per month in 2013 dollars. James and Carol aren't sure how long she'll need their help, but it probably will be for about five years (Exhibit E-1).

James' mother passed away from cancer about two years ago. His father is still alive and has adequate assets to support himself. He is gifting them $10,000 per year and may leave them additional funds when he passes. While they aren't positive how much they will ultimately receive, they decide to include their best estimate in their retirement plan.

James' and Carol's two kids are well established in their careers and are supporting themselves. They have their own families and are engaged in their own retirement planning efforts. James' stepson is also doing fine and is not likely to need any financial support.

Based on all of these changes, especially the increase in the Social Security early retirement and the Medicare normal retirement ages, James and Carol estimate that they may need to delay their retirement somewhat.

In order to assess this, they recomplete the retirement gap model (see Exhibit E-1) assuming a 6 percent average annual rate of return in their savings during their retirement years. This calculation shows that they have an estimated gap of $238,603 in 2013 dollars. Since they can't come up with the additional funds before their planned retirement date, they estimate that they can either delay their retirement for one and a half years or work part-time for three to four years. By delaying their retirement, they will receive higher Social Security benefits when they do retire. In addition, they will add to rather than draw on their retirement savings during their additional working period. They decide they will delay their retirement because they don't want to have to work after they retire.

Elements	Amount
Social Security benefits for first year of retirement:	
James	$24,250*
Carol	$17,750*
Employer-sponsored pension—annual payment:	
James	$0**
Carol	$25,000
Employer-sponsored savings program—401(k)—balance:	
James	$548,388***
Carol	$308,196***
Personal savings—IRA—balance:	
James	$119,143**
Carol	$150,687***
Other retirement savings—balance	$38,958******
Gifts/Inheritance	$146,025*******
Earnings from continued employment:	
James	$0
Carol	$0

*Adjusted for a 15% versus 20% reduction in Social Security benefits.
***These balances assume James and Carol contributed varying 401(k) amounts each year and received a 50% match on their contributions on the first 6% of their pay, and that they earned an 8.5% annual rate of return. Thus, after combining their yearly contributions with their beginning balances, their money grew to the amounts shown.
****This balance results from the growth of James's $20,000 beginning balance and contribution of $2,000 per year for 12 years with an 8.5% annual rate of return.
*****This balance results from the growth of Carol's $20,000 beginning balance and $2,000 annual contribution over 17 years with an 8.5% annual rate of return.
******This balance is the result of the beginning balance of $20,000 and earning a 4% annual after tax rate of return.
*******James and Carol expect this inheritance at about the time of their retirement.

(Continued)

Exhibit E-1 *(Continued)* (Retirement) James' and Carol's complete retirement resources worksheet

Better late than never. At least they will be able to have a reasonable standard of living in their retirement years. They're glad they read that retirement security book in 1996 and decided to follow its plan. They only wish they had started their planning efforts sooner.

While James and Carol have decided to delay their retirement for one and a half years, they are confident that they will enjoy their retirement years when they do retire. This will help both their and their children's piece of mind for many years to come. Have a great retirement James and Carol; you've earned it.

Step 1: Determine the amount needed in savings to fund the detailed budget total for the first year of retirement.

Detailed budget total for first year of retirement	$ 130,728	(Exhibit 14-1—Expenses)
Social Security annual benefit:	− $ 42,000	(Exhibit 14-1—Resources)
Employer-sponsored pension annual payment:	− $ 25,000	(Exhibit 14-1—Resources)
Result—Amount needed in savings to fund first year detailed budget:	$ 63,728	

Step 2: Using the result from Step 1, refer to the chart in Exhibit 11-1 to determine the amount of savings needed to fund annual retirement budget.

Amount: $ 1,175,000

Step 3: Add the value of the supplemental retirement expenses (Exhibit 14-1—translation) to the amount in Step 2.

Amount from Step 2:	$ 1,175,000	
Value of the supplemental retirement expenses:	$ 375,000	*(Exhibit 14-1—Translation)
Sum:	$ 1,550,000	

*This approach assumes that all of the supplemental retirement expenses will be covered in the first year of retirement.

Step 4: Determine the value of current savings.

401(k)	$ 856,584	(Exhibit 14-1—Resources)
IRA	$ 269,830	(Exhibit 14-1—Resources)
Other savings	$ 38,958	*(Exhibit 14-1—Resources)
Inheritance	$ 146,025	*(Exhibit 14-1—Resources)
Sum:	$ 1,311,397	

Step 5: Subtract the sum in Step 3 from the sum in Step 4.

Sum (Step 4)	$ 1,311,397
Sum (Step 3)	$(1,550,000)
Difference = retirement surplus (deficit)	$ (238,603)

Exhibit E-1 *(Continued)* (Retirement) James' and Carol's retirement gap (difference between retirement resources and retirement needs)

Benefit (PIA) Projections

Year Retired	Earnings in Previous Year[1]			Worker's Annual Unreduced Benefit Amount[2]		
	Low	Average	Maximum	Low	Average	Maximum
1996	$ 11,103	$ 24,673	$ 61,200	$ 6,461	$ 10,660	$ 15,016
1997	11,546	25,657	62,700	6,823	11,263	16,004
1998	12,029	26,731	65,100	6,932	11,444	16,390
1999	12,511	27,802	67,800	7,185	11,855	17,103
2000	13,023	28,939	70,500	7,487	12,362	17,984
2001	13,589	30,199	73,500	7,814	12,917	18,937
2002	14,211	31,579	76,500	8,187	13,521	19,974
2003	14,879	33,065	79,800	8,560	14,123	21,022
2004	15,599	34,655	83,400	8,934	14,761	22,117
2005	16,371	36,380	87,300	9,331	15,423	23,262
2006	17,190	38,199	91,500	9,764	16,122	24,490
2007	18,049	40,109	96,000	10,222	16,892	25,826
2008	18,952	42,115	100,800	10,716	17,710	27,246
2009	19,899	44,220	105,900	11,257	18,590	28,764
2010	20,894	46,431	111,300	11,811	19,517	30,341
2011	21,939	48,753	116,700	12,401	20,492	32,002
2012	23,036	51,191	122,700	13,027	21,516	33,760
2013	24,188	53,750	128,700	13,678	22,599	35,602
2014	25,397	56,438	135,300	14,364	23,731	37,541
2015	26,667	59,260	141,900	15,074	24,910	39,503
2016	28,000	62,223	149,100	15,833	26,151	41,562
2017	29,400	65,334	156,600	16,627	27,463	43,705
2018	30,870	68,600	164,400	17,458	28,836	45,944
2019	32,414	72,030	172,500	18,337	30,281	48,256
2020	34,034	75,632	181,200	19,252	31,797	50,677
2021	35,736	79,413	190,200	20,215	33,387	53,241
2022	37,523	83,384	199,800	21,227	35,060	55,914
2023	39,399	87,553	209,700	22,286	36,807	58,719
2024	41,369	91,931	220,200	23,394	38,649	61,656
2025	43,437	96,528	231,300	24,573	40,587	64,739
2026	45,609	101,354	243,000	25,802	42,621	67,978
2027	47,890	106,422	255,000	27,090	44,741	71,385
2028	50,284	111,743	267,900	28,450	46,980	74,949
2029	52,798	117,330	281,100	29,871	49,328	78,694
2030	55,438	123,196	295,200	31,364	51,808	82,619
2031	58,210	129,356	309,900	32,930	54,385	86,748
2032	61,121	135,824	325,500	34,579	57,106	91,094
2033	64,177	142,615	341,700	36,312	59,971	95,646
2034	67,386	149,746	358,800	38,131	62,969	100,402
2035	70,755	157,233	376,800	40,033	66,112	105,386
2040	90,303	200,674	480,900	51,098	84,377	134,186

Benefit projections for steady workers retiring at age 65 (*Source: CCH-Social Security Explained, 1996.*)

Year Retired	Earnings in Previous Year[1]			Worker's Annual Unreduced Benefit Amount[2]		
	Low	Average	Maximum	Low	Average	Maximum
2045	115,252	256,116	613,800	65,209	107,697	171,076
2050	147,094	326,876	783,300	83,233	137,449	218,309
2055	187,734	417,186	999,900	106,229	175,434	278,629
2060	239,601	532,446	1,275,900	135,583	223,907	355,613
2065	305,798	679,551	1,628,700	173,039	285,758	453,860
2070	390,284	867,299	2,078,400	220,861	364,715	579,268

[1] "Low" yearly earnings are defined through 1982 as earnings at the minimum wage for 2080 hours. "Average" earnings are based upon wages reported to the Social Security Administration. "Maximum" earnings are amounts equal to the wage base for each year.

[2] This table projects upreduced benefits for "steady" workers who retire in January of their retirement year. Caution: the unreduced amounts shown are projected from current estimates.

A Brief History of Government Regulation of Private Pensions

Legislation governing private pension plans was only sporadic until passage of the Employee Retirement Income Security Act (ERISA) in 1974. Since then, however, pension law has been subject to incessant revision by Congress.

What follows is only a thumbnail sketch of the evolution of private pension regulation. However, it is sufficient to demonstrate how obsessively Congress has tinkered with the law and how complicated that law has become.

BEFORE ERISA

1. *Revenue Act of 1921.* Deferred tax (until benefit disbursement) on contributions to, and income from, stock bonus or profit-sharing plans established for employees. The *Revenue Act of 1926* extended the concession to other pension plans.

2. *Revenue Act of 1938.* Denied tax-exempt status to any pension plan that revoked pension promises to its participants. This legislation responded to the problem of plans being terminated so that the funds could be used for purposes other than meeting pension obligations.

3. *Revenue Act of 1942.* Responded to concerns about discrimination against rank-and-file employees by establishing participation tests.

4. *Welfare and Pension Plans Disclosure Act of 1958.* Required pension plan documents and annual reports to be submitted to the

Secretary of Labor and to plan participants. The objective was to make fraud and other maladministration of plans more easily detectable.

5. *Self-Employed Individual Retirement Act of 1962 (Keogh Act).* Expanded tax-favored retirement plans to include unincorporated small business and the self-employed.

EMPLOYEE RETIREMENT INCOME SECURITY ACT OF 1974 (ERISA)

1. Concerns addressed by legislation:
   a. Plans were exclusionary, with limits on participation and vesting of benefits.
   b. Some plans were inadequately funded to meet their obligations.
   c. There were insufficient incentives for some employers to offer pension plans.
   d. Some plans were not administered according to acceptable fiduciary standards.
   e. Pension benefits for key employees were sometimes viewed as excessive in relation to perceived retirement needs.
   f. Pensions were not always protected during takeovers or other kinds of company restructuring.

2. Major provisions:
   a. Required more *information* to be provided by employers to plan participants: an easily intelligible plan description, subsequent plan modifications, an annual financial report, and a statement of the participant's accrued benefits upon request. This strengthened the provisions of the 1958 disclosure act, which was formally repealed.
   b. Strengthened *participation* rules. Required that employees 25 years old and over with one year of service could not be excluded from a plan.
   c. Established *vesting* rules. Employers could choose one of three alternative formulas:
      (1) Full vesting after 10 years with no vesting until then.
      (2) Graded vesting, achieving 100 percent after 15 years of service.

(3) The "rule of 45": at least 50 percent vesting when the employee's age and years of service add to 45, increasing by 10 percent each succeeding year until full vesting is attained.

d. Required that a *joint and survivor annuity* be provided to an employee retiring at the normal age unless the employee specifically waived that right.

e. Set *minimum funding* rules, by requiring that the normal cost of a pension plan be funded currently. Past service costs were to be amortized over 30 or 40 years.

f. Set *fiduciary standards.* Plan assets had to be invested prudently and for the sole benefit of plan participants. Relevant financial and participation data must be provided periodically to the government.

g. Allowed a person not covered by a pension plan to establish an *individual retirement account (IRA).* IRA contributions up to the lesser of $1,500 or 15 percent of earned income would be tax-deductible.

h. *Limited contributions* to profit-sharing and money purchase plans to the lesser of 25 percent of annual compensation or $25,000.

i. *Limited annual pension benefits* that could be paid to highly compensated employees to the lesser of $75,000 or 100 percent of average compensation for the three years of highest career earnings.

j. Established the *Pension Benefit Guaranty Corporation (PBGC).* Purchase of insurance was made mandatory for most plans receiving tax concessions. The PBGC guaranteed payment of vested benefits to a certain level. The premium was set at $1 per plan participant.

REVENUE ACT OF 1978

1. Contained incentives to encourage smaller firms to set up pension plans for their employees.

2. Major provisions:

a. Established *cash or deferred arrangements (CODAs)* by adding § 401(k) to the Internal Revenue Code.

b. Established *simplified employee pensions (SEPs),* in which the employer sets up and finances IRAs for eligible employees.

However, the maximum contribution limit, $7,500, was higher than for IRAs.

   c. Created *tax-credit ESOPs*, or *TRASOPs*, a form of employee stock ownership plan whereby an employer could receive a tax credit equal to contributions.

MULTIEMPLOYER PENSION PLAN AMENDMENTS ACT OF 1980 (MEPPAA)

1. This legislation was designed to address underfunding of multi-employer pension plans.
2. Major provisions:
   a. Reduced the incentive for individual employers to withdraw from multiemployer plans by obliging them to continue funding the liability of workers they had hired in the past.
   b. Increased PBGC premiums for multiemployer plans.
   c. Required faster funding of unfunded liabilities.

ECONOMIC RECOVERY TAX ACT OF 1981 (ERTA)

1. Contained further incentives to increase pension saving:
   a. Replaced TRASOPs with *payroll-based ESOPs (PAYSOPs)*, whereby an employer received a tax credit equal to a percentage of payroll.
   b. Commercial lenders facilitating *leveraged ESOPs* were allowed to deduct a portion of their interest income on these loans. This effectively lowered the cost of setting up an ESOP.
   c. Permitted *IRAs for all workers,* and raised the *contribution limit* from $1,500 to $2,000.
   d. Increased *limit on contributions to SEPs* from $7,500 to $15,000 per participant.

TAX EQUITY AND FISCAL RESPONSIBILITY ACT OF 1982 (TEFRA)

1. This legislation signaled a shift in pension policy away from concerns about pension security and the adequacy of retirement income toward measures to reduce tax revenue loss.

2. Major provisions:

a. Reduced *contribution limits for defined-contribution plans* to the lesser of 25 percent of compensation or $30,000.

b. Reduced *maximum annual pensions from defined-benefit plans* from $136,425 to the lesser of 100 percent of average cash compensation in the three years of highest earnings or $90,000.

c. For *defined-contribution plans integrated with Social Security*, contributions based on that part of income *above* the Social Security taxable wage base (the so-called *integration level* or *breakpoint*) could not exceed contributions in respect of income *below* (the *base contribution percentage*) by more than 5.4 percent.

d. Introduced *top-heavy rules*. A top-heavy plan was defined as one in which 60 percent of accumulated benefits had accrued to key employees (officers and highly compensated employees). Top-heavy plans had to comply with special standards for vesting, contributions and benefits, and Social Security integration.

DEFICIT REDUCTION ACT OF 1984 (DEFRA)

1. Major provision:

Delayed *indexing of contribution and benefit limits* until 1988.

RETIREMENT EQUITY ACT OF 1984 (REA)

1. Major provisions:

a. Strengthened *participation rules* by lowering the minimum age a firm can require for enrollment in a plan from 25 to 21; the law also lowered the minimum age for vesting service from 22 to 18.

b. An employee could now have a *break in service* of up to five consecutive years or the period of eligibility or vesting service accumulated prior to the break without losing that eligibility or vesting service. Maternity and paternity leaves were to be treated as though the employee was still at work through the period of absence.

c. Greater *survivor protection:*

(1) Preretirement death benefit was extended to all vested employees.

(2) Written spousal consent was required to exclude death benefits in order to obtain a more generous pension.

(3) On some domestic relations orders, private pensions could be divided upon divorce.

SINGLE EMPLOYER PENSION PLAN AMENDMENTS ACT OF 1986 (SEPPAA)

1. Congress enacted SEPPAA largely because of the moral hazard implicit in the pension insurance system, whereby under existing law, it was possible for a firm to terminate a pension plan and shift the unfunded liabilities onto the PBGC.

2. Major provisions:

   a. Raised *PBGC premium.*

   b. Limited the circumstances under which a *voluntary plan termination* could occur:

      (1) Standard termination: A voluntary termination in which liabilities were covered by assets.

      (2) Distressed termination: Permitted at the discretion of the PBGC. Required the plan administrator to show that the firm was financially unable to continue the plan.

TAX REFORM ACT OF 1986 (TRA)

1. Major provisions:

   a. The minimum *vesting* requirement was now defined by the following two options:

      (1) Five-year cliff.

      (2) Graded, under which participants are 20 percent vested after three years, with an additional 20 percent each subsequent year until full vesting is attained after seven years.

   b. Where plan *vesting* was 100 percent upon enrollment, an employer could now require only *two* years of service before enrolling an employee.

   c. Instituted a 10 percent *tax penalty* on distributions made prior to age 59½.

   d. Established a 10 percent *excise tax on excess pension assets* that reverted to the employer upon termination of a pension plan.

e. For participants in employer-sponsored pension plans whose adjusted gross income was greater than $25,000 ($40,000 for a married couple filing jointly), pretax *IRA contributions* were phased out.

f. Limited the amount of *compensation that could be considered* in contribution or benefit calculations of $200,000, the same as for top-heavy plans.

g. Temporarily capped *contributions to defined-contribution plans* at $30,000.

h. Reduced the limit on employee contributions to *401(k) plans* from $30,000 to $7,000.

i. Changed rules for *integration* of plans with Social Security:

  (1) For a defined-contribution plan, contributions in respect of compensation *above* the integration level could not exceed the base contribution percentage by more than the lesser of the base contribution percentage or 5.7 percent.

  (2) For a defined-benefit *excess* plan, the excess benefit percentage could not exceed the base percentage by more than the lesser of the base benefit percentage or .75 percent.

  (3) For a defined-benefit *offset* plan, the maximum offset could not exceed the lesser of 50 percent of the benefit accrued without regard to the offset or .75 percent of final average compensation multiplied by years of service.

j. New *coverage* rules were introduced. One of three tests now had to be satisfied:

  (1) Percentage test: The plan must cover at least 70 percent of all non-highly compensated employees.

  (2) Ratio test: The percentage of non-highly compensated employees covered under a plan must be at least 70 percent of the percentage of highly compensated employees covered.

  (3) Average benefits percentage test: Both of the following must be satisfied to pass this test:

   (a) The plan must cover a nondiscriminatory classification of employees.

   (b) The ratio of employer-provided benefits or contributions to the participant's compensation for non-highly compensated employees must be at least 70 percent that of highly compensated employees.

k. A new *nondiscrimination* rule was introduced for 401(k) plans. The average ratio of contributions to compensation of the highly compensated group cannot exceed:

   (1) 125 percent of the ratio of the rank-and-file group if the ratio for the latter group is 8 percent or more.

   (2) 200 percent of the ratio of the rank-and-file group if the ratio for the latter group is 2 percent or more.

   (3) 2 percent in all other cases.

l. Profit-sharing plans could no longer apply the unused portion of their prior year contribution limit (15 percent of the cash compensation of plan participants) to exceed their contribution limit in another year.

OMNIBUS BUDGET RECONCILIATION ACT OF 1986

1. Major provisions:

   a. Benefit accruals could no longer be frozen beyond normal retirement age.

   b. Employees hired after age 60 could no longer be excluded from participation.

OMNIBUS BUDGET RECONCILIATION ACT OF 1987 (OBRA87)

1. Major provisions:

   a. Increased the *PBGC premium* from $8.50 to $16 per participant, plus an additional premium of $6 per $1,000 of unfunded liability (although the premium was capped at $50 per participant).

   b. Introduced *quarterly contribution requirements.*

   c. The *period for amortizing* experience gains and losses was reduced from 15 to 5 years.

   d. Introduced a new *minimum contribution standard* for underfunded defined-benefit plans with more than 100 participants. The minimum contribution may henceforth include a "deficit reduction contribution" that would effectively speed up the funding of underfunded plans.

e. The *full-funding limitation* for defined-benefit plans was capped at 150 percent of termination liabilities. As a consequence of rising asset values, many firms were unable to make further deductible contributions.

TECHNICAL AND MISCELLANEOUS REVENUE ACT OF 1988 (TAMRA)

1. Major provision:

Increased the *excise tax* on employer reversion of assets from 10 percent to 15 percent.

OMNIBUS BUDGET RECONCILIATION ACT OF 1989 (OBRA89)

1. Major provision:

Defined-benefit *plan valuations* would now be required annually instead of triennially.

OMNIBUS BUDGET RECONCILIATION ACT OF 1990 (OBRA90)

1. Major provision:

Enabled employers to transfer excess pension assets tax-free to an account for the current health benefit expenses of retirees. Otherwise, the excise tax on asset reversions increased to 20 percent or 50 percent unless the employer transferred a portion of the assets to a replacement plan or increased benefits under the terminating plan.

OMNIBUS BUDGET RECONCILIATION ACT OF 1993 (OBRA93)

1. Major provision:

Reduced *considered compensation* from $235,840 to $150,000.

RETIREMENT PROTECTION ACT OF 1994 (RPA, INCORPORATED IN URUGUAY ROUND AGREEMENTS ACT)

1. The Retirement Protection Act accelerated funding of the liabilities of underfunded pension plans and contained other measures that strengthened the position of the PBGC. The net effect of RPA on government revenues is positive; consequently, it was incorporated as part of the financing package for the General Agreement on Tariffs and Trade (GATT).

2. Major provisions:

   a. Delayed indexation of *dollar limits on contributions and benefits* by stipulating that inflation adjustments be implemented in round dollar amounts, rather than annually in step with the precise rate of inflation. Indexation will now occur in the following increments:

      (1) Benefit limit for a defined-benefit plan: $5,000.

      (2) Contribution limit for a defined-contribution plan: $5,000.

      (3) Limit on elective deferrals under a 401(k) plan: $500.

   b. Strengthened *minimum funding standards* for underfunded defined-benefit plans:

      (1) Increased the required contribution for underfunded new liability.

      (2) Provided for accelerated funding of *unpredictable contingent event benefits.*

      (3) Lowered the maximum interest rate that could be used for calculating plan liability to 105 percent of the weighted average of 30-year Treasury securities, for the four most recent years prior to the plan year.

      (4) Mandated use of the 1983 Group Annuity Mortality Table for determination of current plan liability.

   c. Prohibited certain underfunded plans from changing actuarial assumptions for determining current liability without first gaining approval of the Secretary of the Treasury.

   d. Prohibited an employer in bankruptcy from amending an underfunded plan to increase benefits unless the increase became effective after the planned date of the firm's reorganization.

e. Authorized the PBGC to obtain certain information from sponsors of underfunded plans that would assist the PBGC in determining plan assets and liabilities.

f. Gave the PBGC authority to sue plan sponsors to enforce minimum funding requirements where the amount of the deficient contributions exceeds $1 million.

g. Phased out, over three years, the cap on the variable part of the PBGC premium.

h. Required employers who pay the variable premium to notify plan participants of the plan's funded status and the extent of the PBGC's guaranty in the event of plan termination.

SMALL BUSINESS JOB PROTECTION ACT OF 1996

1. This legislation involved a number of major pension provisions which were designed to:

   a. Simplify existing tax rules relating to qualified pension and savings plans;

   b. Encourage adequate pension savings, including creation of a new "SIMPLE" salary reduction plan for small employers;

   c. Discourage lump sum distributions;

   d. Expand the availability of ESOPs; and

   e. Address certain other policy issues.

2. The major provisions of this bill:

   a. Simplified the tax non-discrimination rules for Section 401(k) plans, including permitting employers to adopt one of two safe-harbor rules that would eliminate the need to perform annual non-discrimination testing and simplifying the definition of highly compensated employee;

   b. Repealed the combined plan benefit limit (i.e., Section 415(e)) effective for years beginning in 2000;

   c. Created new and simplified salary reduction plans (SIMPLE 401(k) plans and SIMPLE IRAs) for employers with 100 or fewer employees under which employees may make deductible contributions of up to $6,000 (indexed). Generally, the employers must match the employees' contributions up to 3 percent of compensation. All employees earning at least $5,000 with 2 years of service would be eligible, contributions are fully

d. Waived the 15 percent excise tax on excess distributions from qualified plans and IRA's for the years 1997–1999;

e. Repealed the 5 year income averaging option for lump sum distributions and the $5,000 death benefit exclusion effective in the year 2000;

f. Extended ESOPs to sub-chapter S corporations;

g. Eliminated the minimum distribution requirement for employees who reach age 70½ and continue to work, except for 5 percent owners and distributions from IRA's effective in 1997. Any payments delayed past age 70½ must be actuarially adjusted.

h. Required certain makeup contributions on behalf of employees returning to an employer following a leave for service in uniform (e.g., Desert Storm) and permits employees to makeup missed salary deferrals.

i. Modified the definition of compensation in connection with the 25 percent of compensation limit to include pre-tax contributions to a cafeteria plan or Code Section 457 plan effective in 1998; and,

j. Extended Section 401(k) arrangements to not-for-profit employers.

(Sources: Who Will Pay for Your Retirement: The Looming Crisis, Committee for Economic Development (1995). Arthur Andersen LLP—Small Business Job Protection Act of 1996.)

Estimated Life Expectancies

Life Expectancy

Age in 1990 (Years)	Expectation of Life in Years				
		White		Black	
	Total	Male	Female	Male	Female
At birth	75.8	73.2	79.8	65.0	73.9
1	75.4	72.8	79.3	65.2	74.1
2	74.5	71.8	78.3	64.3	73.1
3	73.5	70.9	77.3	63.4	72.2
4	72.5	69.9	76.3	62.4	71.2
5	71.6	68.9	75.4	61.4	70.3
6	70.6	67.9	74.4	60.5	69.3
7	69.6	66.9	73.4	59.5	68.3
8	68.6	65.9	72.4	58.5	67.3
9	67.6	65.0	71.4	57.5	66.3
10	66.6	64.0	70.4	56.5	65.4
11	65.6	63.0	69.4	55.5	64.4
12	64.6	62.0	68.4	64.5	63.4
13	63.7	61.0	67.4	53.6	62.4
14	62.7	60.0	66.5	52.6	61.4
15	61.7	59.1	65.5	51.7	60.4
16	60.7	58.1	64.5	50.7	59.5
17	59.8	57.2	63.5	49.8	58.5
18	58.8	56.2	62.5	48.9	57.5
19	57.9	55.3	61.6	48.1	56.6
20	56.9	54.3	60.6	47.2	55.6
21	56.0	53.4	59.6	46.3	54.6
22	55.1	52.5	58.7	45.5	53.7
23	54.1	51.6	57.7	44.6	52.7
24	53.2	50.6	56.7	43.8	51.8
25	52.2	49.7	55.7	42.9	50.8
26	51.3	48.8	54.8	42.1	49.9
27	50.4	47.8	53.8	41.2	48.9
28	49.4	46.9	52.8	40.4	48.0
29	48.5	46.0	51.8	39.5	47.1
30	47.5	45.1	50.9	38.7	46.1
31	46.6	44.1	49.9	37.8	45.2
32	45.7	43.2	48.9	37.0	44.3
33	44.7	42.3	48.0	36.2	43.4
34	43.8	41.4	47.0	35.3	42.4
35	42.9	40.5	46.0	34.5	41.5
36	42.0	39.8	45.1	33.7	40.6
37	41.0	38.7	44.1	32.9	39.7
38	40.1	37.8	43.2	32.1	38.8
39	39.2	36.9	42.2	31.3	37.9

(Continued)

Age in 1990	Expectation of Life in Years				
		White		Black	
(Years)	Total	Male	Female	Male	Female
40	38.3	36.0	41.2	30.5	37.1
41	37.4	35.1	40.3	29.7	36.2
42	36.5	34.2	39.3	28.9	35.3
43	35.6	33.3	38.4	28.2	34.4
44	34.7	32.4	37.5	27.4	33.6
45	33.8	31.5	36.5	26.7	32.7
46	32.9	30.6	35.6	25.9	31.9
47	32.0	29.7	34.7	25.2	31.0
48	31.1	28.8	33.7	24.4	30.2
49	30.2	28.0	32.8	23.7	29.3
50	29.3	27.1	31.9	23.0	28.5
51	28.5	26.3	31.0	22.3	27.7
52	27.6	25.4	30.1	21.5	26.8
53	26.8	24.6	29.2	20.8	26.0
54	25.9	23.7	28.3	20.1	25.3
55	25.1	22.9	27.5	19.5	24.5
56	24.3	22.1	26.6	18.8	23.7
57	23.5	21.3	25.7	18.2	23.0
58	22.7	20.6	24.9	17.6	22.2
59	21.9	19.8	24.1	16.9	21.5
60	21.1	19.1	23.2	16.3	20.8
61	20.4	18.3	22.4	15.8	20.1
62	19.7	17.6	21.6	15.2	19.4
63	18.9	16.9	20.8	14.6	18.7
64	18.2	16.2	20.0	14.1	18.0
65	17.5	15.5	19.3	13.5	17.4
70	14.2	12.4	15.6	11.0	14.3
75	11.1	9.6	12.2	8.9	11.4
80	8.5	7.2	9.2	6.8	8.6
85 and over	6.2	5.3	6.6	5.1	6.3

(*Source:* U.S. National Center for Health Statistics, *Vital Statistics of the United States,* annual; and unpublished data.)

Statistical Abstract of the United States, 1995 (Arthur Andersen Library).

ACCRA Cost-of-Living Index Fourth Quarter 1995

Component Index Weights	100% Composite Index
MSA/PMSA Urban Area and State:	
Anchorage, AK, MSA	
Anchorage, AK	125.6
Nonmetropolitan Areas	
Fairbanks, AK	126.3
Juneau, AK	136.6
Kodiak, AK	150.0
Anniston, AL, MSA	
Anniston/Calhoun County, AL	90.7
Birmingham, AL, MSA	
Birmingham, AL, MSA	98.7
Decatur, AL, MSA	
Decatur-Hartselle, AL	92.8
Gadsden, AL, MSA	
Gadsden, AL	91.9
Huntsville, AL, MSA	
Huntsville, AL	97.7
Montgomery, AL, MSA	
Montgomery, AL	92.3
Nonmetropolitan Areas	
Cullman County, AL	90.3
Fayetteville-Springdale-Rogers, AR, MSA	
Fayetteville, AR	95.3

Component Index Weights	100% Composite Index
MSA/PMSA Urban Area and State:	
Fort Smith, AR-OK, MSA	
Fort Smith, AR	88.5
Nonmetropolitan Areas	
Hot Springs, AR	90.6
Jonesboro, AR	87.2
Flagstaff, AZ-UT, MSA	
Flagstaff, AZ	108.5
Las Vegas, NV-AZ, MSA	
Lake Havasu City, AZ	99.7
Phoenix-Mesa, AZ, MSA	
Phoenix, AZ	101.4
Scottsdale, AZ	103.0
Tucson, AZ, MSA	
Tucson, AZ	98.5
Yuma, AZ	
Yuma, AZ	96.3
Nonmetropolitan Areas	
Prescott-Prescott Valley, AZ	105.2
Bakersfield, CA, MSA	
Bakersfield, CA	105.1
Fresno, CA, MSA	
Fresno, CA	107.3
Los Angeles-Long Beach, CA, PMSA	
Los Angeles-Long Beach, CA PMSA	116.7
Riverside-San Bernardino, CA, PMSA	
Palm Springs, CA	114.5
Riverside City, CA	106.4
San Diego, CA, MSA	
San Diego, CA	120.2
San Francisco, CA, PMSA	
Marin County, CA	160.5
San Francisco, CA	172.0
San Mateo County, CA	149.8
Santa Barbara-Santa Maria-Lompoc, CA, MSA	
Lompoc, CA	111.1
Santa Rosa, CA, PMSA	
Santa Rosa, CA	129.9

Component Index Weights	100% Composite Index
MSA/PMSA Urban Area and State:	
Visalia-Tular-Porterville, CA, MSA	
Visalia, CA	108.1
Boulder-Longmont, CO, PMSA	
Boulder, CO	119.1
Longmont, CO	102.0
Colorado Springs, CO, MSA	
Colorado Springs, CO	100.6
Denver, CO, PMSA	
Denver, CO, PMSA	103.9
Grand Junction, CO, MSA	
Grand Junction, CO	96.1
Pueblo, CO, MSA	
Pueblo, CO	91.1
Nonmetropolitan Areas	
Glenwood Springs, CO	115.2
Gunnison, CO	103.9
Washington, DC-MD-VA-WV, PMSA	
Washington, DC-MD-VA-WV, PMSA	123.4
Dover, DE, MSA	
Dover, DE	102.8
Wilmington-Newark, DE-MD, PMSA	
Wilmington, DE	108.4
Fort Myers-Cape Coral, FL, MSA	
Fort Myers-Cape Coral, FL, MSA	98.3
Fort Walton Beach, FL, MSA	
Fort Walton Beach, FL	100.9
Jacksonville, FL, MSA	
Jacksonville, FL	95.2
Miami, FL, PMSA	
Miami/Dade County, FL	109.3
Orlando, FL, MSA	
Orlando, FL	96.3
Panama City, FL, MSA	
Panama City, FL	96.7
Pensacola, FL, MSA	
Pensacola, FL	95.9

Component Index Weights	100% Composite Index
MSA/PMSA Urban Area and State:	

Sarasota-Bradenton, FL, MSA
| Sarasota-Bradenton, FL | 98.9 |

Tallahassee, FL, MSA
| Tallahassee, FL | 101.8 |

Tampa-St. Petersburg-Clearwater, FL, MSA
| Tampa, FL | 95.6 |

West Palm Beach-Boca Raton, FL, MSA
| West Palm Beach, FL | 105.5 |

Albany, GA, MSA
| Albany, GA | 90.9 |

Atlanta, GA, MSA
| Atlanta, GA | 99.2 |
| Carrollton, GA | 92.9 |

Augusta-Aiken, GA-SC, MSA
| Augusta-Aiken, GA-SC | 92.7 |

Macon, GA, MSA
| Warner Robins, GA | 98.5 |

Savannah, GA
| Savannah, GA | 93.9 |

Nonmetropolitan Areas
Americus, GA	92.7
Bainbridge, GA	91.5
Douglas, GA	89.4
Tifton, GA	93.9
Valdosta, GA	92.1

Honolulu, HI, MSA
| Honolulu, HI, MSA | 177.4 |

Cedar Rapids, IA, MSA
| Cedar Rapids, IA | 95.9 |

Des Moines, IA, MSA
| Des Moines, IA | 95.4 |

Dubuque, IA, MSA
| Dubuque, IA | 98.2 |

Iowa City, IA, MSA
| Iowa City-Coralville, IA | 107.0 |

Waterloo-Cedar Falls, IA, MSA
| Waterloo-Cedar Falls, IA | 94.7 |

Component Index Weights	100% Composite Index
MSA/PMSA Urban Area and State:	
Nonmetropolitan Areas	
Mason City, IA	94.2
Boise City, ID, MSA	
Boise, ID	101.3
Nonmetropolitan Areas	
Idaho Falls, ID	105.3
Twin Falls, ID	99.0
Champaign-Urbana, IL	
Champaign-Urbana, IL	97.4
Davenport-Moline-Rock Island, IA-IL, MSA	
Quad-Cities, IL-IA	97.8
Decatur, IL, MSA	
Decatur, IL	93.0
Rockford, IL, MSA	
Rockford, IL	102.2
Springfield, IL, MSA	
Springfield, IL	96.3
Nonmetropolitan Areas	
Carbondale, IL	93.1
Danville, IL	95.7
DeKalb, IL	101.5
Dixon-Sterling-Rock Falls, IL	97.0
Freeport, IL	102.5
Quincy, IL	97.2
Bloomington, IN, MSA	
Bloomington, IN	96.8
Elkhart-Goshen, IN, MSA	
Elkhart-Goshen, IN	94.8
Evansville-Henderson, IN-KY, MSA	
Evansville, IN	94.5
Fort Wayne, IN, MSA	
Fort Wayne/Allen County, IN	90.8
Indianapolis, IN, MSA	
Anderson, IN	95.5
Indianapolis, IN	93.8
Muncie, IN, MSA	
Muncie, IN	99.8

Component Index Weights	100% Composite Index
MSA/PMSA Urban Area and State:	

South Bend, IN, MSA	
South Bend, IN	89.7
Nonmetropolitan Areas	
LaPorte-Michigan City, IN	96.5
Lawrence, KS, MSA	
Lawrence, KS	99.1
Wichita, KS, MSA	
Wichita, KS	92.4
Nonmetropolitan Areas	
Garden City, KS	99.8
Great Bend, KS	97.4
Hays, KS	100.8
Manhattan, KS	96.4
Salina, KS	92.5
Cincinnati, OH-KY-IN, PMSA	
Covington, KY	92.1
Clarksville-Hopkinsville, TN-KY, MSA	
Hopkinsville, KY	95.1
Evansville-Henderson, IN-KY, MSA	
Henderson, KY	93.5
Louisville, KY-IN, MSA	
Louisville, KY	92.8
Nonmetropolitan Areas	
Bowling Green, KY	92.2
Danville, KY	89.8
Murray, KY	91.6
Paducah, KY	91.8
Pikeville/Pike County, KY	99.5
Alexandria, LA, MSA	
Alexandria, LA	92.8
Baton Rouge, LA, MSA	
Baton Rouge, LA	98.5
Lafayette, LA, MSA	
Lafayette, LA	97.1
Lake Charles, LA, MSA	
Lake Charles, LA	95.0

Component Index Weights	100% Composite Index
MSA/PMSA Urban Area and State:	
Monroe, LA, MSA	
Monroe, LA	93.5
New Orleans, LA, MSA	
New Orleans, LA	94.8
Shreveport-Bossier City, LA, MSA	
Shreveport-Bossier City, LA, MSA	92.1
Boston, MA-NH, PMSA	
Boston PMSA (MA Part)	138.9
Framingham-Natick, MA	133.8
Fitchburg-Leominster, MA, PMSA	
Fitchburg-Leominster, MA, PMSA	100.2
Baltimore, MD, PMSA	
Baltimore, MD	99.1
Cumberland, MD-WV, MSA	
Cumberland, MD	98.8
Hagerstown, MD, PMSA	
Hagerstown, MD	97.9
Nonmetropolitan Areas	
Worcester County, MD	109.8
Benton Harbor, MI, MSA	
Benton Harbor-St. Joseph, MI	105.4
Detroit, MI, PMSA	
Oakland County, MI	115.9
Grand Rapids-Muskegon-Holland, MI, MSA	
Grand Rapids, MI	101.5
Holland, MI	100.8
Lansing-East Lansing, MI, MSA	
Lansing, MI	104.6
Minneapolis-St. Paul, MN-WI, MSA	
Minneapolis, MN	100.9
Rochester, MN, MSA	
Rochester, MN	97.8
St. Cloud, MN, MSA	
St. Cloud, MN, MSA	96.0

Component Index Weights	100% Composite Index
MSA/PMSA Urban Area and State:	
Columbia, MO, MSA	
Columbia, MO	93.0
Joplin, MO, MSA	
Joplin, MO, MSA	87.2
Kansas City, MO-KS, MSA	
Kansas City, MO-KS, MSA	95.5
Lee's Summit, MO	94.1
St. Joseph, MO, MSA	
St. Joseph, MO, MSA	92.7
St. Louis, MO-IL, MSA	
St. Louis, MO-IL, MSA	96.3
Springfield, MO, MSA	
Springfield, MO	91.9
Nonmetropolitan Areas	
Jefferson City, MO	89.0
Kennett, MO	83.4
Kirksville, MO	95.9
Nevada, MO	92.3
Poplar Bluff, MO	89.1
Biloxi-Gulfport-Pascagoula, MS, MSA	
Gulfport, MS,	94.4
Hattiesburg, MS, MSA	
Hattiesburg, MS	90.2
Jackson, MS, MSA	
Jackson, MS	93.3
Billings, MT, MSA	
Billings, MT	102.5
Great Falls, MT, MSA	
Great Falls, MT	97.9
Nonmetropolitan Areas	
Bozeman, MT	101.1
Helena, MT	95.2
Missoula, MT	99.9
Asheville, NC, MSA	
Asheville, NC	101.0
Charlotte-Gastonia-Rock Hill, NC-SC, MSA	
Charlotte, NC	97.4

Component Index Weights	100% Composite Index
MSA/PMSA Urban Area and State:	
Fayetteville, NC, MSA	
Fayetteville, NC	94.3
Greensboro-Winston-Salem-High Point, NC, MSA	
Burlington, NC	92.3
Winston-Salem, NC	97.8
Greenville, NC, MSA	
Greenville, NC	94.6
Hickory-Morganton-Lenoir, NC, MSA	
Hickory, NC	96.5
Raleigh-Durham-Chapel Hill, NC, MSA	
Raleigh-Durham, NC	100.3
Wilmington, NC, MSA	
Wilmington, NC	99.9
Nonmetropolitan Areas	
Marion/McDowell County, NC	90.3
Statesville, NC	97.4
Bismarck, ND, MSA	
Bismarck-Mandan, ND	99.2
Fargo-Moorhead, ND-MN, MSA	
Fargo-Moorhead, ND-MN, MSA	95.9
Grand Forks, ND-MN, MSA	
Grand Forks, ND	95.4
Nonmetropolitan Areas	
Minot, ND	94.8
Lincoln, NE, MSA	
Lincoln, NE	88.4
Omaha, ME-IA, MSA	
Omaha, NE	89.3
Nonmetropolitan Areas	
Grand Island, NE	91.9
Hastings, NE	87.9
Kearney, NE	92.1
Scottsbluff-Gering, NE	94.4
Manchester, NH, PMSA	
Manchester, NH	109.2

Component Index Weights	100% Composite Index
MSA/PMSA Urban Area and State:	
Albuquerque, NM, MSA	
Albuquerque, NM	100.7
Las Cruces, NM, MSA	
Las Cruces, NM, MSA	96.3
Santa Fe, NM, MSA	
Los Alamos, NM	122.8
Santa Fe, NM	110.8
Nonmetropolitan Areas	
Carlsbad, NM	93.0
Clovis-Portales, NM	90.8
Farmington, NM	98.5
Hobbs, NM	86.7
Roswell, NM	88.9
Las Vegas, NV-AZ, MSA	
Las Vegas, NV	102.0
Reno, NV, MSA	
Reno-Sparks, NV	112.3
Nonmetropolitan Areas	
Elko, NV	104.0
Albany-Schenectady-Troy, NY, MSA	
Albany, NY	105.2
Binghamton, NY, MSA	
Binghamton/Broome County, NY	101.7
Dutchess County, NY, PMSA	
Poughkeepsie, NY	113.6
Glens Falls, NY, MSA	
Glens Falls, NY	103.3
New York, NY, PMSA	
New York (Manhattan), NY	219.7
Westchester County, NY	138.8
Syracuse, NY, MSA	
Syracuse, NY	104.2
Utica-Rome, NY, MSA	
Utica-Rome, NY, MSA	103.1
Nonmetropolitan Areas	
Cortland, NY	113.8

Component Index Weights	100% Composite Index
MSA/PMSA Urban Area and State:	
Akron, OH, PMSA	
Akron, OH	95.3
Canton-Massillon, OH, MSA	
Canton/Stark County, OH	93.8
Cincinnati, OH-KY-IN, PMSA	
Cincinnati, OH	98.9
Columbus, OH, MSA	
Columbus, OH	107.3
Newark/Licking County, OH	94.1
Mansfield, OH, MSA	
Mansfield, OH	96.4
Parkersburg-Marietta, WV-OH, MSA	
Marietta, OH	96.1
Toledo, OH, MSA	
Toledo, OH	97.5
Youngstown-Warren, OH, MSA	
Youngstown-Warren, OH, MSA	95.7
Nonmetropolitan Areas	
Findlay, OH	97.0
Lawton, OK, MSA	
Lawton, OK	92.5
Oklahoma City, OK, MSA	
Oklahoma City, OK	92.3
Tulsa, OK, MSA	
Tulsa, OK	90.6
Nonmetropolitan Areas	
Ardmore, OK	87.3
Bartlesville, OK	92.7
Muskogee, OK	89.0
Pryor Creek, OK	87.0
Stillwater, OK	92.8
Eugene-Springfield, OR, MSA	
Eugene, OR	106.9
Portland-Vancouver, OR-WA, PMSA	
Portland, OR, PMSA	107.7
Salem, OR, PMSA	
Salem, OR	104.1

Component Index Weights	100% Composite Index
MSA/PMSA Urban Area and State:	
Nonmetropolitan Areas	
Bend, OR	103.9
Klamath Falls, OR	97.1
Allentown-Bethlehem-Easton, PA, MSA	
Allentown-Bethlehem-Easton, PA	103.6
Altoona, PA, MSA	
Altoona, PA	93.6
Erie, PA, MSA	
Erie, PA	105.7
Harrisburg-Lebanon-Carlisle, PA, MSA	
Harrisburg, PA	101.7
Lancaster, PA, MSA	
Lancaster, PA	101.2
Philadelphia, PA-NJ, PMSA	
Philadelphia, PA	101.2
Scranton-Wilkes Barre-Hazleton, PA, MSA	
Wilkes-Barre, PA	96.3
York, PA, MSA	
Hanover, PA	97.1
York County, PA	95.1
Nonmetropolitan Areas	
Chambersburg/Franklin County, PA	102.6
Providence-Fall River-Warwick, RI-MA, PMSA	
Providence, RI	114.8
Charleston-North Charleston, SC, MSA	
Charleston-N. Charleston, SC, MSA	94.8
Columbia, SC, MSA	
Columbia, SC	94.3
Florence, SC, MSA	
Florence, SC	92.2
Greenville-Spartanburg-Anderson, SC, MSA	
Spartanburg, SC	94.0
Myrtle Beach SC, MSA	
Myrtle Beach SC	96.1
Sumter, SC, MSA	
Sumter, SC	94.1

Component Index Weights	100% Composite Index
MSA/PMSA Urban Area and State:	

Nonmetropolitan Areas
Hilton Head Island, SC — 121.0

Rapid City, SD, MSA
   Rapid City, SD — 99.9
Sioux Falls, SD, MSA
   Sioux Falls, SD — 94.8
Nonmetropolitan Areas
   Vermillion, SD — 98.9

Chattanooga, TN-GA, MSA
   Chattanooga, TN — 91.6
Johnson City-Kingsport-Briston, TN-VA, MSA
   Johnson City, TN — 91.4
   Kingsport, TN — 91.2
Knoxville, TN, MSA
   Knoxville, TN — 88.6
Memphis, TN-AR-MS, MSA
   Memphis, TN — 82.7
Nashville, TN, MSA
   Nashville-Franklin, TN — 93.1
Nonmetropolitan Areas
   Cleveland, TN — 90.3
   Dyersburg, TN — 91.3
   Morristown, TN — 96.3

Abilene, TX, MSA
   Abilene, TX — 92.0
Amarillo, TX, MSA
   Amarillo, TX — 90.8
Austin-San Marcos, TX, MSA
   Georgetown, TX — 95.0
   San Marcos, TX — 96.3
Brownsville-Harlingen-San Benito, TX, MSA
   Harlingen, TX — 91.9
Bryan-College Station, TX, MSA
   Bryan-College Station, TX — 89.4
Corpus Christi, TX, MSA
   Corpus Christi, TX, MSA — 93.5

Component Index Weights	100% Composite Index
MSA/PMSA Urban Area and State:	
Dallas, TX, PMSA	
Coppell, TX	108.2
Dallas, TX, PMSA	98.2
Fort Worth-Arlington, TX, PMSA	
Fort Worth, TX	92.6
Weatherford, TX	90.8
Houston, TX, PMSA	
Houston, TX, PMSA	94.8
Killeen-Temple, TX, MSA	
Killeen, TX	89.8
Longview-Marshall, TX, MSA	
Longview, TX	95.7
Lubbock, TX, MSA	
Lubbock, TX	90.5
McAllen-Edinburg-Mission, TX, MSA	
McAllen, TX	91.7
Odessa-Midland, TX	
Midland, TX	89.7
Odessa, TX	91.2
San Antonio, TX, MSA	
San Antonio, TX	91.9
Texarkana, TX-AR, MSA	
Texarkana, TX-AR	88.5
Tyler, TX, MSA	
Tyler, TX	90.7
Victoria, TX, MSA	
Victoria, TX	89.4
Waco, TX, MSA	
Waco, TX, MSA	90.2
Wichita Falls, TX, MSA	
Wichita Falls, TX, MSA	88.9
Provo-Orem, UT, MSA	88.8
Provo-Orem, UT	99.1
Salt Lake City-Ogden, UT, MSA	
Salt Lake City, UT	96.5
Nonmetropolitan Areas	
Cedar City, UT	93.7
Logan, UT	103.6
St. George, UT	101.7

Component Index Weights	100% Composite Index
MSA/PMSA Urban Area and State:	
Johnson City-Kingsport-Bristol, TN-VA, MSA	
Bristol, VA	90.2
Norfolk-Virginia Beach-Newport News, VA-NC, MSA	
Hampton Roads/SE, VA	99.0
Richmond-Petersburg, VA, MSA	
Richmond, VA	104.0
Roanoke, VA, MSA	
Roanoke, VA	90.9
Washington, DC-MD-VA-WV, PMSA	
Fredericksburg, VA	103.8
Nonmetropolitan Areas	
Christiansburg, VA	94.7
Burlington, VT, MSA	
Burlington/Chittenden County, VT	116.9
Nonmetropolitan Areas	
Barre-Montpelier, VT	106.9
Bellingham, WA, MSA	
Bellingham, WA	106.4
Richland-Kennewick-Pasco, WA, MSA	
Richland-Kennewick-Pasco, WA	100.4
Tacoma, WA, PMSA	
Tacoma, WA	101.2
Yakima, WA, MSA	
Yakima, WA	105.4
Nonmetropolitan Areas	
Pullman, WA	106.7
Skagit County, WA	110.7
Appleton-Oshkosh-Neenah, WI, MSA	
Appleton-Oshkosh-Menasha, WI	96.4
Oshkosh, WI	98.5
Eau Claire, WI, MSA	
Eau Claire, WI	99.6
Green Bay, WI, MSA	
Green Bay, WI	97.4
Janesville-Beloit, WI, MSA	
Janesville, WI	100.8

Component Index Weights	100% Composite Index
MSA/PMSA Urban Area and State:	
Sheboygan, WI, MSA	
Sheboygan, WI	95.7
Wausau, WI, MSA	
Wausau, WI	102.5
Nonmetropolitan Areas	
Fond du Lac, WI	97.1
Marinette, WI	95.8
Marshfield, WI	99.1
Charleston, WV, MSA	
Charleston, WV, MSA	95.4
Huntington-Ashland, WV-KY-OH, MSA	
Huntington, WV	97.0
Washington, DC-MD-VA-WV, PMSA	
Martinsburg/Berkely County, WV	90.2
Casper, WY, MSA	
Casper, WY	99.7
Cheyenne, WY, MSA	
Cheyenne, WY	96.2
Nonmetropolitan Areas	
Gillette, WY	98.0
Saskatoon, SK, CMA	
Saskatoon, SK	97.2

(*Source:* ACCRA Cost of Living Index, 4th Quarter, 1995.)

Income Tax Rates and Exemptions

ALABAMA[1]

First $1,000	2.0%
Next $5,000	4.0%
Over $6,000	5.0%

ARIZONA[2, 3]

First $20,000	3.0%
Next $30,000	3.5%
Next $50,000	4.2%
Next $200,000	5.2%
$300,001 or over	5.6%

ARKANSAS

First $2,999	1.0%
Next $3,000	2.5%
Next $3,000	3.5%
Next $6,000	4.5%
Next $10,000	6.0%
$25,000 or over	7.0%

CALIFORNIA[3, 4]

$0 to $9,662	1.0%
$9,663 to $22,898	2.0%
$22,899 to $36,136	4.0%
$36,137 to $50,166	6.0%
$50,167 to $63,400	8.0%
$63,401 to $219,872	9.3%
$219,873 to $439,744	10.0%
$439,745 and over	11.0%

COLORADO[5]

5% of federal taxable income

CONNECTICUT[6]

First $4,500	3.0%
Over $4,500	4.5%

DELAWARE

$2,001 to $5,000	3.2%
Next $5,000	5.0%
Next $10,000	6.0%
Next $5,000	6.35%
Next $5,000	6.65%
Over $30,000	7.1%

DISTRICT OF COLUMBIA[7]

First $10,000	6.0%
Second $10,000	8.0%
Over $20,000	9.5%

GEORGIA[8]

First $1,000	1.0%
Next $2,000	2.0%
Next $2,000	3.0%
Next $2,000	4.0%
Next $3,000	5.0%
Over $10,000	6.0%

HAWAII[9]

First $3,000	2.0%
Next $2,000	4.0%
Next $2,000	6.0%
Next $4,000	7.25%
Next $10,000	8.0%
Next $10,000	8.75%
Next $10,000	9.5%
Over $41,000	10.0%

IDAHO[3, 10]

First $1,000	2.0%
Second $1,000	4.0%
Third $1,000	4.5%
Fourth $1,000	5.5%
Fifth $1,000	6.5%
Next $2,500	7.5%
Next $12,500	7.8%
Over $20,000	8.2%

ILLINOIS[11]

3% of taxable income

INDIANA[12]

3.4% of adjusted gross income

IOWA[13]

$0 to $1,081	0.4%
$1,082 to $2,162	0.8%
$2,163 to $4,324	2.7%
$4,325 to $9,729	5.0%
$9,730 to $16,215	6.8%
$16,216 to $21,620	7.2%
$21,621 to $32,430	7.55%
$32,431 to $48,645	8.8%
Over $48,645	9.98%

KANSAS[14]

First $30,000	3.5%
Next $30,000	6.25%
Over $60,000	6.45%

KENTUCKY

First $3,000	2.0%
Next $1,000	3.0%
Next $1,000	4.0%
Next $3,000	5.0%
$8,000 and over	6.0%

LOUISIANA[3, 16]

First $10,000	2.0%
Next $40,000	4.0%
Over $50,000	6.0%

MAINE[17]

Less than $4,150	2.0%
$4,150 to $8,249	4.5%
$8,250 to $16,499	7.0%
$16,500 or more	8.5%

MARYLAND

First $1,000	2.0%
Second $1,000	3.0%
Third $1,000	4.0%
Over $3,000	5.0%

MASSACHUSETTS

Interest, dividends, capital gains	12.0%
Five classes of capital gain income	0% to 5.0%
All other income	5.95%

MICHIGAN

4.4% of taxable income[20]

MINNESOTA[21]

$0 to $23,490	6.0%
$23,491 to $93,340	8.0%
Over $93,340	8.5%

MISSISSIPPI

First $5,000	3.0%
Next $5,000	4.0%
Over $10,000	5.0%

MISSOURI

First $1,000	1.5%
Second $1,000	2.0%
Third $1,000	2.5%
Fourth $1,000	3.0%
Fifth $1,000	3.5%
Sixth $1,000	4.0%
Seventh $1,000	4.5%
Eighth $1,000	5.0%
Ninth $1,000	5.5%
Over $9,000	6.0%

MONTANA[24]

$0 to $1,800	2% less $0
$1,801 to $3,700	3% less $18
$3,701 to $7,400	4% less $55
$7,401 to $11,100	5% less $129
$11,101 to $14,800	6% less $240
$14,801 to $18,400	7% less $388
$18,401 to $25,800	8% less $572
$25,801 to $36,900	9% less $830
$36,901 to $64,600	10% less $1,199
Over $64,900	11% less $1,845

NEBRASKA[25]

First $4,000	2.62%
Next $26,000	3.65%
Next $16,750	5.24%
Over $46,750	6.99%

NEW HAMPSHIRE[26]

	5%

NEW JERSEY[27]

First $20,000	1.4%
Next $30,000	1.75%
Next $20,000	2.45%
Next $10,000	3.5%

Next $70,000	5.525%
Over $150,000	6.37%

NEW MEXICO[3, 28]

Not over $8,000	1.7%
$8,001 to $16,000	3.2%
$16,001 to $24,000	4.7%
$24,001 to $40,000	6.0%
$40,001 to $64,000	7.1%
$64,001 to $100,000	7.9%
Over $100,000	8.5%

NEW YORK[29]

First $11,000	4.0%
Next $5,000	5.0%
Next $6,000	6.0%
Over $22,000	7.0%

NORTH CAROLINA[30]

Up to $21,250	6.0%
Next $78,750	7.0%
Over $100,000	7.75%

NORTH DAKOTA[31]

First $3,000	2.67%
Next $2,000	2.0%
Next $3,000	5.33%
Next $7,000	6.67%
Next $10,000	8.0%
Next $10,000	9.33%
Next $15,000	10.67%
Over $50,000	12.0%

OHIO

First $5,000	0.743%
Next $5,000	1.486%
Next $5,000	2.972%
Next $5,000	3.715%
Next $20,000	4.457%
Next $40,000	5.201%
Next $20,000	5.943%
Over $200,000	7.5%

OKLAHOMA[33]		VIRGINIA	
First $2,000	0.5%	First $43,000	2.0%
Next $3,000	1.0%	Next $2,000	3.0%
Next $2,500	2.0%	Next $12,000	5.0%
Next $2,300	3.0%	Over $17,000	5.75%
Next $2,400	4.0%		
Next $2,800	5.0%	WEST VIRGINIA[43]	
Next $6,000	6.0%	First $10,000	3.0%
Remainder	7.0%	Next $15,000	4.0%
		Next $15,000	4.5%
OREGON[34]		Next $20,000	6.0%
First $1,250	5.0%	Over $60,000	6.5%
Next $3,240	7.0%		
Over $5,400	9.0%	WISCONSIN[3, 44]	
		$0 to $10,000	4.9%
PENNSYLVANIA		$10,001 to $20,000	6.55%
	2.8%	$20,001 and over	6.93%

CITIES (Over 125,000)

RHODE ISLAND
27.5% of federal liability

Akron	2.0%
Baltimore	50% surtax
Birmingham	1.0%

SOUTH CAROLINA

		Cincinnati	2.1%
First $2,250	2.5%	Cleveland	2.0%
Next $2,250	3.0%	Columbus	2.0%
Next $2,250	4.0%	Dayton	2.25%
Next $2,250	5.0%	Detroit:	
Next $2,250	6.0%	Residents	3.0%
$11,250 and over	7.0%	Nonresidents	1.5%
		Flint:	
TENNESSEE[38]		Residents	1.0%
	6.0%	Nonresidents	0.5%
		Grand Rapids:	
		Residents	1.0%
UTAH[39]		Nonresidents	0.5%
First $1,500	2.55%	Kansas City, MO	1.0%
Next $1,500	3.5%	Lansing, MI:	
Next $1,500	4.4%	Residents	1.0%
Next $1,500	5.35%	Nonresidents	0.5%
Next $1,500	6.0%	Lexington-Fayette Urban	
Over $7,500	7.0%	County Government	2.25%
		Louisville	2.2%
VERMONT		Newark	1.0%
25% of federal income tax			

CITIES (Over 125,000)		Portland, OR[60]	0.6176%
New York City[57]	From 2.6% to	St. Louis	1.0%
	3.4%	San Francisco[62]	1.0% to 1.5%
Philadelphia[58]	4.86%	Toledo	2.25%
Pittsburgh (City)	1.0%	Yonkers[66]	15% surtax
Pittsburgh (School Dist.)	1.875%	Youngstown	2.0%

[1] Alabama: Rates shown are for married persons filing jointly. Single persons, heads of families, married persons filing separately, and estates or trusts are taxed at 2% of the first $500 of taxable income, 4% on the next $2,500, and 5% on any excess over $3,000. Certain multistate businesses with gross sales volumes not over $100,000: 0.25% of such sales volume.

[2] Arizona: Rates shown are for married persons filing jointly and heads of households. For single taxpayers, the rates change from 3% of the first $10,000 of taxable income to 5.6% of taxable income over $150,000.

[3] Community property state in which, in general, one-half of the community income is taxable to each spouse.

[4] California: The rates shown are the 1995 rates for residents who are joint taxpayers or surviving spouses with dependents. For single taxpayers, married persons filing separately, and fiduciaries, the rates range between 1% on the first $4,831 of taxable income and 11% on taxable income over $219,872. For unmarried heads of households, the rates range between 1% on the first $9,662 of taxable income and 11% on taxable income over $299,279. 1996 rates will be set administratively, based on inflation. A 7% alternative minimum tax is imposed.

[5] Colorado: Alternative minimum tax imposed. Qualified taxpayers may pay alternative tax of 0.5% of gross receipts from Colorado sales.

[6] Connecticut: The tax rates shown are for married individuals filing jointly. For unmarried individuals and married individuals filing separately, the rates are 3% on the first $2,250 of Connecticut taxable income and $67.50 plus 4.5% of the excess over $2,250. For heads of households, the rates are 3% of the first $3,500 of Connecticut taxable income and $105 plus 4.5% of the excess over $3,500. For trusts or estates, the rates are 4.5% of Connecticut taxable income. For tax years beginning after 1996, the tax rates are (1) for unmarried individuals and married individuals filing separately, 3% on the first $4,500 of Connecticut taxable income and $135 plus 4.5% of the excess over $4,500; (2) for heads of households, 3% of the first $7,000 of Connecticut taxable income and $210 plus 4.5% of the excess over $7,000; (3) for married individuals, 3% of the first $9,000 of Connecticut taxable income and $180 plus 4.5% of the excess over $9,000; and (4) trusts or estates, 4.5% of Connecticut taxable income.

Additional state minimum tax imposed on resident individuals, trusts, and estates is equal to the amount by which the Connecticut minimum tax exceeds the Connecticut basic income tax (the less of (a) 19% of adjusted federal tentative minimum tax or (b) 5% of adjusted federal alternative minimum taxable income). Separate provisions apply for nonresident and part-year resident individuals, trusts, and estates.

[7] District of Columbia: The tax on unincorporated businesses is 9.975%; minimum tax, 100%.

[8] Georgia: The rates shown are for married persons filing jointly and heads of households. Single persons pay at rates ranging from 1% on taxable net income not over $750 to 6% on taxable net income over $7,000. Married persons filing separately pay at rates

ranging from 1% on taxable net income not over $500 to 6% on taxable net income over $5,000.

[9] Hawaii: Rates shown are for taxpayers filing jointly and surviving spouses. Special rate tables are provided for heads of households, unmarried individuals, and married individuals filing separately and estates and trusts.

[10] Idaho: Each person (joint returns deemed one person) filing return pays additional $10.

[11] Illinois: Additional personal property replacement tax of 1.5% of net income is imposed on partnerships, trusts, and S corporations.

[12] Indiana: Counties may impose an adjusted gross income tax on residents at 0.5%, 0.75%, or 1%, and at 0.25% on nonresidents or a county option income tax at rates ranging between 0.2% and 1%, with the rate on nonresidents equal to one-fourth of the rate on residents.

[13] Iowa: An alternative minimum tax is imposed equal to 75% of the maximum state individual income tax rate for the tax year of the state alternative minimum taxable income.

[14] Kansas: The rates shown are for married individuals filing joint returns. For all other individuals, the rates are 4.4% of the first $20,000 of Kansas taxable income, 7.5% of the next $10,000, and 7.75% of the excess over $30,000.

[16] Louisiana: These are the maximum tax rates for individuals. For joint returns, the tax is determined as if net income and the personal exemption credits were reduced by one-half. Actual tax is determined from tax tables.

[17] Maine: Rates shown are 1995 rates for single individuals and married persons filing separately. For unmarried or legally separated individuals who qualify as heads of household, the tax rates range between 2% if taxable income is less than $6,200 and 8.5% if taxable income is $24,750 or more. For married individuals filing jointly and widows or widowers permitted to file a joint federal return, the tax rates range between 2% if taxable income is less than $8,250 and 8.5% if taxable income is $33,000 or more. 1996 rates will be set administratively, based on inflation. Additional state minimum tax is imposed equal to the amount by which the state minimum tax (27% of adjusted federal tentative minimum tax) exceeds Maine income tax liability, other than withholding tax liability.

[20] Michigan: Persons with business activity allocated or apportioned to Michigan are also subject to a single business tax of 2.35% on an adjusted tax base.

[21] Minnesota: The rates shown apply to married individuals filing jointly and surviving spouses. For unmarried individuals, the tax is 6% on the first $16,070, 8% on all over $16,070 but not over $52,790, and 8.5% on all over $52,790. For unmarried heads of households, the tax is 6% on the first $19,870, 8% on all over $19,870 but not over $79,500, and 8.5% on all over $79,500. A 7% alternative minimum tax is imposed.

[24] Montana: Rates shown are 1995 amounts; minimum tax, $1. 1996 rates will be set administratively, based on inflation.

[25] Nebraska: Rates shown are for married couples filing jointly and qualified surviving spouses. Rates for married couples filing separately range between 2.62% of the first $2,000 and 6.99% of taxable income over $23,375. Rates for heads of household range between 2.62% of the first $3,800 and 6.99% of taxable income over $35,000. Rates for single individuals range between 2.62% of the first $500 to 6.99% for taxable income over $15,150.

[26] New Hampshire: Limited to interest and dividends.

[27] New Jersey: Rates shown are for married persons filing jointly, heads of households, and surviving spouses. The rates for married persons filing separately, unmarried

individuals, and estates and trusts range between 1.4% of the first $20,000 of taxable income and 6.37% of taxable income over $75,000.

[28] New Mexico: Rates shown are for married persons filing jointly and surviving spouses. For married persons filing separately, the rates range between 1.7% on the first $4,000 of taxable income and 8.5% on taxable income over $50,000. For heads of household, rates range between 1.7% on the first $7,000 of taxable income and 8.5% on taxable income over $83,000. For single individuals, estates and trusts rates range between 1.7% of the first $5,500 of taxable income and 8.5% of taxable income over $65,000. Qualified taxpayers may pay alternative tax of 0.75% of gross receipts from New Mexico sales.

[29] New York: The rates shown are the figures for married individuals filing jointly and surviving spouses. Separate schedules are set out for heads of households (ranging between 4% on the first $7,500 of taxable income and 7% on taxable income over $15,000) and for unmarried individuals, married individuals filing separately, and estates and trusts (ranging between 4% of the first $5,500 of taxable income and 7% of taxable income over $11,000). The rates are reduced for tax years beginning after 1996. In addition, individuals, estates, and trusts are subject to a 6% tax on minimum taxable income. A tax table benefit recapture supplemental tax is imposed equal to a taxpayer's tax table benefit multiplied by a fraction, the numerator of which is the lesser of $50,000 or the excess of the taxpayer's New York adjusted gross income for the tax year over $100,000 and the denominator of which is $50,000.

[30] North Carolina: Rates shown are for married persons filing jointly. For heads of households, the rates are 6% on the first $17,000, 7% of next $63,000, 7.75% of excess over $80,000. For unmarried individuals other than surviving spouses and heads of households, the rate is 6% of first $12,750, 7% of next $47,250, 7.75% of excess over $60,000. For married persons filing separately, the rate is 6% of first $10,625, 7% of next $39,375, 7.75% of excess over $50,000.

[31] North Dakota: Individuals, estates, and trusts are allowed an optimal method of computing the tax. The optional tax is 14% of the taxpayer's adjusted federal income tax liability for the tax year.

[33] Oklahoma: Rates shown are for heads of households, married persons filing jointly, and a surviving spouse not deducting federal income taxes. Single persons, married persons filing separately, and estates and trusts not deducting federal income taxes pay at rates ranging from 0.5% on the first $1,000 of taxable income to 7% on taxable income over $10,000. Optional rates (ranging from 0.5% to 10%) are enacted for taxpayers who deduct federal income taxes.

[34] Oregon: Rates shown are 1995 amounts. Rates for joint filers, heads of households, and qualifying widow(er)s are 6% of the first $4,300, 7% over $4,300 but not over $10,800, and 9% of taxable income over $10,800.

[38] Tennessee: Individuals are taxable only on interest and dividends.

[39] Utah: Rates shown are for married persons filing jointly and heads of households. Married taxpayers filing separately, single taxpayers, and estates and trusts pay at rates ranging from 2.55% on taxable income not over $750 to 7% on taxable income over $3,750. After 1996, rates for married persons filing jointly or heads of households range from 2.3% of the first $1,500 of taxable income to 7% of taxable income over $7,500. After 1996, rates for single taxpayers, estates and trusts, and married couples filing separately range from 2.3% of the first $750 of taxable income to 7% of taxable income over $3,750.

[43] West Virginia: A minimum tax is also imposed equal to the excess by which an amount equal to 25% of any federal minimum tax or alternative minimum tax for the tax year exceeds the total tax due for the tax year.

[44] Wisconsin: Rates shown are for married persons filing jointly. Rates for married persons filing separately range between 4.9% of the first $5,000 of taxable income and 6.93% of taxable income over $10,000. The rates for fiduciaries and single individuals range between 4.9% or the first $7,500 of taxable income and 6.93% of taxable income over $15,001. Alternative minimum tax is imposed. For the tax year ending after April 1, 1991, April 1, 1992, and April 1, 1993, and for the tax years beginning in 1994, 1995, and 1996, a surcharge is imposed on individuals, estates, trusts, and partnerships, except an entity with gross receipts of less than $1,000, at the rate of the greater of $25 or 0.4345% of net business income. The maximum surcharge is $9,800. An individual, estate, trust, or partnership engaged in farming with a net farm profit of $1,000 or more is subject to a surcharge of $25, regardless of whether the entity is otherwise subject to a surcharge. (The Department of Revenue must establish annual surcharge rates necessary to generate a sufficient level of revenue to fund appropriations from the recycling fund.)

[57] New York City: For 1997, tax rates range from 2.7% to 3.4%; after 1997, tax rates range from 1.35% to 1.7%. Nonresidents, 0.25% (0.45% for 1971 through 1997) of wages; 0.375% (0.65% for 1971 through 1997) of net earnings from self-employment; unincorporated business, 4%. Minimum tax, 2.85% (2.5% after 1997) of city minimum taxable income. A graduated surtax is imposed for tax years 1990 through 1996. An additional tax is imposed for tax years beginning after 1990 but before 1998 equal to 14% of the sum of the basic city income tax and tax surcharge.

[58] Philadelphia: The rate shown is for residents; nonresidents are subject to a rate of 4.2256%.

[60] Portland, OR: The tax is imposed on employers paying wages for services performed and is levied in Washington, Clackamas, and Multnomah Counties (including Portland).

[62] San Francisco: A payroll expense tax is imposed on employers in the city and county of San Francisco at the rate of 1% to 1.5%, depending on character of business and payroll expenses and/or salary distributions.

[66] Yonkers, NY: Nonresidents subject to 0.5% tax on earnings. Tax in effect only through 1997.

NOTE: Missing footnote numbers should be ignored. The missing numbers represent reserve numbers which are not currently in use due to the frequent and many changes in this listing over time.

(*Source:* CCH Incorporate, Volume 1, 12/95 State Tax Guide.)

Glossary

American Association of Retired Persons (AARP): A Washington based service and lobbying association for individuals aged 50 and over.

Accrued Benefit: The amount of benefits that an individual has earned based on their service to date. This is equal to a calculated amount for traditional defined benefit plans, typically based on the plan's provisions and the employees service and compensation to date. The accrued benefit in a defined contribution plan is normally equal to the participant's account balance. All accrued benefits may not be fully vested.

Administrative Services Only (ASO) Arrangement: An outsourcing arrangement relating to an employer-sponsored employee benefit plan, typically a health or welfare benefit plan, whereby an insurance company provides certain administrative services (e.g., claims payments) but does not assume any risk for the payment of the related benefits (i.e., no insurance relationship exists).

Annual Trustees' Report: The annual report(s) of the Social Security and Medicare Boards of Trustees.

Annuities: A type of contract issued by an insurance company that agrees to pay an amount periodically (e.g., monthly) for a stated period (e.g., until death or for a stated number of years) in exchange for a lump sum payment on issuance of the contract. The payment amounts can either be fixed (nonparticipating) or variable (participating). Under fixed contracts, the periodic payment amount is set for the entire term of the contract. Under variable contracts, the periodic payment amount can vary based on the performance of certain related investments chosen by the individual or plan trustees..

Annuity Form: Receiving the value of an accrued pension benefit or other amount in the form of periodic payments for life or a stated period of time versus as a lump sum.

Anti-Cutback Rule: The provision under the Internal Revenue Code (i.e., Section 411(d)(6)) that prevents employers from retroactively reducing an accrued benefit amount or form of benefit.

Asset Allocation: The process of deciding how to invest an individual's or institution's (e.g., pension fund) assets between various asset classes.

Asset Classes: The various types of investment categories (e.g., stocks, bonds, cash equivalents, real estate) that individuals and institutions consider in deciding how to invest their assets.

Baby Boomers: Individuals born between 1946 and 1964.

Baby Busters: Those individuals born between 1965 and 1980.

Balanced Fund: An investment fund (e.g., mutual fund) that is designed to invest in both equity and fixed income securities.

Cafeteria Plan: An employer-sponsored health and welfare benefit plan arrangement whereby employees choose between a menu of benefit choices, some or all of which may be provided with a tax-favored basis.

Contract with America: A political contract entered into by most Republican candidates for Congress in 1992 stating their primary objectives if they, and a Republican Congress, were elected.

COBRA: The federal Consolidated Omnibus Budget Reconciliation Act of 1987 which, among other things, provided employees and certain other individuals (e.g., spouse, dependants) who are covered under employer-sponsored health benefit plans with the ability to purchase health insurance at group rates if they change jobs or if certain other events occur (e.g., divorce).

Defined Benefit Pension Plans: A type of employer-sponsored retirement income plan that provides employees or their beneficiaries with a stated amount of income per month, typically based on the employee's age, length of service, and income. The investment risk under these plans is borne by the employer and most defined benefit plans are insured by the federal Pension Benefit Guaranty Corporation (PBGC). Defined dollar benefit plans are also considered to be defined benefit plans.

Defined Contribution Plans: A type of employer-sponsored retirement or savings plan that provides for fixed or variable contributions by the employer that are allocated to individual accounts of plan participants (i.e., employees participating in the plan). The investment risk under these plans is borne by the plan participants and these plans are not insured by the Pension Benefit Guaranty Corporation (PBGC). Defined contribution plans include money purchase plans, profit-sharing plans, thrift/savings plans, stock bonus plans, and employee stock ownership plans.

Defined Dollar Benefit Plans: A type of defined benefit plan under which the employer promises to make a stated contribution and pay a stated rate of return on accumulated contributions.

Demographics: The study of population trends.

Disability Insurance (DI) Program: The federal insurance program for the disabled that is administered by the Social Security Administration. The DI Program is funded by a payroll tax on employers and employees and all receipts and payments are made via the DI Trust Fund.

Distribution Planning: The process of determining when to begin to withdraw assets from tax-favored or other savings vehicles for retirement income purposes. Distribution planning also involves consideration of the order of withdrawal from various savings vehicles (e.g., tax-favored versus nontax-favored) in order to minimize taxes and maximize the long-term economic value to the individual.

Duration: The average number of years remaining in the term of a bond based on its cash flows (i.e., interest and principal payments). The duration of a bond, other than a zero coupon bond, is always shorter than its remaining term due to the effects of interim interest payments on the calculation of the average remaining cash flows.

Early Retirement Age (ERA): The age, before the normal retirement age, at which individuals are eligible to retire, typically with a reduction from their normal retirement benefit due to payment of their accrued benefit over a longer period of time.

Employee Retirement Income Security Act (ERISA): The federal labor law passed in 1974 that establishes the regulatory framework for most employer-sponsored pension and welfare benefit plans. This law is designed to provide a number of protections for workers in connection with their pension and welfare benefit programs (e.g., minimum standards, fiduciary responsibility provisions, reporting and disclosure requirements, PBGC insurance program).

Employee Stock Ownership Plans (ESOPs): A type of stock bonus plan that is designed to invest primarily in employer securities (i.e., common or convertible preferred stock). ESOPs can either be leveraged or unleveraged.

Equity Securities: Stocks and ownership participations in different types of entities (e.g., corporations).

Expectation Gap: The difference between what an individual expects to occur and what will likely occur in connection with a particular subject matter (e.g., the future of Social Security, Medicare, or employer-sponsored pension and retiree health programs).

Fixed Income Securities: Bonds and similar instruments (e.g., GICs).

Generation X: Those individuals born between 1965 and 1980.

Global Fund: An investment fund (e.g., mutual fund) that is designed to invest in securities of both U.S. and non-U.S. based enterprises.

Guaranteed Investment Contracts (GICs): A contract with an insurance company that provides for the repayment of principal and the periodic payment of fixed or minimum interest amounts for a stated term.

Health Care Financing Administration (HCFA): The federal agency within the U.S. Department of Health and Human Services that has the primary responsibility for administering Medicare (i.e., HI and SMI) programs.

Hospital Insurance (HI) Program: The portion of the Medicare program that is primarily designed to pay inpatient hospital charges to seniors and the disabled.

Individual Retirement Account (IRA): A type of tax-favored retirement savings vehicle for individuals.

Internal Revenue Service (IRS): For the purposes of this book, the IRS is the federal agency that is responsible for administering and enforcing the tax qualification requirements applicable to tax-favored pension and welfare benefit plans.

International Fund: An investment fund (e.g., mutual fund) that is designed to invest in securities of non-U.S. based enterprises.

Investment Horizon: The period of time over which an individual or entity (e.g., pension fund) is expected to invest.

Joint and Survivor Annuity: An annuity that makes payments over the life of the employee and his or her spouse. Typically spousal benefits are reduced, typically by 50%, after the employee dies.

Junk Bond: A high-yield, noninvestment grade fixed-income instrument.

Keogh Plan (HR 10 Plan): A type of pension plan for self-employed individuals.

KSOP—A 401(k): Plan that is combined with an ESOP feature. Typically these plans give employees the ability to save on a tax-deferred basis with employer matching contributions being made in the form of employer securities (i.e., common or convertible preferred stock).

Leveraged: The use of borrowing to purchase employer securities in connection with an ESOP.

Looming Retirement Crisis: The combined implications of projected demographic trends, current and projected Social Security and Medicare financial imbalances, private pension and retiree health trends and personal savings and investment trends on the future retirement security of Americans.

Lump Sum: Payment of an accrued benefit amount in a single sum as opposed to in annuity form.

Market Timing: Attempts to predict changes in selected market conditions (e.g., equity markets, interest rates, commodity prices).

Means Testing: The process of reducing benefit levels (e.g., Social Security or Medicare benefits) for individuals with higher levels of income or net worth. Full means testing would include the elimination of all benefits for individuals with incomes or net worths in excess of stated levels even if they had paid any applicable payroll taxes during their entire working lifetimes.

Medicaid: The federal health insurance program for the poor that is regulated by the Department of Health and Human Services and administered by the states.

Medicare: The nation's health insurance program for senior citizens and the disabled, enacted in 1965 during President Lyndon Johnson's administration. Medicare is divided into two programs—the Hospital Insurance Program (Part A) and the Supplementary Medical Insurance Program (Part B).

Medigap Policies: Private health insurance policies designed to fill the gap not paid for by Medicare.

Multiple-Employer Plan: A collection of single-employer plans of unrelated companies that have combined certain investment and plan administration functions in order to take advantage of the related economies of scale.

Multiemployer Plan: A type of pension or welfare benefit plan that is sponsored by a union for the benefit of union members who work for a number of different employers.

Non-investment Grade: A fixed income instrument that is viewed to be speculative based on the credit risk relating to the issuer.

Normal Retirement Age (NRA): The age specified under a pension or other retirement plan at which an individual is eligible reduced retirement benefits. This age is currently sixty-five for the OASI program and is currently set to gradually increase to sixty-seven over time.

Old Age Survivors Insurance (OASI) Program: The federal retirement income program that is administered by the Social Security Administration.

OASDI: The combination of the OASI and DI programs administered by the Social Security Administration.

Qualified Retirement Plans: Pension plan (both defined benefit and defined contribution plans) that are designed and operated in accordance with applicable Internal Revenue Code provisions. Qualified retirement plans allow employers a deduction for contributions subject to certain limits, tax free build-up of assets within a related trust fund, and deferral of individual taxation of any benefits under the plan until they are paid.

Part A Program: The Hospital Insurance (HI) program under Medicare.

Part B Program: The Supplementary Medical Insurance (SMI) program under Medicare.

Participant-Directed Investment Arrangements: A feature under a defined contribution plan that allows plan participants to decide how all or part of their individual account will be invested. Typically, individuals will be allowed to choose between at least three pooled investment funds and have the ability to change their investment elections at least quarterly.

Pension Benefit Guaranty Corporation (PBGC): The government corporation that insures certain employer-sponsored defined benefit pension plans, subject to certain rules and limits.

Pension Benefit Plan: A defined benefit or defined contribution plan sponsored by an employer(s) or a union.

Pension and Welfare Benefits Administration: The agency within the U.S. Department of Labor that is responsible for the administration and enforcement of Title I of ERISA.

Plan Sponsor: An employer or union who sponsors a pension or welfare benefit plan.

Primary Insurance Amount (PIA): The calculated normal retirement benefit for an individual under the OASI program.

Privatization: The process of converting enterprises that were previously owned entirely or in part by the government to private ownership. In the context of Social Security reform, it refers to movement from the current government run defined benefit plan arrangement to a full or partial defined contribution arrangement with investments in non-government securities.

Public Trustees: The two individuals who are appointed by the President and confirmed by the U.S. Senate to serve as public watchdogs over the Social Security and Medicare Trust funds, including preparation of the related annual reports.

Qualified Plan: A pension plan that meets the design and operational requirements of the Internal Revenue Code for tax-favored treatment.

Retirement Gap: The difference between the amount of assets that individuals need at retirement to meet their retirement objectives and the amount of assets they are currently expected to have based on their current assets and planned savings, spending, and investment patterns.

Reverse Mortgage: A means to borrow against the equity in a home whereby the loan does not have to be repaid until the home is sold or the borrower moves out or dies.

Right of First Refusal (ROFR): A feature of a stock bonus plan, including an ESOP, which gives the employer the right to purchase any stock distributed to participants before they can sell it to any other party.

Risk Tolerance: The process of determining the degree of fluctuation (or volatility) that an individual will accept in the value of their investments and the related investment returns.

Seniors: Generally deemed to refer to individuals 65 years and over.

SFAS No. 106: An accounting and reporting standard promulgated by the Financial Accounting Standards Board (FASB) which established the current accounting treatment for employer-sponsored postretirement benefit programs (e.g., retiree health programs).

Section 403 and 457 Plans: Types of employer-sponsored pension plans, named after the related provisions of the Internal Revenue Code, that apply to certain governmental and not-for-profit employers.

Section 404(c) Plan: A type of participant-directed defined contribution plan that complies with the requirements of the provision of ERISA for which it is named. Compliance with this ERISA provision will serve to reduce, but not eliminate, an employer's fiduciary responsibility in connection investment results relating to participant directed investment programs.

Section 401(k) Plan: A feature of a defined contribution plan, named after the related provision of the Internal Revenue Code, which allows employees to save a portion of their salary on a tax-deferred basis. These salary reduction amounts may be matched all or in part by the employer.

Single-Employer Plan: A pension or welfare benefit plan sponsored by a single employer of a group of employers within a single, controlled group of companies.

Single Life Annuity: An annuity that makes payments over the life of the employee.

Social Security: In this book, it refers to the retirement income program for seniors enacted into law in 1935 during President Franklin Roosevelt's administration (i.e., the OASI program).

Social Security Administration (SSA): The independent federal agency that administers the OASI and DI programs. SSA also provides certain assistance to HCFA in enrolling Medicare beneficiaries.

Stable Value Fund: A category of investment fund which is designed to preserve principal and provide with a fixed or minimum rate of return that will not go below zero. Typical stable value funds are funded with GICs or similar instruments.

Standard Deviation: A probability measurement whereby 66 ⅔% of all outcomes (e.g., annual rates of return for a particular asset class) are likely to fall within one standard deviation and 90 percent of all outcomes are likely to fall within two standard deviations of a stated amount (e.g., estimated annual rate(s) of return).

Sub-Asset Clauses: Various sub-categories of investments within an overall asset class (e.q., value growth). Small cap and large cap are all subclasses of the stock (equities) asset class.

Supplementary Medical Insurance (SMI) Program: The portion of the Medicare program that is designed to provide outpatient and other related services to seniors and the disabled.

Third Party Administrator (TPA): An individual or entity that performs certain plan administration functions (e.g., claims processing, benefit payments) for a pension or welfare benefit plan.

Title I: The provisions of ERISA which outline the minimum standards, fiduciary responsibility and reporting and disclosure provisions which apply to ERISA covered plans.

Title II: The provisions of ERISA that outline the minimum standards that employer-sponsored pension plans must meet in order to receive tax-favored treatment under the Internal Revenue Code.

Title III: The provisions of ERISA that outline the division of responsibilities for administering ERISA between various federal agencies (i.e., DOL and IRS).

Title IV: The provisions of ERISA that outline the federal defined-benefit plan insurance program administered by the PBGC.

Three-legged Stool Model: The nation's current retirement income security model that assumes that individual's retirement security can be achieved based on a combination of Social Security (OASI) benefits, employer sponsored pension benefits, and personal savings.

Vesting: The process by which employees earn an irrevocable right to certain benefits (e.g., pension), typically based on their years of participation in the plan. Individuals who are fully vested have earned the right to any related accrued benefits even if they leave their employer.

Volatility: The degree of fluctuation (variance) in annual returns of different asset classes. Volatility is normally measured in standard deviation terms.

Welfare Benefit Plan: A health, severance, life insurance, disability, or other type of nonretirement income-related plan sponsored by an employer of a union.

Zero Coupon Bond: A Treasury, fixed-income security that is purchased at a discount of its face value and does not pay principal or interest payments until maturity.

Index

Active duration, 167
Adjusted gross income (AGI), 154
Administrative costs, pension and savings
  plans, 80
Administrative services-only arrangement
  (ASO), 92–93
After-tax contributions, 71
Airline industry, pension plans, 78
Alzheimer's Disease, incidence of, 3
A-M-Best Company, 106, 211
American Express Company, 62
American Institute of Certified Public
  Accountants, 84
Annual reports, 32, 37, 39, 75
Annuities:
  CDs vs., 210
  distributions from, 137
  earnings from, 25
  joint, 143
  as personal savings vehicle, 100, 102, 106
  survivor, 143
  tax-deferred, 72
  two-tiered defined benefit plans and,
    38
  variable, 210–211
Arthur Andersen:
  Institution Investment Consulting Group,
    176
  Retirement Manager Software, 195
  services provided by, 213
Asset allocation:
  focus on, 165–168
  investment considerations, 205–206
  planning framework and, 113
  strategic, 168
  targeted, 212
Asset classes:
  diversification among, 177, 191–192
  historical returns, 170
  listing of, 166–168
  projected risk and return, 177
  returns, 175
  volatility of, 176
Asset management:
  employee-sponsored pension and savings
    plan, 68, 85
  ERISA provisions, 75–76

Assets:
  allocation, see Asset allocation
  closely held, 167–168
  management, see Asset management
  Medicare program, 51
  OASI Trust Fund, 29–31
Association of Private Pension and Welfare
  Plans, 84
AT&T, 97
Attorney:
  role of, 202, 206
  selection factors, 214

Baby boom generation:
  Medicare program and, 56
  mutual fund investment, 209
  population statistics, 12
  retirement security for, 2
  Social Security benefits for, 136
Baby bust generation, 2, 12, 136
Baker, James, 29
Banker, role of, 202
Barbour, Haley, 54
Beneficiaries, Social Security benefits for, 24.
    See also Estate planning
Benefits administration department, 205
Biotech industry, 195
Bismarck, Otto von, 16–17
Board of trustees, OASI Trust Fund, 28–29
Boilermakers, 64
Bond(s):
  corporate, 100
  intermediate volatility, 182
  market crashes, 197–198
  monthly volatility, 183
  municipal, 25, 100
  portfolios, 18, 170–171
  rate of return, 202
  state, 100
  tax treatment, 147
  zero coupon, 195
Break-even analysis, tax-deferred, 162
Broad domestic fixed income, 167
Brochures, as information resource, 205
Broker:
  function of, 206
  selection factors, 207